072

D0421314

Essential Articl

Articles, opinions, arguments, personal accounts, opposing viewpoints

In print in this book & online as part of Complete Issues

FOR REFERENCE ONLY

CANCELLED

Complete Issues
articles · statistics · contacts

Complete Issues
articles · statistics · contacts

www.completeissues.co.uk

Your log in details:

Username: _____

Password: _____

NOT TO BE TAKEN AWAY

CANCELLED

CANCELLED

West Lothian College Library

34129 400261266

Essential Articles 2015

Essential Articles 2015 is part of Complete Issues, a unique combination of resources in print and online.

Complete Issues

Complete Issues gives you the articles, statistics and contacts to understand the world we live in.

The unique format means that this information is available on the shelf and on the screen.

How does Complete Issues work?

Using www.completeissues.co.uk you can view individual pages on screen, download, print, use on whiteboards and edit to suit your needs. It makes Essential Articles even more flexible and useful.

As well as being able to access all these articles in both PDF and editable formats, there are references and links to other parts of Complete Issues - the archive of articles, the statistics and the website and contact details of relevant organisations.

The articles in the Essential Articles series, the statistics in Fact File and online contacts work beautifully together on the Complete Issues website to produce a choice of relevant writing, figures and links.

When you search for a topic you instantly generate a list of relevant articles, figures and organisations with a thumbnail of the page and a short description.

The **advantages of Complete Issues** over just googling are:

- **varied & reliable sources**
- **moderated - so appropriate for student use**
- **properly referenced**
- **beautifully presented**
- **adaptable for classroom use**
- **cleared for copyright**
- **links that are checked for safety and relevance**

Users can search and browse individual elements of Complete Issues or all the parts together, past and present editions.

Students can research a topic secure in the knowledge that they will find reputable sources and considered opinions.

In addition to the online service, you have this attractive printed version always available. Its bright, magazine-style format entices readers to browse and enjoy while learning about current issues and dilemmas, making even difficult issues approachable.

Because you have both the book and online access you can use Essential Articles in different ways with different groups and in different locations. It can be used simultaneously in the library, in the classroom and at home.

Your purchase of the book entitles you to use Complete Issues on one computer at a time. You can find your access codes on your covering letter or by contacting us. It is useful to record them on page 1 of this volume.

You can also buy an unlimited site licence to make the service and the material available to **all** students and staff at **all** times, even from home.

If you do not yet have the other resources in Complete Issues - the statistics and the contacts - you can sample the service and upgrade here:

www.completeissues.co.uk

Complete Issues
articles • statistics • contacts

> *Even if it's not a positive solution, we have to have some solution so these children do not suffer*
>
> Page 28

© Virginia Mayo/AP/Press Association Images

Contents

Photo: Featureflash / Shutterstock.com

> " It's the way that families and friends talk about food and weight which will have the biggest impact on shaping the way they think and act around food. "
>
> Page 34

Contents

FAMILY & RELATIONSHIPS

FINANCIAL ISSUES

> " Kids don't always make decisions that are healthy, sensible or safe "
>
> Page 64

> " ...I was lucky: my brother, aged 16, had to sleep in a telephone box for a week before the council would place him anywhere. "
>
> Page 87

Contents

" If slaughterhouses had glass walls, we would all be vegetarians "

Page 94

Photo: © Jonathon Reed

Contents

66 Every time I criticised her, she would post screenshots and get more support which would make me even angrier... 99

Page 132

Contents

> " By allowing her daughter to have a baby so young, she has wrecked what is left of her childhood "
>
> page 167

Photo: Rena Schild/Shutterstock.com

Contents

66 ... this was a powerful image of resilience and hope, where you would think there was none to be found 99

page 199

Photo: © Jan Grarup/laif/Camera Press

Alcohol, drugs & smoking

It's not harming anyone, so why is Brussels trying to remove my robot cigarette?

You can take my fake smokes from my warm, blood-beating hands   Laurie Penny

SOME ISSUES:

Do you think e-cigarettes are a safe alternative to real cigarettes?

Why do you think people have an issue with them?

Would it bother you if someone was smoking an e-cigarette near you?

What should be done to encourage people to stop smoking?

Do we have a right to comment on a person's health?

See also Smoking outside the hospital, p118

The glory days of fake smoking are nearly over. Soon, if the EU and several American states have their way, electronic-cigarette nerds will no longer be able to sit smugly indoors, breathing out clean nicotine vapour, toying with our silly cyberpunk drug-delivery-devices and feeling sorry for the ordinary smokers shivering in the cold. The proposed EU regulations will make it far harder to buy, sell and use e-cigarettes, and might pull them off the shelves altogether.

I've been using electronic cigarettes for some time, because I love to smoke but am less than thrilled by the prospect of

choking to death in my sixties. I'm unreasonably cross about the proposed legislation as only an addict can be. Imagine the howling rage of a toddler having its teething ring snatched away and combine that with the shaky, instinctive spite of a junkie anticipating withdrawal. That's the kind of cross I am.

It was just getting to the point where I could enjoy a fake smoke in peace without having to explain to interested bystanders five or six times a day how the device in my hands actually works: a nicotine-glycerine liquid with a battery that super-heats when you draw on it, plus a nifty

Smoking is responsible for more deaths annually than road accidents, alcohol, heroin, cocaine, murder and suicide combined...

little flashing light that lets you pretend you're a robot assassin from the future. I love my robot cigarette and I don't want anyone to take it away.

Foot-stomping aside, the raft of legislation against electronic cigarettes is preposterous and illogical. E-cigarettes are one of the most effective ways of reducing the amount of damage Britain's 10 million smokers are doing to their bodies every day, aside from going cold turkey, which not everybody is ready to do.

Smoking is responsible for more deaths annually than road accidents, alcohol, heroin, cocaine, murder and suicide combined, so a nicotine delivery system that allows people to avoid the major health risks of smoking while continuing to enjoy their vice would seem eminently sensible, unless you are of the opinion that smoking is a failure of character that should be stamped out.

The problem a lot of people seem to have is simply that electronic cigarettes are cheating, which, of course, they are. You get the basic kick of smoking without having to suck thousands of poisons into your tortured lungs. There are few conclusive studies on the long-term health effects of "vaping" but it's largely agreed that it's much better for you than tobacco, and a bit worse for you than not sucking on a stick of nicotine all day. I'm a fan of that sort of cheating. I believe in using technology to save lives, which for confirmed smokers is just what e-cigs are doing.

Micro-tyrannies such as this might not seem to matter much, but for millions of people who find it hard to quit, e-cigarettes have been a lifeline. Nicotine is one of the world's most addictive substances. It would have to be, since it has to work against millions of years of evolution telling us not to put burning things in our mouths on a regular basis.

... so a nicotine delivery system that allows people to avoid the major health risks of smoking while continuing to enjoy their vice would seem eminently sensible

The idea that e-cigarettes should be subject to the same restrictions as the leaf-burning variety once again confuses ethics with petty moral panic...

Smoking is an absurdly dangerous thing to do. That, of course, is part of the reason smokers do it. This is not the 1960s and few, if any, smokers can have failed to understand, when they took the first few musty head-spinning drags on their first cigarette, that the habit would kill them one day. Anti-smoking advocates tell us that young people don't really understand what smoking will do to our bodies but I don't think my generation have ever believed ourselves "immortal". We just want a bit more control over the horrible things that will eventually happen to us, and part of being young is believing that you can have that control.

Compassion is the most important feature of public-health policy. I'm no David Hockney, obstinately demanding that smoking legislation of any kind is "the most grotesque piece of social engineering". In fact, I supported the 2007 smoking ban. The bloodlessness of bureaucracy certainly made elements of the ban vindictive – particularly restrictions on the use of tobacco in mental-health wards and care homes, whose inmates can hardly pop outside for a cheeky one.

Overall, though, I'm a firm believer that humans should be permitted to do as much damage to their own bodies as they like, provided they aren't hurting others in the process – I would no more light a cigarette in front of a child than I would poison a public fountain for my own pleasure. And that's where the prospect of a ban on e-cigs, whose vapour is lighter than tobacco smoke, and rarely reaches the lungs of another person, makes no sense. It's not about public health. It's about morality.

The idea that e-cigarettes should be subject to the same restrictions as the leaf-burning variety once again confuses ethics with petty moral panic. To encourage addicts not to indulge their addiction where it might cause harm to children or the sick is ethical. To claim, as some do, that evidence of addiction is itself offensive and unsightly is simple prudishness. I find it unsightly when otherwise attractive young men grow ridiculous hipster moustaches but I would stop short of regulating public display of facial hair. I just avoid certain bars during Movember*.

You can take my fake smokes from my warm, blood-beating hands. No, really, you probably can take them, if "you" are the EU, or the state of New York. We cannot have a compassionate, effective policy on drugs and addiction without starting from a place of compassion, and if our stance on smoking stops with an idea of moral weakness, we have forfeited compassion. Now, stick that in your flashing electronic pipe and smoke it.

New Statesman, 12 December 2013

* During November each year, men volunteer to grow a moustache to raise funds for a global men's health charity, The Movember Foundation

E-cigarettes

The current situation:

They are not banned in Britain and they are not subject to the same legislation as ordinary cigarettes, so they can be used indoors in public places. Some organisations, however will not allow the use of e-cigarettes on their premises

The new EU rules:

A maximum nicotine level.

Containers will have to be child and tamper-proof.

Ingredients must be pure.

A similar level of nicotine with each inhale.

Packets must have health warnings and information on addiction risks and nicotine content.

Manufacturers will have to take full responsibility for the quality and safety of the product.

Advertising will be restricted.

The controversy:

Action on Smoking and Health (ASH) is a public health charity that campaigns against tobacco. It supports rules on electronic cigarettes but is not in favour of prohibiting them in public places. It argues that they are helpful to people who want to stop smoking and don't endanger others through second-hand smoke - which was the reason for the public ban on tobacco products.

In contrast the British Medical Association supports a ban on the use of e-cigarettes in public places because the risks are not yet established and so that smoking is not seen as normal behaviour.

The feeling of drinking alcohol without hangovers, disease or addiction? Bring it on!

We stubbornly refuse to engage in a proper debate about the health effects of alcohol
Nat Guest

SOME ISSUES:

Do you think there could be any negative effects of being able to get drunk without getting a hangover?

Should scientists be focussing on this?

Might this encourage more people to drink alcohol?

Why do you think so many people drink alcohol knowing its negative side-effects?

Ah, Science. From the discipline that brought us classics like penicillin, light bulbs, and adorable mice with ears implanted into their backs, comes possibly its greatest achievement yet: alcohol without the hangovers. Happy news for our proud nation of p**sheads!

Of course, it isn't really "alcohol" as such that we're talking about – rather, it's a compound that mimics the positive effects of being drunk (relaxation, increased sociability, lowered inhibitions, dancing terribly in your lounge to Ke$ha at 4am). More importantly for society, it also removes the negative effects of drinking – and I'm not talking about just those mind-curdling hangovers that eat up entire Sundays, but also the health effects that pickle your body from the inside, and the addictive properties that can destroy lives and families. There's even potential to "switch off" its effects by using an antidote – meaning you can return to your usual sober state in the same amount of time you'd usually have to wait for a painkiller to kick in.

The potential drug is being called a "serious revolution in health", and is pioneered by former Government drugs advisor Professor David Nutt, who has identified five potential compounds and is now putting them through tests. The compounds work by targeting the neurotransmitter system gamma aminobutryric acid (Gaba), which works to keep the brain calm and has previously been identified as the main target for alcohol. This means that other drugs which increase the Gaba function could work as an alcohol surrogate, providing us with the same pleasurable effects but without the adverse health effects.

Of course, we can expect some moralising and finger-wagging about this from people who will see it as little more than another "legal high" - albeit one that's been researched, tested and peer-reviewed by the scientific community. But Nutt's no stranger to controversy; he was famously ejected from his position as chairman of the Advisory Council on the Misuse of Drugs (ACMD) in 2009 after trying to inject

> There's really no reason for us to be unnecessarily risking our health just to get a few jollies

dangerous ideas like "science" and "logic" into the political debate surrounding drugs by pointing out that marijuana isn't actually very dangerous.

For some reason (presumably nostalgic attachment to our history as booze-swilling ale-chasers), using alcohol is deemed an acceptable way of altering our mental states in a way that nothing else is, despite it being enormously dangerous. We now have as many words for being drunk as eskimos purportedly have for snow: tipsy, p**sed, wasted, wrecked, trolleyed, battered, three sheets to the wind (I could go on); despite this, we stubbornly refuse to engage in a proper debate about its health effects.

Alcohol is highly toxic to all bodily systems, locks about 10 per cent of users into addiction and is responsible for more deaths worldwide than either malaria or AIDS. Estimates suggest alcohol-related harm in England costs the NHS £3.5bn

a year. But when it comes to decreasing the potential for harm, minimum pricing strategies aren't exactly vote-winners with the public – and we already know that prohibition fails miserably.

The truth is, alcohol or otherwise, we're never going to be able to stop people from chasing altered states; we've been doing it ever since the moment we first crawled out of the swamps and stumbled upon some dodgy looking mushrooms. But in this age of biological enlightenment and advanced neuroscience, there's really no reason for us to be unnecessarily risking our health just to get a few jollies; which is why Nutt's idea of an alternative, legal inebriant deserves due and proper consideration, not to mention some capital investment. To do otherwise would be nothing short of irresponsible.

In the interim, Prof, if you're looking for volunteers for testing then I'll happily offer up my body and my services. I can

promise you over-enthusiastic angry ranting about the current government, ordering of takeaway in the early hours of the morning, and a sterling rendition of Black Velvet by Alannah Myles. It's all in the name of science, after all.

The Independent, 13 November 2013

> When it comes to decreasing the potential for harm, minimum pricing strategies aren't exactly vote-winners with the public – and we already know that prohibition fails miserably.

One way to solve an alcohol problem: drink from a smaller glass

Scotland's health minister has suggested that pubs and clubs should offer wine in smaller measures to help their customers drink responsibly. He says it is a "simple yet effective" part of measures to tackle the problem of alcohol misuse. But will it work?

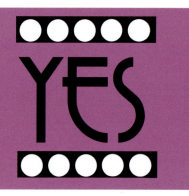

A large glass of wine can contain more than three units of alcohol. That's the full recommended daily amount for men and more than the recommendation for women.

Many places only offer medium and large glasses - this makes people drink more - they don't even realise how much they are drinking.

It gives people more choice if there are small glasses on offer.

Even if they drink the same amount, having to get a refill will mean people have the chance to notice what they are drinking. It will make them think about the amount of alcohol they are consuming.

Wine and other alcoholic drinks are often stronger than they used to be. A small amount is better.

Drinking too much damages people's health and costs the health service a lot of money - anything that prevents this should be welcomed.

People in the drinks industry support the idea.

SOME ISSUES:

Who do you think should be responsible for setting the 'correct' amount of alcohol?

What are the negative effects of drinking too much alcohol?

Do you think providing smaller glasses would help people monitor how much they drink?

What would you do to reduce the amount of alcohol people drink?

Is wine really the root of the drinks problem? Shouldn't time and money be spent encouraging people to drink halves instead of pints of beer?

One large glass might contain your daily amount of alcohol - but that only matters if you are drinking every day, not on the odd night out.

The cost of a small glass won't be half the cost of a large glass because it still costs the pubs the same in wages, lighting etc. to serve small measures.

Bar staff and waiters know that they are supposed to 'up-sell' - that means to get people to order extra or larger amounts. There won't be any incentive for them in offering small glasses.

It's a chance for pubs to make more money by serving smaller amounts at a time but people won't want to pay more.

This is just political interference - a campaign that looks good but doesn't do any good. What has this got to do with the government anyway? The public aren't stupid.

Even if they drink the same amount, having to get a refill will mean people have the chance to notice what they are drinking.

The cost of a small glass won't be half the cost of a large glass... People won't want to pay more for less.

Sources: Various

Cannabis in Colorado: The ups and downs of legalising highs

With more cannabis shops than branches of Starbucks and further liberalisation to come - why hasn't the trade in legal marijuana decreased the number of dealers on the street in Colorado?

Julie Bindel

There are now more cannabis shops in Colorado than there are branches of Starbucks. Since 1 January, it has been legal to sell cannabis for recreational use on licensed premises, three years after the drug was cleared for medical use. The recreational stores sprang up and 37 were granted licences to begin trading on New Year's Day.

With the help of the Cannabis Map of Colorado, I find my way to the Native Roots Apothecary dispensary on the eighth floor of a soulless building in downtown Denver. The shop looks like a cross between a GP's waiting room and a homoeopathic clinic. It is bare and painted white, apart from a coffee machine decorated in the Rastafarian colours.

Courtney Phillips is behind the counter, fielding calls from customers. "Lots of reporters from all over the States have been asking questions about this," she tells me. "I think it's great that Colorado is leading the way in being accepting of pot as both a medicinal aid as well as the fact that some people just prefer it to alcohol."

Before being allowed a doctor's prescription, patients have to apply to the state for a certificate of eligibility that costs between $60 and $100. On prescription, it is possible to buy up to two ounces a day per person. It costs between $150 and $400 an ounce, including tax at 8.5 per cent.

The price of weed when not buying on prescription can range between $400 and $500 an ounce, and all you need to make your purchase is a piece of ID to prove you are over 21.

Despite decriminalisation, there is still an illegal market for weed which sells the drug at half the price of legal retailers. According to one police officer I spoke to, the legislation could, paradoxically, lead to an increase in the involvement of criminal drug dealers. He believes the normalisation of weed-smoking will increase overall demand and that users will soon turn to cheaper black-market suppliers.

But the new law has found support in unexpected places. Steven Foster, the senior rabbi at Temple Emanuel in Denver, endorsed the law, arguing that poor and black Americans are disproportionately targeted by drugs law enforcement. This is also one of the arguments taken up by the state chapter of the United Food and Commercial Workers trade union, one of the largest in the United States.

SOME ISSUES:

What reasons are there for making the sale and use of marijuana legal?

How could the system in Colorado be improved?

Do you think this country will ever follow this example?

What's the going rate for an ounce?

Despite decriminalisation, there is still an illegal market for weed which sells the drug at half the price of legal retailers

Photo: Susan Montgomery / Shutterstock.com

The legal cannabis market is tightly governed. Until October this year, recreational marijuana stores have to grow almost all the cannabis they sell, a policy that will shortly be reviewed. Retailers can't advertise in places where children might see it and must sell their product in opaque, child-resistant packages. They will be inspected regularly by the Colorado Marijuana Enforcement Division and surveillance cameras will track sales to identify each customer.

In the hour I spend at the LoDo Wellness Centre, another cannabis retailer in central Denver, at least 300 people come through the door, ranging from young men in pairs to older women on their own. There are carloads of tourists from as far away as New Jersey, California and Ohio, some of whom ask Elizabeth, the receptionist, which weed-friendly hotels she considers the best value. Elizabeth checks each customer's ID and then directs the client either to the dispensing room or to the commercial storeroom.

I speak to Al (not his real name) who is a regular cannabis smoker. Al tells me that he has visited the store out of curiosity but will continue to buy his usual stash off his dealer. "It is much cheaper, quicker and easier." Two grammes from the store, he tells me, costs him $37, "more than twice as much as I usually pay".

Washington is preparing to liberalise its cannabis laws this year to bring it up to speed with Colorado, and activists in several other states are preparing to follow the Coloradan model. But federal organisations are trying to reverse the law.

Many Colorado businesses are cash-only, as the banks, controlled by the federal government, are refusing to open accounts for cannabis retailers. This makes them a target for organised crime, and the Internal Revenue Service is unhappy that such affluent businesses have no clear money trail.

In Colorado, however, many argue that the new laws are helping the state out of a bad recession. The Tax Foundation, a think tank, estimates that the state will raise almost $70m in new taxes this year.

Weed lovers and libertarians are united in their support for Colorado's approach, but is there enough attention being paid to the lows as well as the highs of legalisation? One thing is certain: with more than half of all Americans supporting legal pot, this issue is unlikely to disappear in a puff of smoke.

New Statesman, 27 February 2014

If cannabis is legal, more teenagers will smoke it – and that can't be good

People who want to legalise drugs talk about harm reduction, and they are right to

JOHN RENTOUL

SOME ISSUES:

Do you think that legalising cannabis would encourage more people to use it?

What would be the negative side-effects of this?

What benefits can you see to society if cannabis were legal?

Would legalising cannabis reduce crime or increase it?

Might using cannabis lead to more harmful drug use?

I know all right-thinking people are supposed to be delighted that Colorado has legalised cannabis, the first American state to do so. We are supposed to say, "When, oh, when will our government realise that it is losing the war on drugs and should take a lesson even from Americans, who can be surprisingly liberal sometimes?" But let us pause.

The idea that the existing policy on drugs in this country, and almost everywhere in the world apart from Colorado and Uruguay, is a self-evident failure is not a truth that is self-evident to me. In particular, the "war on drugs", and the notion that it is being "lost", is a cliché that helps to shut down thought rather than encourage it.

Illegal drug use in this country has decreased, is decreasing and ought to decrease further. In particular, young people in Britain drink less alcohol, smoke less tobacco and use fewer illegal drugs than they did. Those are good trends. If the Government is waging a war on drugs, it is winning it.

People who want to legalise drugs talk a lot about harm reduction, and they are right to do so. Let us then, while we are pausing, ask two questions. One, is cannabis harmful? Mostly, no. Mostly, its effect is to make people boring. But it is possible that, in some cases, it acts as a trigger for serious mental illness, especially for male teenagers.

Is cannabis harmful? Mostly, no. Mostly, its effect is to make people boring. But it is possible that, in some cases, it acts as a trigger for serious mental illness, especially for male teenagers.

Whether cannabis has been shown to be a trigger for people who are susceptible, or whether such people tend to try cannabis, is disputed, and the proportion of people who might be susceptible is small. But it would seem an unwise idea to do anything that might encourage more people to try cannabis unless we are sure.

So the next question is whether legalising cannabis would lead to more young people trying it. Well, what do you think?

It is at this stage that supporters of legalisation tend to drive the argument into the bowling-alley gutters by saying, "What about the harm done by alcohol?" It is serious, is the answer to that. And it is certainly more serious, on aggregate, than the harm done by cannabis. But that is an attempt to change the subject. Do something about attitudes to alcohol by all means. Rush out and buy Alastair Campbell's much-admired novel, My Name Is. Give up for January. Or for life. But none of this answers the question about how to minimise the harm of cannabis.

Then there is the harm done by the control of the production and supply of drugs by criminals. Yes, it is a problem. But we are mainly talking about cocaine and heroin, if we mean organised crime and drugs, and a lot of the harm in those cases is suffered in Colombia and Afghanistan. I don't have the answers to that; but then, neither do the advocates of legalising cannabis, who tend not to propose legalising "harder" drugs, yet.

Finally, legalisers sometimes say that it is jolly confusing that cannabis is illegal in theory but that the police tend to concentrate on more important things in practice. It's a compromise. It is so sensible that it is the most common legal position all over the world: illegal but not stringently enforced for small amounts. It is intellectually unsatisfactory, but it is winning. The people who want to change it have to make a better case.

The Independent, 7 January 2014

It would seem an unwise idea to do anything that might encourage more people to try cannabis unless we are sure.

Assisted dying

Supporting the right to die always runs the risk of diminishing the right to live

Deborah Orr

Frances Inglis should not have been jailed for killing her brain-damaged son – but still, one person cannot decide whether or not another person's life is worth living

SOME ISSUES:

Do you think anybody has the right to choose when a person should die?

Do you think Francis Inglis should have been sent to prison?

When someone can't say what they want, who should make the decision about whether they should go on living?

Frances Inglis is out of jail now, having served five years in prison for the murder of her 22-year-old son, Tom. Now 61, she does not regret ending her son's life. She doesn't believe she should have been sent to prison for doing so, and says that the law needs urgent review. She's right, but in a limited way. Judges need to be able to reject sentencing guidelines in extraordinary cases. It was right that a jury found Inglis guilty of murder. But it wasn't right to jail her for it. She had already killed the only person she is ever likely to kill, and was no threat to the public. Sometimes, people do the wrong thing for the right reasons, and Inglis is one of them.

If one thing in particular makes Inglis's story compellingly awful, it's the way that another "if only" comes relentlessly after the last. Inglis is a woman whose crime was a response to a long catalogue of terrible misfortunes, none of them in the smallest way due to her own choices, mistakes or turpitudes.

If only Tom Inglis, aged 21, hadn't decided to intervene in a fight outside an Essex pub in July 2007. If only he hadn't hit his head as he did so and become concussed. If only paramedics had not insisted that he should go to hospital with them in an ambulance, when he didn't want to. If only he hadn't tried to escape

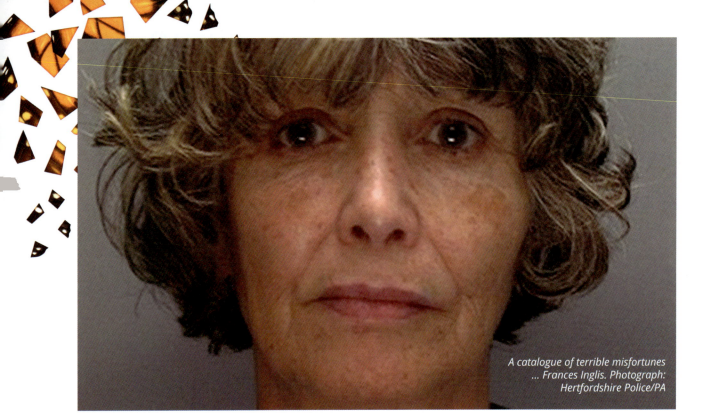

A catalogue of terrible misfortunes ... Frances Inglis. Photograph: Hertfordshire Police/PA

from the ambulance. If only Tom hadn't jumped from the vehicle when it was travelling at 30mph.

If only, having done so, he hadn't sustained such serious further injuries. If only an emergency operation, in which a piece of skull was removed to ease pressure of fluid on the brain, hadn't had the worst possible outcome instead of the best. If only someone had explained to Inglis that her brain-damaged son wouldn't suffer, had a legal application to withdraw food and water been successful, because morphine could still be prescribed.

Horrified by the idea of Tom being starved and dehydrated to death, Inglis decided for herself that an opiated drift to oblivion would be the best thing for her boy. She hung around needle exchanges, a respectable middle-aged

lady, asking suspicious addicts where she could buy heroin. They had enough sense not to tell her. So she went to King's Cross instead, until someone eventually sold her some.

Inglis tried to claim that she had not murdered Tom because she had conducted an assisted suicide

Inglis injected it into her son in hospital, sitting with him until she thought he had died. But he sustained a heart attack, and was

resuscitated, his disabilities yet more profound. Two weeks later, Inglis was arrested, heroin having been found in Tom's body. She was released on bail, on the condition that she didn't see her son. More than a year later, Tom having been transferred to a rehabilitation unit in Hertfordshire, she posed as his aunt, again injected him with heroin, and this time glued the lock of the room they were in, barricaded the door and made sure Tom had died before opening it to the police.

Inglis tried to claim that she had not murdered Tom because she had conducted an assisted suicide. But her son could not have asked his mother to assist him in his suicide because he could not communicate at all. She calls her action a mercy killing. But in truth it's unclear whether that

She must have known that no human life is more valuable than another...

overwhelming urge to end his life was merciful towards Tom or towards Frances. Inglis says she couldn't bear his suffering. Yet, since Tom couldn't communicate, it's hard to say whether he was suffering at all. Some medical opinion even asserts that before the first attack from his mother, there was a chance of some limited recovery. It's possible that Tom may have reached a point where he himself could decide whether he wanted to live or wanted to die. That can never be known.

One of the troubling aspects of this case is that Inglis had spent many years of her life working with children and adults with physical and neurological problems. She must have known that the lives of the people she helped were precious to them, and that no human life is more valuable than another. She must have known that it's wrong to start grading the value of lives according to the relative abilities of different human beings, and how hurtful it is to people with disabilities, when others take it upon themselves to decide whose life is worth living and whose isn't. She must surely have known that people generally want to make the best of their circumstances, however hard.

Of course, there are exceptions to this. Some people kill themselves over matters that can seem to outsiders trivial or fixable, even inexplicable. Others cling to life through immense adversity and suffering. What campaigners for euthanasia often fail to realise is that, however noble it is in theory, conferring the right to die always runs the risk of diminishing the right to live. People who need lots of care and support often worry that they are a "burden" and need reassurance about it. Lauding as heroes those who decide they don't want to be a burden may feel like the right thing to do. But it's the less heroic among us who need compassion. We need to know that there is nothing anti-heroic about rejecting such nobility.

One person simply cannot take it upon themselves to decide whether another person's life is worth living, however much they love them. Inglis rejects the idea that she was making decisions about the worth of her injured son's life based on grief and shock. I don't see how she could have made a distinction between her own suffering, and the suffering she imagined – possibly accurately or possibly not – that her boy was experiencing. But I do know that it isn't right to punish people for being mistaken. I do know that if five years of imprisonment hasn't changed a person's mind, then their mind is unlikely to change.

If anyone deserved mercy in this case, it was Inglis herself. A murderer as benign as Inglis shouldn't have an automatic custodial sentence following a guilty verdict. And when the relatives of someone as profoundly injured as Tom are strongly of the opinion that he would consider death preferable to life, were he able to make that judgment, then they should be able to apply for the withdrawal of food and fluid, safe in the knowledge that palliative painkilling can and will continue.

It seems to me that everyone who needs nursing care in order to survive should have the right to refuse sustenance while accepting pain-management drugs, as long as there are safeguards in place to ensure that a general right doesn't ever feel like an individual obligation. These are not tumultuous changes. They merely enshrine in law what happens at the end of many lives anyway. Inglis suffered so very greatly, and the law made her suffer so much more. That can't be right.

The Guardian, 13 December 2013
© Guardian News & Media 2013

We should all have the same right to die as Cody Curtis

A moving Coronation Street storyline brought the issue into millions of people's homes

Christopher Bucktin

It was with a heavy heart viewers said their final farewells to Coronation Street's Hayley Cropper after the cancer-stricken cafe owner decided to take her own life. Julie Hesmondhalgh's moving portrayal of her character's battle against the cruel disease highlighted the harsh reality faced by thousands of sufferers each year.

Although Hayley eventually opted for suicide and husband Roy played no part in helping her die, the storyline inevitably brought the debate of assisted suicide to the forefront in the UK, pitting public opinion against that of the Church and medical professionals.

It was previously a subject I'd rarely considered despite losing several loved ones to cancer. Having seen loved ones go through untold suffering after all medicine has been stopped, as it currently stands in Britain, we as friends or relatives are left to watch as their lives just slowly ebb away. Too often those dark final days overshadow the years of enjoyment we have shared with each other.

SOME ISSUES:

Do you think people have the right to choose to end their own life?

Should there be specific limitations on who can do this and how it can happen?

What might be the negative effects if assisted dying became legal?

Who has the right to make this decision?

> Too often those dark final days overshadow the years of enjoyment we have shared with each other.

Yet unlike Britain, here in America, three States – Oregon, Washington and Vermont – allow those with a terminal illness with less than six months to live the right to be given help by their relatives, friends and doctors to end their lives at a time of their choosing.

After meeting one of those who watched their loved ones choose to "die with dignity", I firmly believe each and every one of us should be given the same choice in Britain.

I understand not all will agree with my feelings. In fact I am sure some of you will be outraged. But after spending time with widowed Stan Curtis, I would defy anyone not to reason with his, or more importantly his late wife's, belief.

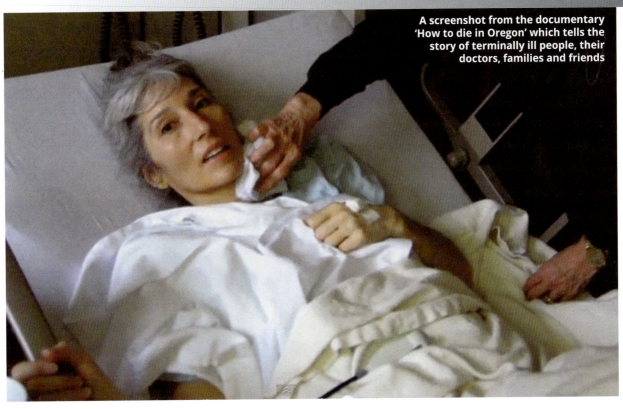

A screenshot from the documentary 'How to die in Oregon' which tells the story of terminally ill people, their doctors, families and friends

Dying people should have the right to compassionate help from a doctor at their time of greatest need, without having to endure a painful, uncomfortable death because of someone else's religious beliefs or fears.

For two years he watched helplessly as his wife Cody suffered cholangiocarcinoma cancer. The debilitating disease, one of the most aggressive which attacks the bile duct, left the mum-of-two's quality of life all but gone.

For her family and friends it was unbearable to watch yet it was Cody, supported by her family, who chose to end her life.

So in December 2009, 12 years after Oregon introduced its Death with Dignity Act and surrounded by her loved ones at her home, she drank a cocktail of legally prescribed drugs to end her life. It placed her in to coma which ultimately ended her suffering. But more importantly she died knowing those she left behind would not be prosecuted for assisting in her death.

Stan told me: "I'm still very proud of her. It wasn't hard for me. She was saying to me 'I can create happily ever after' and she did. For us it was not a medical choice, it was a lifestyle choice. Cody wanted to be in control of her destiny that was the most important thing to her and Death with Dignity allowed for that to happen." In Britain a new Assisted Dying Bill is likely to go before the Lords in May*.

If passed it could finally put an end to dying British patients having to travel to Switzerland's Dignitas centre to end their suffering and instead provide them with the comforts of their own home they should be given.

Dying people should have the right to compassionate help from a doctor at their time of greatest need, without having to endure a painful, uncomfortable death because of someone else's religious beliefs or fears. One of the biggest benefits of the law in Oregon is the comfort it gives to so many patients, knowing that they can die peacefully if they face extended suffering at the end.

A peaceful death, in sound mind and surrounded by loved ones, is a choice that surely should be respected, honoured and treated with the dignity every person so rightly deserves.

Manchester Evening News, 30 January 2014

18th July 2014: The bill to legalise assisted dying passed its second reading in the Lords after a ten hour debate. This means it will be given further consideration, but it does not mean it is likely to become law.

Child euthanasia in Belgium: World first as doctors are allowed to help children with terminal illness die

Charlotte McDonald-Gibson

Belgium has become the first country in the world to allow euthanasia for any age group, after its parliament backed amendments to the existing law which would in very rare cases permit doctors to help end the life of a terminally ill child.

Paediatricians and politicians fighting for the amendment argued that sick children in Belgium should have the same rights at the end of their lives as adults, who since 2002 have been able to ask doctors to help them die with dignity when faced with unbearable and irreversible suffering.

But religious groups and other doctors said such cases were so rare in children that there was no need to rush through new rules. They said guidelines on assessing a child's capacity for making such life-and-death decisions were ill-defined, which they feared could lead to misuse.

After an emotional two-day debate, the lawmakers followed the lead of the Senate and overwhelmingly approved the amendments, which will come into force as soon as Belgium's monarch, King Philippe, signs the law. He is not expected to oppose it.

In the Chamber of Representatives, also known as the "lower house" of parliament, 86 lawmakers voted in favour, 44 against and 12 abstained. Most opposition parties supported it, as well as the governing socialists and liberals. One member of the public in the gallery shouted "murderers" in French when the vote was passed, Reuters reported.

Under the amendments, any terminally ill child can request euthanasia, but such a request would only be granted if the child was close to death and a team of psychologists, doctors

SOME ISSUES:

Do you think that assisted suicide is ever the best option for a person?

Should there be an age limit for assisted suicide?

Does age matter when it comes to ending a person's suffering?

See also A better way of death, p124

Under the amendments, any terminally ill child can request euthanasia

Even if it's not a positive solution, we have to have some solution so these children do not suffer

and other medical professionals agreed that he or she was mature enough to understand the meaning of euthanasia. Any request would also require the approval of the parents.

"As a paediatrician, the first thing we want to do is cure children and babies and make them better as soon as possible," said Dr Gerlant van Berlaer, from the University Hospital Brussels. "We're just talking about the things we cannot resolve. And then, even if it's not a positive solution, we have to have some solution so these children do not suffer."

Belgium, The Netherlands and Luxembourg are the only countries with legal euthanasia – although some nations, including Switzerland, permit assisted suicide. In The

Netherlands, children as young as 12 can request assistance to end their lives; in Luxembourg the minimum age is 18.

For Dr Stefaan Van Gool, a paediatrician at the University of Leuven, the new laws in Belgium amount to "giving lethal injections to children". He was one of more than 170 paediatricians who signed an open letter this week urging parliament to postpone its decision.

"I have never had such a type of question so I don't see the urgency," he told The Independent, adding that he also feared that vulnerable children could become victims of misinterpretations of the law: "If one opens the door, you have no control any more of what is going through this door."

Paediatricians in favour of the amendment agree that young patients requesting euthanasia are rare. But they are thankful they can now openly discuss all the options when such a request is made, knowing that medical teams and the relatives of the child need not fear legal action.

"I can bear them suffering if that's their wish; what I can't bear is that I can't talk about other solutions and discuss with my patients what they think about this," said Dr Jutte Van der Werf Ten Bosch, a paediatric oncologist from University Hospital Brussels. "That makes me feel that I'm a coward and I'm not giving them all the possibilities."

The Independent, 13 February 2014

Protestors at an anti-euthanasia demonstration in Brussels. The red cards stand for a 'no' vote.
© Virginia Mayo/AP/Press Association Images

Body image

The hidden truths behind a transformation pic!

Check out my transformation! It took me 15 minutes. Wanna know my secret?

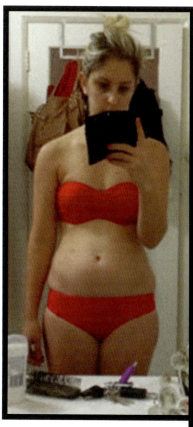

After a big breakfast one morning I chucked on my bather bottoms (that are a bit on the snug side), I stood with my feet together, pushed out my stomach, pulled out my hip phat (yes with a ph), hunched my shoulders forward, looked sad and took a few snaps.

Then I underwent my transformation- Using these fat loss supplements:

FAKE TAN, HAIR EXTENSION, BLACK SWIMSUIT BOTTOMS, PHONE WALLET (DITCHED)

Well firstly I ditched the phonewallet, swapped my bather bottoms to black (cause they're a size bigger & black is slimming), Smothered on some fake tan, clipped in my hair extensions, stood up a bit taller, sucked in my guts, popped my hip, threw in a skinny arm, stood a bit wider, pulled my shoulders back and added a bit of a cheeky/'I'm so proud of my results' smile. Zoomed in on the before pic, zoomed out on the after & added a filter. Cos filters make everything awesome.

I believe my image illustrates my point, that images can be deceiving. But I really want to touch on another point that I feel is

SOME ISSUES:

Do you think these types of images online are encouraging or damaging to people's self-esteem?

Is the writer here doing a good thing by debunking the myth?

Why do you think so many people are concerned with their appearance?

Is this an issue about health or only about body image?

I believe my image illustrates my point, that images can be deceiving

the bigger concern: what a before and after shot doesn't tell you is how the person achieved it. It doesn't tell you if they did it a healthy way or if they starved themselves for weeks on end to get there. It also doesn't show you the person's mental state, their self worth, how many hours of exercise they did, the lifestyle changes, the early mornings, the skipped lunches or how they handled social situations.

To illustrate this, let me give you the very honest low down on my own real life transformation photo. That took a whole lot more effort then a few hair extensions and some fake tan. Although, I certainly utilized some fancy lighting in my after shot.

This first one was taken in 2010 on a family holiday shortly after I had returned from exchange in America. Whilst there I gained around 7-8kg because I had THE GREATEST TIME OF MY LIFE! I went to Vegas twice, I tried all the food, I

This first one was taken in 2010 in America... I gained 7-8kg because I had THE GREATEST TIME OF MY LIFE!

enjoyed a drink or two, I went out dancing, I had desserts, and really had the most amazing time. Although I remember feeling unhappy about my body in that photo, to be honest I didn't really care that much - I knew I would lose the weight eventually. I had lots of friends, I was confident, I went out all the time and people just gathered around me to soak up my awesomeness. Haha ok ok, maybe not, but I was pretty carefree!

The second one was taken 3 years later. During that time I had become obsessed with fitness, I was a fitness instructor taking upwards of 8 classes a week and had recently become a personal trainer. I decided that I could get a six pack in eight weeks and, to do that, I had to completely over-haul my life. I stuck to a very strict diet plan, I socially isolated myself, I avoided certain restaurants, I stopped drinking on the weekends, I went out – but I drove and usually left early. I avoided my Nonna's house so I didn't have to eat her AMAZING food.

The tricks of the trade: Transformation tools – fake tan, hair extension, black swimsuit bottoms, phone wallet (ditched)

I had become obsessed with fitness … I looked good on the outside - but I was a mess on the inside.

I become totally obsessed with my progress, I had my skin folds done weekly, I trained like a dog and rescheduled my photo shoot 2 times so that I would have 'more time' to get leaner. By the time the photo shoot finally happened It was almost 6 months later, I was exhausted, Yeah I looked good on the outside- but I was a mess on the inside. I was tired, moody, I'd tainted good friendships and I actually really hated the person I had become.

It is now almost a full year later, and I can now say I have a much healthier relationship with myself and with food. I still train 4-5 times a week, and I still eat a very healthy diet, but I am much more relaxed about my meals. Now don't get me wrong, I'm all about having a big goal and achieving it, and doing what I did has taught me so much about food, exercise and myself, but was it all worth it? I'm honestly not sure it was.

I can safely say, I finally feel like the old, bubbly, self confident, smart ass me is back and although my booty

has grown, and my jeans are a little tighter, I'm actually living again. So my advice to you if you want to change your physique, is to make small changes towards your goals. Stop wanting results in a week, or a month, make changes you can sustain- be patient and consistent. Don't stop going out with your friends. Learn about food, come up with an achievable plan for you and most importantly enjoy how you exercise and live your life.

Oh and transformation shots are great, but let it be clear – that being thinner doesn't always mean you'll be happier, transformations take time, and good lighting can make buddah have a six pack.

Mel xx

melvfitness.com.au
www.facebook.com/melvfitness
Instagram: @melvfitness

Melanie Ventura is a personal trainer living in Melbourne, Australia. She has worked in the fitness industry since 2009. She is the author of an e-book "Have your cake and get lean too – a guide to counting macros".

I can safely say, I finally feel like the old, bubbly, self confident, smart ass me is back and although my booty has grown, and my jeans are a little tighter, I'm actually living again

Don't blame celebrities or pro-ana websites for the rise in eating disorders

More has to be done to work on prevention and early intervention in cases of eating disorders – and that isn't simply about banning websites

Ilona Burton

SOME ISSUES:

Do you think the rise in eating disorders can be tackled?

How can people best develop a healthy relationship with food and eating?

Do you think celebrity culture plays a role in eating disorders?

How can newspapers report eating disorders responsibly?

I am not 'pro-ana', far from it; but when it's blamed for the massive rise in the total number of people being treated for eating disorders, I will defend it.

'Pro-anorexia' websites are sickening; the result of a minority of people affected by eating disorders piling their obsession with food and weight loss onto vulnerable individuals. They share 'tips and tricks' of the depressing trade and serve to encourage the existing element of fierce competition. Then there are the pictures, or 'thinspiration'. We're aware of what these look like – images of dead-eyed catwalk models, a stack of ribs in spotlights, or emaciated young women contorted and stretched to show off their spines like prize xylophones.

We've seen these images, but we certainly haven't all developed a fascination with them through 'pro-ana' websites.

More than 6,500 children and teenagers were treated in hospital in 2010/11 – 150 of those aged nine or under - for conditions such as anorexia, compared with 1,718, in 2007/8. These figures have been revealed amidst growing worries that there is not enough treatment for those with eating disorders and, for those who are lucky enough to access treatment, the waiting times are often so long that conditions deteriorate rapidly, resulting in longer, more costly hospital stays. Many are turned away, told that their BMI isn't low enough – with a mental illness which instils the belief that you're never thin enough, you're worthless, this kind of 'treatment' only serves to feed into that belief, worsening the illness both mentally and physically.

More has to be done to work on prevention and early intervention of eating disorders – and that isn't simply about banning websites.

Some reports on these figures blame 'pro-ana' websites and celebrity culture,

> Some reports on these figures blame 'pro-ana' websites and celebrity culture, but those publications are the ones that re-post these dangerous images

but those publications are the ones that re-post these dangerous images, that include graphic detail of how their case studies got to their lowest weight, that obsess over the most extreme cases of anorexia, all of which read like a how-to guide, and they incessantly analyse images of bikini-clad celebrities. Too thin, too fat, pouring curves, containing curves… We're bombarded much more intensely, on a much more regular basis not by 'pro-ana', but by publications that hypocritically blame eating disorders on anything but themselves.

My anorexia began at seven, and I continued to find new, inventive ways to dispose of my food without people noticing. It's clear through my 20 years of eating disorders, that my illness had nothing to do with celebrity culture or the internet. In hospital, the majority of patients disagreed that the media and fashion worlds played a part in their eating disorders.

During my illness, I was far too wrapped up in my own world of starvation to notice what was going on around me, but through recovery, I became aware that 'normal' people seemed increasingly worried about what they were allowing to pass their lips. Impressionable children and teens were being taught what's 'good', 'bad' and 'naughty'. People were being judged on food choices. Calories were inescapable; on packaging and scrawled across restaurant menus, taking any element of fun or enjoyment out

> It's the way that families and friends talk about food and weight which will have the biggest impact on shaping the way they think and act around food. 'Good' and 'bad' need to be replaced with 'balance' and 'enjoyment'.

of eating out. There's constant analysis and judgement of everything we eat and that is more catching than we might think. Good health and nutrition is important – but that shouldn't ever induce feelings of guilt for daring to indulge in pudding.

Young people absorb and echo the beliefs and behaviours that exist around them, but rather than blaming the Rihannas and Delevignes, we should look closer to home. It's the way that families and friends talk about food and weight which will have the biggest impact on shaping the way they think and act around food. 'Good' and 'bad' need to be replaced with 'balance' and 'enjoyment'.

Eating disorders develop through complex combinations of factors and pressures which differ from person to person. The fact that so many young people are now requiring hospital treatment proves that not enough is being done to pick up on these illnesses early enough;

even more education, awareness and understanding is needed at every level.

We need to stop scapegoating and start taking responsibility. There are no easy solutions to the seemingly unstoppable rise in cases of eating disorders, but if one thing is true, we need to look closer to home than Hollywood to find the answers.

The Independent, 3 December 2013

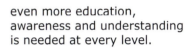

More education, awareness and understanding is needed at every level.

WHY MEN NEVER DISCUSS BODY IMAGE ISSUES

Quentin Vennie

An American writer and speaker on wellbeing and fitness

SOME ISSUES:

Do you think body image issues affect men as well as women?

Does he have an accurate view of what women expect in a man?

Why do you think men and women feel differently about their body image?

What things do you think contribute towards people's ideas about body image?

What can be done to help people have a more positive body image?

During a recent conversation with my close friend Daryl, a very interesting topic came up. A topic that I've never really touched on, thought about or discussed prior to that conversation - body image.

It's no secret that women have been battling this for years and even today, with all of our modern advancements, it's evident that we still have a long way to go.

With society's hand on the pulse of popularity, I'm often left to wonder - why don't men ever talk about body image issues?

Would we be deemed sensitive or weak if we discussed the dissatisfaction of our appearance? Would we not be looked at as protectors and/or leaders if we honestly admitted that we have physical insecurities? Has pop culture demoralized morality and influenced masculinity to the point that men have disassociated themselves with the authenticity of vulnerability?

Again, I'm left to wonder.

Body image issues have never been an easy topic to discuss. Proudly, women have started fighting back against antagonistic criticism, while men have yet to admit that an issue actually exists. The problem is there are way too many men suffering in silence.

Let's face it, as much as men hate to admit it, we are very self-conscious about our bodies!

As a trainer, I've helped countless men and women vanquish their self-doubt and regain their confidence. I've had male clients admit to their fears of being nude around women. I've had guys confess to having lacklustre sex lives due to the anxiety associated with their perceived body image.

In fact, body image issues are very common amongst men despite popular opinion, and I'm no exception. I've battled my own body image issues from childhood into my adult life.

Growing up, I was always the short, skinny kid. I like to think I was a popular child, but that didn't stop me from being singled out and castigated. Kids would jump in front of me in the line for recess and make fun of me because I was short.

EVEN AS AN ADULT I FACED UNCERTAINTY. I'M NOT AS SUAVE AS IDRIS ELBA, OR AS TALL AS WILL SMITH!

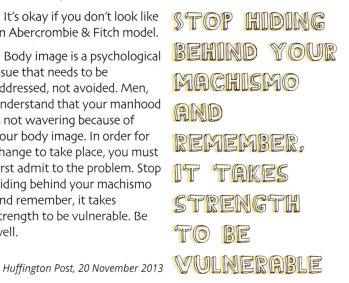

Idris Elba at the 2014 Palm Springs International Film Festival Awards
Image: Jaguar PS / Shutterstock.com

I've gotten into quite a few altercations in my adolescent years because people thought they could intimidate or bully me due to my size.

Even as an adult I've faced uncertainty. I was never the guy that women swooned over. I'm not as suave as Idris Elba or as tall as Will Smith. During the conversation with my friend, he and I laughed about how we were always considered the cute guys - only recently graduating to handsome. We're both members of the Under Six Feet Tall Club.

In fact, prior to adopting a regular exercise routine, I was only 128 pounds soaking wet with Timberland work boots on. If the wind blew too hard, I would be flying alongside pieces of debris (I'm exaggerating, but you get the point).

It was only five years ago that I started to embrace who I was. I saw what I didn't like about myself and I changed what I had control over.

When it comes to relationships, women tend to look for a man to be a provider, a protector, a leader and a partner. The typical woman's man is generally tall with a muscular physique. In the paleolithic age they would've been known as the hunter gatherers - the guys chopping firewood, building forts and killing cattle.

But what about the 26-year-old account executive that's 5-feet, 9-inches tall, slim, toned and weighs 148 pounds? How about the 6-foot, 3-inch, overweight, 41-year-old construction worker? Have you considered the 58-year-old schoolteacher with back hair and an untrimmed beard?

Since they don't fit the conventional physical attributes that media would consider "hot," are they excluded from being protectors, providers and leaders? Not at all, but I bet some think they are.

Men often combat their dilemma with body image by becoming exercise dependent, which can lead to overtraining and increased injury. Some will indulge in steroid use or entertain ambiguous fad diets for quicker (short-term) results.

Others become immersed in their sorrows, seeking refuge from public events and social gatherings. Both are behavioural pitfalls that I've seen a number of times.

It doesn't matter what body type you fall under - skinny, thick, tall or short, at some point I'm sure you have been self-absorbed with your body image. Stop being afraid to address it! Stop living in misery! Change what you can control and embrace what you cannot change.

It's okay if you don't look like an Abercrombie & Fitch model.

Body image is a psychological issue that needs to be addressed, not avoided. Men, understand that your manhood is not wavering because of your body image. In order for change to take place, you must first admit to the problem. Stop hiding behind your machismo and remember, it takes strength to be vulnerable. Be well.

Huffington Post, 20 November 2013

STOP HIDING BEHIND YOUR MACHISMO AND REMEMBER, IT TAKES STRENGTH TO BE VULNERABLE

Paloma Faith on how to be confident in the spotlight

Singer Paloma Faith shares her secrets with Rachæl Dove

Prepare your mind

Before I go on stage, everyone has to leave my dressing-room to give me a quiet moment to myself. I run through my forthcoming performance in my head while doing my own hair and make-up. Taking time to think ahead is important preparation for any nerve-racking event, whether it's a big presentation or meeting your boyfriend's parents for the first time.

Look the part

Go into a vulnerable situation feeling your absolute best. For me, that means getting dressed up and wearing a bit of glam make-up. I really make an effort to accentuate my best features and always wear nice underwear - even if no one is going to see it - because I think it makes me stand more boldly. Looking confident on the outside helps you to feel confident on the inside.

SOME ISSUES:

Do you think the clothes you wear can affect the way you behave and your mood?

What do you think of the advice given here?

What advice would you give to others to make the best of themselves?

How important is it to be happy and confident?

Image: Featureflash / Shutterstock.com

Find supportive friends

I was very shy as a child. I had a dominating friend who often put me in situations where I didn't feel comfortable. Breaking off our friendship marked the point where I started to think for myself and feel much more confident. It's important to stand on your own two feet.

Look people in the eye; looking down is like putting yourself beneath them.

I act as if I am proud of my flaws.

Be certain of your flaws

If you harbour uncertainty about yourself and your actions, it makes other people feel uncertain about you too. For example, I'm a messy eater and I always spill food. Even if I feel embarrassed, I will point it out and confidently ask for a serviette so that people find it endearing or funny rather than awkward or weird. I act as if I am proud of my flaws; it's better than being self-deprecating, which makes you feel worse.

Stand tall

Look people in the eye; looking down is like putting yourself beneath them. When I enter a room, I make eye contact straightaway and follow it with some sort of physical contact. I find people who try too hard to be loud and have swagger irritating. I'd steer clear of acting like that. Being a confident person is not as superficial as having a loud voice.

I try not to compare myself to others; it can breed negative feelings.

Focus on your own path

I like to be pleased for my friends' successes but I try not to compare myself to others; it can breed negative feelings. Validation from others has its place, but I don't rely on it. It's good to know who you can turn to for an honest opinion. For me, it's my mum.

Keep calm and carry on

The playwright Antonin Artaud describes how we all play a role in society: a fireman adopts the role of a fireman, a secretary becomes a secretary. Remember that beneath the surface of their roles others feel insecure too. There are a lot of brave faces. Regardless of what is going on, I must play my part, even if I'm not at my most confident. The show must go on.

I must play my part, even if I'm not at my most confident. The show must go on.

The Daily Telegraph, 8 December 2013
© Telegraph Media Group Limited 2013

Britain &
its citizens

Photo: William Perugini / Shutterstock.com

WHAT ARE YOU LIKE?

WHAT'S THE TRUTH ABOUT YOUNG PEOPLE TODAY?

In February 2014 the think tank, Demos, published a report about young people. It began: "Today's teenagers will shape the future of our country and our planet. If you believed the headlines, our outlook would look distinctly gloomy."

For their analysis, the Demos researchers looked at 10 years' worth of articles mentioning young people. They examined six different papers - the Guardian, the Telegraph, the Times, the Sun, the Daily Mail and the Daily Mirror. They found that the most common words, across all the publications, included crime (six mentions), those related to alcohol and drunkenness (eleven mentions), smoking and drugs (six mentions), and sex and pregnancy (five mentions). Some of the most frequently occurring words and phrases included 'binge drinking', 'yobs', 'immature', 'riots', 'crime' and 'alcohol'.

This is the portrait of today's youth in the newspapers. But how close does it come to the reality?

Demos conducted a survey of 1,000 14–17-year olds in England and Northern Ireland, as well as a separate survey of 500 secondary school teachers across the UK and their findings were quite different to that of the newspapers. Their research, in fact, caused them to label today's young people Generation C: C for caring, community minded, connected, concerned. In short they are Generation Citizen.

SOME ISSUES:

Why do you think the media present such a negative image of young people?

Should the media consider how their reporting affects young people?

Which description of young people matches your experience of your generation?

If people your age have 'a strong moral compass' where did that come from?

TOP TEN FINDINGS OF THE DEMOS REPORT:

1 SOCIAL ISSUES

Both the teenagers themselves and their teachers thought that teenagers now were more concerned about social issues, more active about them and more likely to volunteer for good causes and organisations than previous generations.

> **SOME OF THE MOST FREQUENTLY OCCURRING WORDS TO DESCRIBE TEENAGERS IN NEWSPAPERS INCLUDED 'BINGE DRINKING', 'YOBS', 'IMMATURE', 'RIOTS', 'CRIME' AND 'ALCOHOL'.**

2 TRADITIONAL POLITICS

Young people do not think that traditional politics is the most effective means of tackling social issues. Despite this, 84% said they intended to vote when they turned 18.

They are open to being engaged in politics and still see voting as a civic duty but they are committed to effecting change in different ways.

3 ACTING FOR POSITIVE CHANGE IN LOCAL COMMUNITIES

They have a strong sense of individual responsibility and are not looking to government to make a difference. They see positive change in their communities coming from charities, social enterprises, campaigners and businesses. 64% of teenagers thought that by getting involved themselves they could make a difference in their local community.

4 VOLUNTEERING AND SOCIAL ACTION

The Community Life Survey for 2012–13 showed a significant increase in volunteering rates among 16–19-year-olds compared with 2010-11.

Over half of teenagers in the Demos survey reported that they had raised money for charity; 35% had signed a petition to support local or national issues; and a third helped an organisation such as a local charity. Three out of four teenagers said they wanted to take part in a social action and volunteering programme.

5 VOLUNTEERING HAS BENEFITS

Among those who did volunteer, over 90% said it made them 'feel better about themselves', 'care more about others', 'work better in a team' or 'improved their self-confidence'.

The majority felt that volunteering gave them a better chance of getting a job and made them work harder at school and want to go further in their education. An added benefit was that they became friends with people they would otherwise never have met.

Teachers were very positive about the effects of volunteering on the social and personal development of their students, (though less than half thought there was any improvement in learning.)

6 USING SOCIAL MEDIA FOR SOCIAL ACTION

Substantial proportions of teenagers reported using social media for activities like raising awareness and funds for charity, and expressing support for political causes:

38% had signed a petition online; 29% had used Facebook or Twitter to raise awareness of a cause; 21% had 'liked' a political cause or group that they agreed with. 19% had donated money online.

Most teenagers agreed that using social media was an effective way to gain momentum behind social issues and that social media were just as important as more traditional ways for raising awareness of social issues.

7 WHAT CONCERNS TEENAGERS THE MOST?

Demos found that the social issues that teenagers are most concerned about are:

- unemployment and access to work (43%)
- living costs (34%)
- bullying (28%)
- crime (27%)
- student debt (23%)

TEACHERS DISAGREED STRONGLY WITH THESE STEREOTYPES AND WERE MUCH MORE LIKELY TO DESCRIBE TEENAGERS IN POSITIVE TERMS

9 SOCIAL CONSCIENCE IN CAREERS AND CONSUMING

Teenagers express their social conscience through the choices they make as consumers and in the careers that they aspire to:

- 77% said that being happy with the ethical record of their employer was essential.
- 70% said that it was important that they were involved in a career that helped change the world for the better.
- Three out of five teenagers specifically would like a career that helped people less fortunate than themselves.

While making money was still important to most, they are clearly still strongly motivated for careers that go above and beyond financial security.

10 INSPIRATIONAL LEADERS AND ROLE MODELS

Demos wanted to know who in the public eye teenagers look up to most as role models:

Nelson Mandela was by far the most mentioned individual, followed by Barack Obama and David Beckham.

While one in four teenagers mentioned celebrities, such as singers, actors, TV presenters, comedians and footballers as their role models, they usually chose those who have used their fame to back worthwhile social causes. The actress Jennifer Lawrence, for example, was often cited as promoting a healthy body image and David Beckham was described as being a family man alongside his thriving career.

Teenagers also mentioned a wide variety of other role models, including politicians, royals, parents, teachers, entrepreneurs and people who do something worthwhile for society.

One in five teenagers stated that they had no role models in the public eye and many stated specifically that they did not admire celebrities.

The report concludes that today's teenagers may not be politically active in the same way as other generations but "they have a strong moral compass and desire to make positive impacts in their communities ...It is time that we as a society recognise this and give credit where credit is due, and support where support is needed. Our future depends on it."

Source: Demos, Introducing Generation Citizen,
February 2014
www.demos.co.uk

> **MOST TEENAGERS AGREE THAT SOCIAL MEDIA ARE JUST AS IMPORTANT AS MORE TRADITIONAL WAYS FOR RAISING AWARENESS OF SOCIAL ISSUES.**

8 NEGATIVE MEDIA PORTRAYALS HAVE A BAD IMPACT

Teenagers feel they are too often negatively stereotyped and this affects how they connect with the world around them.

A large majority considered that the negative view from the media was having an adverse impact on their lives by:

- affecting employment opportunities
- making them less willing to reach out to those outside of their peer group
- making them less actively engaged in their community.

More than half of teachers thought that the media portray teenagers as 'lacking in respect'; 'lazy'; and 'anti-social'. They disagreed strongly with these stereotypes and were much more likely to describe teenagers in positive terms.

THESE MIGRANT FIGURES ARE GOOD FOR OUR ECONOMY

STRINGENT TARGETS FOR NET MIGRATION COULD DAMAGE LONDON'S AND BRITAIN'S PROSPERITY

VINCE CABLE, BUSINESS SECRETARY

SOME ISSUES:

Why do you think some newspapers have so many negative stories about immigration?

How does immigration help the country and its economy?

What should be done to make sure the facts about immigration issues are printed, and not false stories?

Do you ever want to travel, study or work abroad?

London illustrates the broadly positive impact of immigration on Britain. Thirty-four per cent of the city's population is foreign-born.

In the capital, successive waves of migrants have provoked a negative reaction before being absorbed. Freed slaves, Huguenots and Asian seamen in the Port of London. Jewish refugees from the pogroms of Tsarist Russia. Irish construction workers. Black Caribbeans who manned the buses and the NHS. Sikhs in Southall. Bangladeshis in Tower Hamlets. Asians fleeing Kenya and Uganda. Then, in the 1990s, refugees from the Balkans. Latterly, Polish and Lithuanian workers following EU accession (and French tax refugees). Perhaps Ukrainians next?

The immigration debate has seen a subtle shift from arguments about race to arguments about net migration of (mainly white) Europeans. In fact, racism is in welcome retreat. Mixed marriages are now commonplace. The population of white British people who would "mind a lot" about having black boss has fallen from almost 30 per cent three decades ago to under 10 per cent. That figure is still 10 per cent too high, but it shows attitudes are changing.

As for net migration, until recently the number of immigrants roughly balanced the number of emigrants. In the 1960s and 1970s, when immigration was an especially toxic issue, net immigration was actually negative: more people left than arrived. But they had a different complexion. The anti-immigration backlash, captured most notoriously in Enoch Powell's speeches, was essentially about colour and culture.

In the past decade and a half, however, net immigration has averaged about 200,000 per annum. New arrivals from Eastern Europe are not conspicuous in the streets. But the rising numbers have added to anxieties about housing, public services, jobs and welfare benefits. No politician could possibly be unaware of public concern. After five years of economic hardship, people are feeling insecure.

Politicians should start by sticking to the facts. The proportion of foreign nationals in our population from immigration this century is actually lower than in Germany, Sweden, Norway, Belgium, Spain and Switzerland. Roughly two million Brits reside on the Continent, about the same as continental Europeans living here: one of the liberating achievements of the EU.

In the decade since 2001, recent migrants from the EU paid in 34 per cent more tax than they took out in benefits

THE PROPORTION OF FOREIGN NATIONALS IN OUR POPULATION FROM IMMIGRATION THIS CENTURY IS ACTUALLY LOWER THAN IN GERMANY, SWEDEN, NORWAY, BELGIUM, SPAIN AND SWITZERLAND.

and services. Far from being a mass of unskilled people, a third of European immigrants and 43% of non-European migrants have university degrees, compared with 21 per cent of British adults. And overseas students make up around 17 per cent of the student population of 2.5 million and contribute £9 billion to the UK economy - making them one of our leading exports.

The evidence is that, overall, immigrant workers do not displace British workers. Last year 90 per cent of new jobs - almost 400,000 - went to British workers, despite rising immigration. During the recession, youth unemployment - which is a genuinely worrying problem - grew faster in areas with lower immigration rates.

"Benefit tourism" arouses understandable resentment but is very small in practice: fewer than 3% of jobseekers allowance claimants are from other EU countries.

Inflationary pressures in the London housing market are undoubtedly fuelled by rising numbers of people but the biggest damage is being done by marketing property overseas to people who don't actually live here.

The current political debate centres on net immigration numbers. Almost 80 per cent of the public say they want a reduction, though their ire is directed at asylum seekers and illegal immigrants, not students and skilled workers who make up most of the net immigrants. The policy focus on stemming this flow of skilled people and students does not address the public's concerns and damages our economic recovery.

Last week's immigration numbers caused serious embarrassment for the Conservative side of the Coalition. Net immigration in the year to September 2013 rose to 212,000, making their target of "tens of thousands" look

unrealistic. Let me be clear - the Coalition Government has no such target. It is a Conservative manifesto pledge and frankly, if they had any sense, they would drop it. Leading Conservatives such as Liam Fox seem to agree. Either they will have egg on their faces next year as the target is missed, or they will undermine the UK economy as they try to meet it.

is hit. There has recently been a crackdown on the undoubted abuse of visas by some private colleges but the consequence of tightening the rules has been to drive away bona fide students, especially from India, to the US, Canada and Australia. Universities, and Britain, are poorer as a result.

Among this Government's stated aims is the creation of

'BENEFIT TOURISM': FEWER THAN 3% OF JOBSEEKERS ALLOWANCE CLAIMANTS ARE FROM OTHER EU COUNTRIES

The net immigration target makes no sense. Net immigration rises if emigration - Britons leaving the country - falls. Surely that is a good thing? Surely we want British people to stay in Britain? Then, a significant number - around 100,000 "immigrants" - are British people returning from overseas. Surely we don't want to keep them out?

One of the biggest categories of "immigrants" is overseas students - 176,000 last year, over a third of the total. They are not immigrants but they are defined as such because they are here for more than a year. Take them out of the figures and the "tens of thousands" target

an open, innovative, exporting economy. To achieve this we need the skills and experience of migrant workers and overseas visitors. But we must also enforce the National Minimum Wage, give young people the skills they need and protect employment rights. Ideally, migrants come here and help us grow and help more Brits into work in the process. Last week's figures suggest that our approach is the right one.

*London Evening Standard,
3 March 2014*

MIGRANTS COME HERE AND HELP US GROW AND HELP MORE BRITS INTO WORK IN THE PROCESS

As Britain becomes more multi-ethnic, what will happen to 'Englishness'?

The Policy Exchange report on Britain's ethnic minority population, A Portrait of Modern Britain, is a first-class bit of work, full of important and interesting facts about us and our nation. I heartily recommend reading the whole thing, but there's one aspect I'd like to focus on: national identity.

James Kirkup

This has always been a complicated subject in a country that has been multinational for centuries: England, Wales and Scotland are all nations that are part of another nation-state. And let's not even talk about Northern Ireland for now.

As someone who grew up near the Border and has lived and worked on both sides of it, I've always been intrigued by the blurring of British and English identities. For generations, England effectively submerged itself in Britain: people from England were apt to use the two as synonyms. Scots, meanwhile, knew and felt the difference. (That's recent, of course: not so very long ago a lot of Scots celebrated their imperial status and proclaimed themselves North British.)

SOME ISSUES:

Which nationality do you identify with?

What do you think is the difference between Englishness and Britishness?

Why do you think more non-white people identify with Britishness?

Is nationality all that important?

So figures highlighted by Policy Exchange on Englishness, Britishness and ethnicity are fascinating.

To be clear, Policy Exchange is not saying that an increasingly non-white population poses some sort of threat to Englishness, and neither am I. The

> While non-white people were keen to embrace the notion of Britain and call themselves British, the English identity is largely the preserve of white people

In summary: While non-white people were keen to embrace the notion of Britain and call themselves British, the English identity is largely the preserve of white people, the paper suggests.

Some 64 per cent of white people describe themselves as solely "English" with no other national identity.

Far fewer non-white people identify themselves as English: only 12 per cent of Indian Britons described themselves as English. Among those of Pakistani origin, the figure was 15 per cent, and 26 per cent for black people of Caribbean descent.

Some 71 per cent of Banglasdeshi-heritage people described themselves as British with no other nationality. For those of Pakistani descent, it is 63 per cent, and 58 per cent for Indians.

By contrast, only 14 per cent of white people described themselves only as "British", with most preferring to identify with one of the nations of the UK.

report makes clear that far from undermining our predominant national identity — Britishness — Black Minority Ethnic people generally reinforce it.

Nevertheless, there is clearly a demographic challenge to Englishness here. If the UK population is to become steadily less white, how viable will Englishness be if only white people subscribe to it? How can England persuade many of its non-white residents to fly its flag? And what will happen to it

Would it really be such a bad thing if Englishness withered while Britishness flourished?

if they do not? Would it really be such a bad thing if Englishness withered while Britishness flourished? The Victorians certainly would not have thought so; attachment to individual nationalities within the Union is relatively recent thing, after all.

And remember, all this is without even touching on the challenge to Englishness from below, the sub-national level: the Cornish are increasingly asserting themselves, and the number of counties flying their own flags is rising; before long, my Northumbrian brethren will surely rise and be a nation once again.

What happens to England in the increasingly multi-ethnic, multinational Britain of the mid-21st century? It's a big, important and yes, sensitive question. Policy Exchange should be commended for a report that is thought-provoking in the best way.

Daily Telegraph, 6 May 2014
© Telegraph Media Group Limited 2014

What happens to England in the increasingly multi-ethnic, multinational Britain of the mid-21st century?

Benefits Street: How it feels for those of us who are judged because of our background

Many watch with a comfortable sense of distance. They forget that you are only ever a bad decision away from having to rely on state support

Dom Anderson

SOME ISSUES:

Do you think that TV programmes can be responsible for how people are viewed in society?

Do TV companies have a responsibility to show people in a fair light?

Why do you think society is so quick to judge those who are not as privileged as others?

What should be done to help people be more kind towards each other, regardless of circumstance?

A lot has been written about Channel 4 class warfare reality show Benefits Street*. My issue wasn't just with the show; I grew up and hung around an estate much like the one depicted on the programme, what really got to me is the reaction on social media.

I looked down both my Twitter and Facebook timelines with despair as I saw people pouring scorn on the 'scum' that feature on the show. It must be great to live a privileged enough existence to be able to sit in judgement of people less fortunate.

I grew up in a place called Sinfin in Derby, which has a high rate of people who claim some sort of state support. A large amount of the housing there is or has been local authority. The houses that are former housing association are generally owned by people who have a large property portfolio and have never lived in the area.

It's the same old story of people with no link to a community getting rich from properties that were built to be state assets. There is a stigma even in Sinfin around the people who live in houses owned by the council. Stigma that is fed by government narratives of scroungers and skivers and by programmes like Benefits Street.

The tweets about the addictions of some of the residents were heartbreaking to read. Addiction is terrible, but I don't believe that it is something anyone would choose to have. Addiction is a condition much like and often linked to depression, and often the result of difficult circumstances that people have suffered.

Watching the show was tough, as it filled me with fear and anguish for the people in it. And then you had people like Joey Barton tweeting his disgust for the lifestyles of the people on

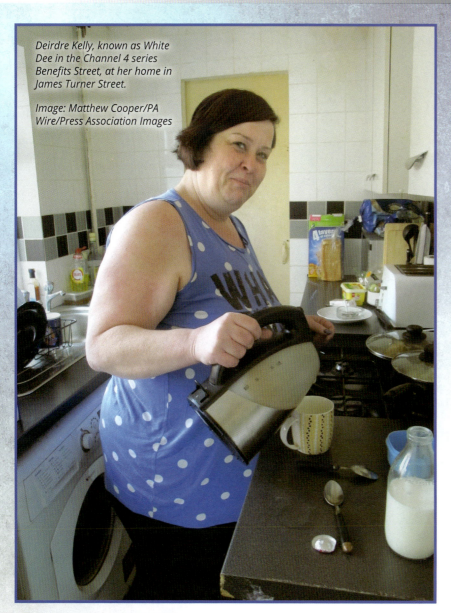

Deirdre Kelly, known as White Dee in the Channel 4 series Benefits Street, at her home in James Turner Street.

Image: Matthew Cooper/PA Wire/Press Association Images

There is a stigma around the people who live in houses owned by the council. Stigma that is fed by programmes like Benefits Street

that you are only ever a bad decision away from having to rely on state support. Some people I grew up with refuse to acknowledge their upbringing and roots, and this programme builds on the notion that you should be ashamed to be raised on a housing estate with poor people.

It makes me and others feel that we are inferior to those around us from 'better stock'. It is bad enough that at times and in certain settings I am already made to feel acutely like I don't belong there - this programme and the reactions to it spread far and wide by social media only serve to make that worse.

The Independent, 21 January 2014

*Benefits Street: According to Channel 4 "This documentary series reveals the reality of life on benefits, as the residents of one of Britain's most benefit-dependent streets invite cameras into their tight-knit community."

The five-episode series proved to be extremely controversial. It provoked strong views both in support of and against this community and sparked debates about welfare. Some residents felt that they had been misrepresented and exploited by the makers of the programme.

the show: "Strong evidence to support the breeding licence theory...", tweeted the footballer, among other judgmental remarks.

It seems money can buy you a nice house and nice things but it cannot buy you empathy. Let's hope that for the rest of his life he is squeaky clean.

And what about White Dee? She has two children with dual ethnic heritage. I watched my Twitter feed fill with words like 'slob', 'tramp' and 'skank' as she came on screen. I watched in disgust as people

suggested she should just 'get off her fat arse and get a job'. There seemed a palpable undertone of racism to the way people viewed her children being dual heritage. I was brought up by a white mother and white grandparents and I can tell you first hand that I always found confusion when considering my own ethnicity, imagine how those young people feel seeing the tweets about them.

People seemed to be watching the programme with a comfortable sense of distance. They forget

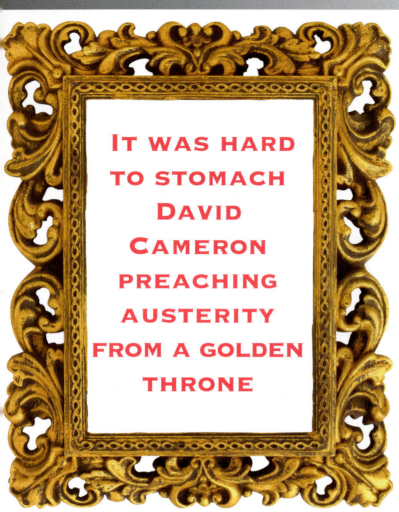

IT WAS HARD TO STOMACH DAVID CAMERON PREACHING AUSTERITY FROM A GOLDEN THRONE

AS A WAITRESS AT THE LORD MAYOR'S BANQUET, THE CONTRAST BETWEEN WHAT CAMERON WAS SAYING AND WHERE HE WAS SAYING IT FELT PARTICULARLY CHILLING

RUTH HARDY

At a state banquet for the new Lord Mayor on Monday, David Cameron gave a speech about his commitment to the cause of permanent austerity. He stood up to speak from a golden chair, and read his notes from a golden lectern.

As it happens, I was at the banquet too and heard the news about permanent spending cutbacks for myself. Sadly I was not there as a dignitary, a foreign diplomat, a captain of industry or the director of a big City firm. I was there as a waitress. The contrast between what he was saying and where he was saying it seemed initially almost too laughable to get worked up about. But actually, it reflected something chilling in Cameron's attitude towards the people he purports to be working for.

I work evenings and weekends at an events company. The company is great and the hours are flexible, which allows me to combine it with my main job of an internship. It's tough, and I've been in a state of semi-tiredness for the last two months. I do get to work at interesting events, though, and the fanciness of the Guildhall banquet was breathtaking. Although, as one of my colleagues said: "I thought Boris Johnson was the lord mayor, that's the only reason I agreed to work!"

The guests enjoyed a champagne reception, and then were served a starter ("a celebration of British mushrooms"), a fish course and main course of fillet of beef, all served with wine of course. In the break before dessert, coffee, dessert wine, port, brandy and whisky were served, Cameron gave his speech. We retreated downstairs to a steam-filled kitchen, where we polished the cutlery. Most of us were exhausted by this point. Dinner service is physically demanding, and I am by no means the only person who combines two or three jobs. The contrast of the two worlds was striking; someone said it was like a scene from Downton Abbey.

Maybe Cameron didn't see the irony; perhaps he forgot about the army of waiting staff, cleaners, chefs and porters who were also present at the banquet. Perhaps he thought he was in a room of similarly rich people, who understood the necessity for austerity.

SOME ISSUES:

What do you think about the Prime Minister's speech?

Is it important for the Lord Mayor's Banquet and other events to be grand ceremonies?

This is one person's viewpoint. Should such personal views always be balanced by giving the opposing opinion?

THE GUESTS ENJOYED A CHAMPAGNE RECEPTION...CAMERON GAVE HIS SPEECH

Perhaps it didn't occur to him that this message might not be as easily comprehended by those who hadn't just enjoyed a four-course meal. Perhaps he forgot about those of us, disabled or unemployed or on the minimum wage, for whom austerity has had a catastrophic and wounding effect.

In his speech, Cameron talked about a "leaner, more efficient, more affordable state". He argued that austerity could be a permanent government policy; a way of trimming down the administrative excesses of some public services. He framed it in the context of the current tough living conditions – a minimising of state spending, as it "comes out of the pockets of the same taxpayers whose living standards we want to see improve".

No word yet, of course, on what changes will be made to the banquet he was speaking at. Perhaps next year there will only be three courses, or the dessert wine will be ruthlessly culled.

I wonder how Cameron and his government can do these things. Aside from the idiocy of calling for cuts while wearing a white tie – has the man never heard of Twitter – does he not see what welfare cuts are doing to the vulnerable in society? He enjoys a banquet, while the number of people using food banks has tripled in the past year. As someone on the shift with me said, "It gets annoying that we always serve free food to the people who really don't need free food."

The political content of what Cameron is saying is obviously more important than where he was saying it, but I don't think the latter is irrelevant. I have a fundamental problem with a man who sits on a golden throne and lectures us about spending less, like a modern-day, white-tie clad sheriff of Nottingham. And all around him, the insidious stain of austerity creeps across the country, manifesting in the bedroom tax, rising tuition fees and the closure of public services that vulnerable people depend on.

Each of us has just one chance at existence, and so many people's lives are being blighted by these cuts. If this is the cruel and damaging reality of permanent austerity, then we should be telling Mr Cameron we don't want it.

The Guardian, 13 November 2013
© Guardian News & Media 2013

PERHAPS NEXT YEAR THE DESSERT WINE WILL BE RUTHLESSLY CULLED

Yui Mok/PA Archive/Press Association Images

Photo: Fourman films, YouTube

Owen Jones's 'Agenda for Hope': We want a fairer society – and here's how we can achieve it

SOME ISSUES:

Do you think Britain is an equal and fair country?

What do you think about Mary's situation as outlined here?

Is Owen Jones right that the government and media promote an agenda of fear?

What do you think about his Agenda for Hope?

What would you have in your own Agenda for Hope?

Social and economic inequality blights Britain. Here's my nine-point manifesto for change

The alarm goes off. It's dark outside, and Mary wakes to get ready for work at the checkout of a local supermarket. Like most of Britain's poor, she has a job that leaves her and her children trapped below the poverty line. She finds herself competing with colleagues for overtime, just to earn a few more pounds to spend on her kids. Even though her employer makes hundreds of millions of pounds of profit a year, it is the taxpayer who has to step in and subsidise those poverty wages to give Mary a chance to pay the bills and feed her children.

Mary had a rough night's sleep because it's nearly time to pay the rent. She would love nothing more than a secure,

Because her rent is so extortionate, the taxpayer has to step in again, to make sure her landlord gets the rip-off sum he demands.

affordable home for her family but, like 5 million others, she's stuck on a council housing waiting list. Because her rent is so extortionate, the taxpayer has to step in again, to make sure her landlord gets the rip-off sum he demands.

On her way downstairs, Mary knocks on the door of her 19-year-old son, Michael. He is one of nearly a million unemployed young people. Michael sends in CV after CV, to supermarkets and call centres, and often does not even get a response. The odds are that being unemployed at such a young age will leave him with a lower wage, and an increased risk of being out of work, for the rest of his life.

As she approaches the front door, Mary glimpses another reason for her sleepless night: an unopened energy bill lying on her kitchen table. As the bills have soared, so the hot meals she eats have declined in number. And so Mary leaves for a gruelling shift at the supermarket, working hard to earn her poverty.

Mary isn't a real person, but there are millions of people in this country who share aspects of their lives with someone like her. We all have to pay, literally, as poverty-paying bosses and rip-off landlords milk our welfare state.

The Government and much of the media have answers for people like Mary. "Instead of being angry at your situation," Mary is told, "be angry at unemployed people, immigrants, public sector workers, or disabled claimants instead." It is an Agenda of Fear. The bankers who plunged Britain into disaster, the politicians in the pockets of the wealthiest, the rich tax-dodgers, the poverty-paying bosses and rip-off landlords – all are let off the hook. The Agenda of Fear makes sure that the real solutions to the problems faced by someone like Mary – and the nation as a whole – are never even discussed.

But we desperately need an Agenda of Hope. It is a series of policies that the next Government must implement if it is going to transform our country. They are not plucked out of nowhere. Polls show the British people overwhelmingly support a minimum wage that is a living wage, public ownership of our utilities, letting councils build houses, and tax justice. These are common-sense, mainstream ideas that are ignored by our political and media elite. When Ed Balls suggested restoring the 50p tax on the top 1 per cent of earners, he provoked near-hysteria among the political and media elite, and yet the polls show the British people support going even further.

The Government and much of the media have answers for people like Mary.
"Instead of being angry at your situation," Mary is told, "be angry at unemployed people, immigrants, public sector workers, or disabled claimants instead."
It is an Agenda of Fear.

The gentleman's agreement of British politics, which ensures that our national political debate is kept on the terms of the wealthy and powerful, has to end. But our history shows that change is never given: it has to be demanded. The polls show that some of these demands are backed even by Conservative voters. And no wonder. This isn't about left or right. It's about building a country run in the interests of those who keep it ticking, not run in the interests of the elite. That's what an Agenda of Hope can offer [see page 54].

Agenda for hope: A nine-point manifesto

1) A STATUTORY LIVING WAGE with immediate effect, for large businesses and the public sector, and phased in for small and medium businesses over a five-year Parliament. This would save billions spent on social security each year by reducing subsidies to low-paying bosses, as well as stimulating the economy, creating jobs because of higher demand, stopping pay being undercut by cheap labour, and tackling the scandal of most of Britain's poor being in work. An honest day's pay for an honest day's work would finally be enshrined in law.

2) RESOLVE THE HOUSING CRISIS by regulating private rents and lifting the cap on councils to let them build hundreds of thousands of houses and in doing so, create jobs, bring in rent revenues, stimulate the economy and reduce taxpayers' subsidies to landlords.

3) A 50 PER CENT TAX ON ALL EARNINGS ABOVE £100,000 – or the top 2 per cent of earners – to fund an emergency jobs and training programme for young unemployed people, including the creation of a national scheme to insulate homes and businesses across Britain, dragging millions of people out of fuel poverty, reducing fuel bills, and helping to save the environment. All such jobs will be paid the living wage, supported with paid apprenticeships rather than unpaid "workfare" schemes.

4) AN ALL-OUT CAMPAIGN TO RECOUP THE £25BN WORTH OF TAX AVOIDED BY THE WEALTHIEST EACH YEAR, clamping down on all possible loopholes with a General Anti-Tax Avoidance Bill, as well as booting out the accountancy firms from the Treasury who help draw up tax laws, then advise their clients on how to get around them.

5) PUBLICLY RUN, ACCOUNTABLE LOCAL BANKS. Transform the bailed-out banks into regional public investment banks, with elected taxpayers' representatives sitting on boards to ensure they are accountable. Give the banks a specific mandate to help small businesses and encourage the green industries of the future in each region.

6) AN INDUSTRIAL STRATEGY TO CREATE THE "GREEN JOBS" AND RENEWABLE ENERGY INDUSTRIES OF THE FUTURE. It would be focused on regions that have been damaged by deindustrialisation, creating secure, skilled, dignified jobs, and reducing unemployment and social security spending, based on an active state that intervenes in the economy, learning from the experiences of countries such as Germany.

7) PUBLICLY OWNED RAIL AND ENERGY, DEMOCRATICALLY RUN BY CONSUMERS AND WORKERS. As each rail franchise expires, bring them back into the public sector, with elected representatives of passengers and workers to sit on the new management boards, ending our fragmented, inefficient, expensive railway system. Build a publicly owned energy network by swapping shares in privately run companies for bonds, and again put elected consumers' representatives on the boards. Democratic public ownership instead of privatisation could be a model for public services like the NHS, too.

8) A NEW CHARTER OF WORKERS' RIGHTS FIT FOR THE 21ST CENTURY. End all zero-hour contracts, with new provisions for flexible working to help workers. Allow all unions access to workplaces so they can organise, levelling the playing field and giving them a chance to improve wages and living standards. Increase turnout and improve democratic legitimacy in union ballots by allowing workplace-based balloting and online voting.

9) A UNIVERSAL CHILDCARE SYSTEM that would pay for itself as parents who are unable to work are able to do so, and which would take on the inequalities between richer and poorer children that begin from day one.

The Independent, 26 January 2014

Education

Daughter inspires ambulance driver to go to university

A mature student tells his story of combining ambulance driving with a course in history

David Lucas

Parents are frequently inspired by their children, but it's not often that they follow in their educational footsteps like I did. My daughter inspired me to go and pursue a degree at university – something I never thought was possible at 52 years old.

I left school at 16 without any qualifications and went straight into full-time employment. Born to working-class parents in London, I started work at a newspaper wholesaler company and subsequently had several driving jobs; from vans, to lorries, to being a London taxi driver.

Throughout this time, I always had an interest in history, particularly social history and how people's lives changed in the course of big historical events such as WWII and the Industrial Revolution.

But I had never really considered pursuing this interest any further. I had a family, bills to pay and a full-time job to consider. For me, my time in education was in the distant past and the thought of returning to it was very alien.

It was only when my daughter, Sarah, started a BA in history and archaeology at Birkbeck, University of London, studying part-time and working full-time as a legal secretary, that my opinion changed. I started to consider a degree as an option for me.

But would I have what it takes? I had been out of education a long time and had never been particularly academic at school.

My daughter's experiences on her course, particularly

SOME ISSUES:

Is there anything that you do that has inspired your parents/ guardian?

What stops people continuing with their education?

Is there an advantage to coming into higher education later in life?

My daughter's experiences on her course, particularly the support she was given by the university, gave me the confidence to take the leap.

I was completely computer illiterate when I began, too, so I had to learn everything

the support she was given by the university, gave me the confidence to take the leap. The next year I enrolled to study a part-time history degree, during my daughter's final year.

Now I'm in my third year of a four-year course, and my daughter has been there to help every step of the way. It's been great to have someone to show me the best way to take notes in lectures, and get hints for writing essays from someone who has been through it. She continues to inspire me and has helped make something I thought might be impossible, possible.

That's not to say it's all been smooth sailing. I work for the London Ambulance Service, which means long 12-hour shifts that sometimes run into the evening and clash with lectures. I fit in university around work and I've even tried studying out of the back of an ambulance.

I'd never really written an essay before I started the course and had no idea of the amount of analytical reading I'd need to do. It's been a struggle to get to grips with the work load and go back to basics.

I was completely computer illiterate when I began, too, so I had to learn everything, from using

a Word document to researching historical texts from an online library catalogue.

The ambulance service team have been fantastic at helping me pursue this ambition, with colleagues swapping shifts with me and even on one occasion having a special period of leave for an important deadline. It's been a comfort to know my bosses are onboard with what I'm doing.

I was lucky enough to be able to fund my own way through my degree, but other part-time students, including mature students, have found they are eligible to access financial support.

In a year I will have a BA in history and will be over the moon about it. My degree will allow me to apply for roles I would not have been previously eligible for, and while I enjoy my current job, who

knows what the future holds?

Instead of driving past landmarks and wondering how they came to be there, I now go and find out more to expand my knowledge. It just goes to show that age really doesn't matter. If you want to do something and put your mind to it then it's possible – even if your children get there first.

The Guardian, 28 January 2014
© Guardian News & Media 2014

My degree will allow me to apply for roles I would not have been previously eligible for

We need to accept not all our kids are A* students

Not everyone is cut out to be an A student. I certainly wasn't but my ambition to be an actress was acknowledged and nurtured by my wonderful drama teacher and my parents – Denise Welch

SOME ISSUES:

Why do you think we focus so much on grades?

Do you think high grades are the most important thing to gain in your education?

What useful skills are not reflected in high school grades?

How can other types of skills be nurtured and developed?

Good luck to all those anxious teenagers picking up their A-level results. I hope you will all get the grades you no doubt worked very hard to achieve.

However, I'm saddened to hear reports from the excellent Prince's Trust that the fear of low grades is causing widespread depression and leading to increases in mental health problems for a large percentage of young people.

These vulnerable teenagers feel that if the desired grade is not achieved at A-level they are destined for a life on benefits and this may well be the message that their school is conveying.

A few years ago I took part in a BBC documentary called Playing The Part. The premise was that as I played Steph Haydock (the rubbish French teacher in an under-achieving school in the TV series Waterloo Road) I would take on the challenge of becoming a "real teacher" in my old real-life grammar school.

The fear of low grades is causing widespread depression

It was a terrifying experience as I was thrown in at the deep end and followed by cameras as I taught several classes over a week to see how I coped.

I have always had the utmost respect for teachers, but this respect grew as I realised how hard the job was. The pressure on the staff to reach the goals set in the school league tables means that the under-achievers get left behind in my opinion.

Not everyone is cut out to be an A student. I certainly wasn't but my ambition to be an actress was acknowledged and nurtured by my wonderful drama teacher Terry Cudden and my parents. Although I was encouraged to try my best academically it was obvious I wasn't Oxbridge-bound.

But during the TV documentary I got to spend time with one particular class and the teachers and the BBC were very keen to see how I fared with these pupils who were struggling academically and not expected to achieve much.

I loved every moment with them and there were tears from them and me when I left. They had not been given any alternatives for careers that could be obtained without A* grades and they felt they were on the scrapheap so early in their lives.

I asked them what they would like to do when they left school and as they grew to trust me their passions came to the fore. One boy, a very athletic lad, said he was determined to be a stuntman. One girl said she would love to try stand-up comedy and "why not?" I told them. Aim for the sky and you'll reach the mountain tops.

There is a huge demand for skilled manual workers – plumbers, bricklayers, carpenters, plasterers – and we need to encourage businesses to take on more apprentices so these kids can take pride in learning a trade.

The plumbers I know are making a damn sight more money than those I know stressed to hell in the City.

It's not the teachers' fault. Their schools are penalised if not enough A-level passes are achieved, but university is not for everyone.

*Manchester Evening News,
16 August 2013*

Aim for the sky and you'll reach the mountain tops

Untouchable, unwelcome and uneducated...

Why India's poorest children are not receiving an education

A new Human Rights Watch report shows how teachers and school officials fail to provide a welcoming environment for children from the lowest rungs of Indian society.

India researcher Jayshree Bajoria talks with Amy Braunschweiger about what needs to change.

SOME ISSUES:

What should be done to tackle the discrimination children face in schools?

Should the schools or the government be responsible for tackling this problem?

What cultural factors are affecting attendance?

How will the lack of an education for some affect society in general, now and in the future?

Who is dropping out?

Children from the poorest and the most marginalised communities such as Dalits – so-called "untouchables," at the bottom of India's caste system – Muslims and tribal members. Often these children are among the first generation in their families to have ever stepped inside a classroom, and very few of them make it to grade 8.

Why are they dropping out?

A number of reasons. The widespread problems of child labour and early marriage for girls are clearly factors. But our research shows the insidious and damaging impact of ingrained discrimination at school. Teachers will tell students from marginalised communities to sit at the back of class and then basically ignore them. They are often served their free school lunch only after all the other students. They are even asked to do tasks considered degrading, like cleaning the toilet – something that never happens to privileged kids. Teachers make derogatory remarks, or don't stop more privileged children from ostracising them. An unfriendly environment can make a child reluctant to attend classes, putting them at risk of dropping out.

Didn't India enact a law guaranteeing education?

The Right of Children to Free and Compulsory Education Act was an important step, though of course the challenges are enormous, considering the inequities built into Indian society for centuries. Since the law went into effect in 2010, primary school enrolment has shot up to nearly 100%, from 83% enrolment in 2001– a huge achievement for a country that six decades ago had staggering illiteracy levels. But while the law calls for a "child-friendly" classroom setting – one where each student is treated equally – this is clearly not happening in many places. And no one is being held responsible for creating unwelcoming environments.

What is the level of discrimination?

I had an eye-opening conversation in Uttar Pradesh state with the principal from a school attended by children from the Ghasiya tribe. The principal said that Ghasiya children are a big problem. She complained that they didn't wear school uniforms, and that their parents were illiterate. She said they didn't mix well and that they ruined the class for the other children – that nothing could be done with them. As I sat with her, we watched the Ghasiya kids walk into the school, and she pointed at them, saying, "See how dirty they are?" She complained that their eating habits were different, noting that these children ate meat, unlike the majority Hindus, many of whom are vegetarian. She even suggested that these children be put in a separate school.

Clearly, she did not like these children.

But here's what really struck me: going over the school records, I saw that 59 Ghasiya children attended the school, and 58 of them, irrespective of their ages, were in the 2nd grade. There was clearly a kind of segregation happening. So I travelled to the hamlet where the community lived to hear their side of the story.

What did the children say when you met them?

I spent a lot of time with the children and after a while they opened up to me. They said that the teachers made them sit in a corner. If one of the Ghasiya kids touches another child who wasn't Ghasiya, there's a ruckus, complaints, and a scolding from the teacher. They said they want to learn, but they rarely had a teacher in their classroom – no one was even teaching them properly.

The children are routinely called dirty and told to take a bath. But their settlement has no water or electricity. The children have to walk a kilometre to fetch water, which makes them late for school if they bathe before class.

What else did you learn?

My conversations with a girl we are calling "Meena" really affected me. One year after my first visit I returned to the school, and saw that none of the Ghasiya kids were there. So I went back to their village and spoke with Meena. She is 9 now, and when I first met her she was determined to learn but at the same time sad and angry about her treatment at school. A year later Meena told me that all the Ghasiya children were now rarely going to the government school and were attending a nearby charitable school. "Why should we go to government school when we don't learn anything?" she said. "We will go to a school where they treat us with love." Many are still at risk of dropping out.

Does the government know how many children are dropping out?

India doesn't keep accurate track of children who have dropped out. One Indian state defines a dropout as a student with three months of unexplained absences, but other states say it's one month or even seven days. How can the government set guidelines for intervening when students are in danger of dropping out if they don't have a common definition for a dropout? Additionally, three school principals admitted to us that they were inflating attendance records because of the pressure they felt from education authorities.

But teachers must know?

They do, but they aren't sure how to address the problem. When I asked principals and teachers at what point they worry about a child not coming

to school, many said they didn't know, and asked me how they should be addressing it. Many also said they had been told to never delete anyone's name from the register. A key step to fixing this problem is that teachers should accurately record attendance, and there should be a common definition of when a child is considered to have dropped out of school. This would pressure educational authorities to act in time.

What do you want to see happen?

Thanks to the Right to Education Act, nearly all Indian children are getting enrolled in school. We want them to stay there until graduation, and to do so, India needs to create a classroom atmosphere that inspires all children to learn, regardless of their backgrounds. Teachers are often a child's first role model, and a teacher's attitude can go a long way to keeping children in class. Teachers and principals need to be trained in inclusion. It's important for teachers who do discriminate to incur appropriate disciplinary measures. And India's education authorities are not being held to account for failing to enforce the law properly. There just isn't enough oversight.

Do you really think you can fix a problem as entrenched as discrimination with a law?

These are age-old attitudes. It will take time. But enforcing the education law will be an important step along the way.

Source: Human Rights Watch, "They Say We're Dirty,"
www.hrw.org

Libraries should survive if only to enlighten us

A vital part of the public realm will be run down because no one in Government can make a decent case otherwise – RICHARD GODWIN

What are libraries for? It's not an easy question. The Department for Culture seems so confused it has just commissioned its 263rd review to establish "delivery models" and "core principles". The Arts Council has launched its own investigation, focusing on libraries' "economic contribution".

But while we wait for the long answers, a short one is forming. What are libraries for? The history books.

Campaigners this week declared a state of emergency. It is estimated that cuts to local authorities will force 100 libraries to close by the end of 2015, with another 200-300 becoming reliant on volunteers. The Bookseller warns that we will lose a level of service that can never be restored. It is a familiar story of under-investment leading to decline, then decline cited as a reason for their inevitable demise. A vital part of the public realm will be run down because no one in government can make a decent case otherwise.

It's not that they're anti-libraries. No one's manifesto ever said: "Oh, and btw, you know libraries? WE HATE 'EM!" No investigation has revealed that, actually, Danny Alexander has £305.27 of unpaid library fines and this is a roundabout way of not paying them.

It's not like we can't afford libraries either. We aren't engaged in total war. We haven't had any tsunamis or earthquakes. For all the economic chaos, we are richer as a country than at most points in our history.

It is true the digital age poses challenges — but it also offers new roles. For the unemployed, for example, the local library is often the only place to search for work online. Still, for pensioners, small children, the woman opposite me on the Tube this morning, a library may remain a source of free reading material. The fact is, different people use different libraries for different things at different points in their lives.

I suspect that it isn't the technology that is forcing obsolescence so much as ideology. The Arts Council is at least trying to make the case for libraries in terms that the Treasury might understand — quantifying how much the British economy receives back for every pound invested long term.

Still, the fact that they resort to utilitarian talk of GDP and financial return is telling. The idea that there might be some worth in a public space that does not make a profit for someone or other is baffling to our ministers. It's almost ideologically offensive. It undermines the whole philosophy behind the transformation of Britain over the past 30 or so years, where everything and everyone must justify themselves in economic terms. What if libraries simply provide pleasure, enlightenment, civilisation, respite? I can think of no better reason to save them.

London Evening Standard, 26 February 2014

> It's not like we can't afford libraries, we are richer than at most points in our history.

SOME ISSUES:

Why do you think libraries are not more popular?

What can be done to encourage people to use their local library?

What sort of services would you like a library to provide?

Who should be responsible for the survival of libraries?

Family & relationships

Mums, I spy on my kids on Facebook and so should you

Actress Julianne Moore admits she spies on her children through Facebook and Instagram. Beverley Turner, another snooping mum, says the parents who care are the ones who spy

SOME ISSUES:

Do you think it is a good idea for parents to 'spy' on their kids online?

How can parents make sure their children are using the internet safely?

What sort of dangers are there online?

How would you promote internet safety?

See also Do you know where your children go online? p128

I always knew Julianne Moore was the smartest actress in Hollywood. She's the red-headed mother-of-two in her 50s who still bags the best movie roles; The New York Times described her as "peerless in her portraits of troubled womanhood"; she's a pro-choice activist, Planned Parenthood supporter and ambassador for Save The Children. She speaks out against Botox and plastic surgery; supported Barack Obama and absolutely nailed a scathing portrayal of Sarah Palin in HBO movie, Game Change. When asked by one interviewer what God would say upon her arrival in heaven she replied: "Well, I guess you were wrong, I do exist." If you ignore the immense wealth, success and beauty, I like to think we'd have a lot in common.

That suspicion was confirmed this week when she confessed to checking up on her kids: "In my opinion you don't get to have privacy when you're only 16!" Cue shocked intake of breath from all those parents who are afraid to say 'no' to their kids and have forgotten

This the modern day equivalent of the diary under the mattress

that children are children and do not have adult privileges until they are, say, adults.

Perhaps it is different for her. Caleb, 16 and Liv, 12, who do, after all, have a mother who is a mega-star which perhaps renders them a more likely target for ingenuine 'friends' and weirdos. But what Moore describes are the feelings of any caring parent. Talking specifically about online freedom she said: "It's a scary world out there. I'm all over it with my kids. My son has a Facebook page which he uses but he also knows that his father and I – what they call, lurk – on it so that if we see something untoward we can talk to him about it."

This the modern day equivalent of the diary under the mattress, except that more extrovert teenagers now have a larger audience to impress with their shenanigans and the more introverted feel pressured to play along. In a completely unregulated theatre of showing-off, prying parents may be the only thing that stops the 'look-at-me' generation from broadcasting the fact that they lost their virginity – or indeed, the actual act of doing so. The previous generation's 'neglected' children were the 'latch-key kids': the ones who let themselves in because no parent was ever home. Today's equivalent are the ones who flick from webpage to webpage completely un-policed. The parents who care are the ones who spy.

Private communication has always been the thrill of choice for kids and teenagers: the scribbled note in the classroom, whispering behind a cupped hand, the curly telephone cord pulled into the coat cupboard. Being a grown up could largely be defined as finally being able to have a conversation without your mum listening in at the door. And with good reason – kids don't always make decisions that are healthy, sensible or safe and access to potentially problematic images, issues and ideas has never been easier than it is today.

The tragic irony is that more and more parents are shielding their kids from the imaginary horrors of the real world, whilst allowing them private intercourse with the cyber version. I'm almost alone amongst my peers in letting my 10-year-old son walk round to the local park (without his own mobile phone – shock horror!). He adores the sense of independence and freedom – and, no doubt, a break from his nagging mother. I reckon he'll accept a bit of snooping when he's older in exchange for this sense of responsibility.

But when I ask my friends why they won't let their children do the same, they can't really explain it except for looking ashen and mouthing: "Paedos." Yet their kids are allowed largely unmonitored internet access and they'll be the ones letting their teenagers Instagram, Facebook and tweet to their private heart's content once the hormones kick in. Perhaps because this is all so new, it is as though today's mums and dads just haven't thought this stuff through.

Worrying about physical dangers is of course completely normal. Moore admits to following Caleb on the New York underground to check he is safe. She says: "When my son first started to take the subway, my husband and I used to follow him to make sure he was all right, and then we had to stop following him and let him do it by himself."

That's not prying, that's sensible. My son and I have crossed the road to that park a thousand times as I bang on about stopping, looking and listening. I trust his judgement. But it will be a long time until I trust his judgement on relationships and the moral maze of living in a big city in the twenty-first century. Luckily, he has me and his dad to spy on him for that.

Daily Telegraph, 18 February 2014
© Telegraph Media Group Limited 2013

Kids don't always make decisions that are healthy, sensible or safe

Just one little tattoo

When Tess Morgan's son came home with a tattoo, she was grief-stricken. She knew her reaction was OTT (he's 21) but it signalled a change in their relationship

Put out the bunting, crack open the beers, stand there in the kitchen smiling from ear to ear, because he's home – our student son is home and the family is together again. And after supper, after the washing up is done, the others – his younger siblings – drift off to watch television, and he says: "Would you like to see my tattoo?"

I say, "You're joking."

He says, "No, I'm not."

But still I wait. Any minute he's going to laugh and say, "You should see your faces" because this has been a running joke for years, this idea of getting a tattoo – the hard man act, iron muscles, shaved head, Jason Statham, Ross Kemp. He's a clever boy. Maybe during his school years he thought a tattoo would balance the geeky glory of academic achievement.

His father says, "Where?"

"On my arm," he says, and touches his bicep through his shirt.

His lovely shoulder.

In the silence, he says, "I didn't think you'd be this upset."

After a while, he says, "It wasn't just a drunken whim. I thought about it. I went to a professional. It cost £150."

£150? I think, briefly, of all the things I could buy with £150.

"It's just a tattoo," he says, when the silence goes on so long that we have nearly fallen over the edge of it into a pit of black nothingness. "It's not as if I came home and said I'd got someone pregnant."

It seems to me, unhinged by shock, that this might have been the better option.

His father asks, "Does it hurt?"

"Yes," I say, cutting across this male bonding. "It does. Very much."

For three days, I can't speak to my son. I can hardly bear to look at him. I decide this is rational. The last thing we need, I think, is an

SOME ISSUES:

Do you agree with the mother's point of view?

At what age do you think parents should stop having a say in their child's life?

Should the son have had a tattoo knowing it would upset his mother so much?

Do you think her reaction is justified?

explosion of white-hot words that everyone carries around for the rest of their lives, engraved on their hearts. In any case, I'm not even sure what it is I want to say. In my mind's eye I stand there, a bitter old woman with pursed lips wringing my black-gloved hands. He's done the one thing that I've said for years, please don't do this. It would really upset me if you did this. And now it's happened. So there's nothing left to say.

I know you can't control what your children do. Why would you want to, anyway? If you controlled what they did, you'd just pass on your own rubbish tip of imperfections. You hope the next generation will be better, stronger, more generous. I know all you can do as a parent is to pack their bags and wave as you watch them go.

So I cry instead. I have a lump in my throat that stops me from eating. I feel as if someone has died. I keep thinking of his skin, his precious skin, inked like a pig carcass.

My neighbour says, "There's a lot of it about. So many teenagers are doing it." I stare at pictures of David Beckham with his flowery sleeves, Angelina Jolie all veins and scrawls. Tattoos are everywhere. They seem no more alternative than piercings these days. But I still don't understand. Sam Cam with her smudgy dolphin, the heavily tattooed at Royal Ascot – these people are role models?

"My niece had doves tattooed on her breasts," says a friend, "And her father said, you wait, in a few years' time they'll be vultures."

It's the permanence that makes me weep. As if the Joker had made face paints from acid. Your youthful passion for ever on display, like a CD of the Smiths stapled to your forehead. The British Association of Dermatologists recently surveyed just under 600 patients with visible tattoos. Nearly half of them had been inked between the ages of 18 and 25, and nearly a third of them regretted it.

I look up laser removal. Which is a possibility, I think miserably, that only works if you want a tattoo removed. And I'm not in charge here. My son is.

My husband asks, "Have you seen it yet?"

I shake my head. Like a child, I am hoping that if I keep my eyes tightly shut the whole thing will disappear.

"It's his body," he says gently. "His choice."

"But what if he wants to be a lawyer?"

"A lawyer?"

"Or an accountant."

"He'll be wearing a suit. No one will ever know. And he doesn't want to be a lawyer. Or an accountant."

I know. I know.

I know you can't control what your children do. Why would you want to, anyway?

I meet a colleague for lunch. "He knew how much it would hurt me," I say, tears running down my face. "For years I've said, don't do it. It's there for ever, even after you've changed your mind about who you are and what you want to look like. You're branded, like meat. It can damage your work prospects. It can turn people against you before you've even opened your mouth."

She says, "Tell him how you feel."

But I can't. For a start, I know I'm being completely unreasonable. This level of grief is absurd. He's not dying, he hasn't killed anyone, he hasn't volunteered to fight on behalf of a military dictatorship. But I feel as though a knife is twisting in my guts.

I get angry with myself. This is nothing but snobbery, I think – latent anxiety about the trappings of class. As if my son had deliberately turned his back on a light Victoria sponge and stuffed his face with cheap doughnuts. I am aware, too, that I associate tattoos on men with aggression, the kind of arrogant swagger that goes with vest tops, dogs on chains, broken beer glasses.

Is this what other women feel? Or perhaps, I think, with an uncomfortable lurch of realisation, just what older women feel. I stand, a lone tyrannosaurus, bellowing at a world I don't understand.

Tattoos used to be the preserve of criminals and toffs. And sailors. In the 1850s, the corpses of seamen washed up on the coast of north Cornwall were "strangely decorated" with blue, according to Robert Hawker, the vicar of Morwenstow – initials, or drawings of anchors, flowers or religious symbols ("Our blessed Saviour on His Cross, with on the one hand His mother, and on the other St John the Evangelist"). "It is their object and intent, when they assume these signs," says Hawker, "to secure identity for their bodies if their lives are lost at sea."

He says, "I'm upset that you're upset. But I'm not going to apologise"

Tattoos, then, were intensely practical, like brightly coloured smit marks on sheep.

Perhaps even then this was a fashion statement, a badge of belonging. Or just what you did after too much rum. Later, the aristocracy flirted with body art. According to the National Maritime Museum in Greenwich (they know a lot about tattoos), Edward VII had a Jerusalem cross on his arm while both his sons, the Duke of Clarence and the Duke of York (later George V), had dragon tattoos. Lady Randolph Churchill, Winston's mum, had a snake on her wrist.

But you can do what you like if you're rich.

On day three, still in a fog of misery, I say to him, "Shall we talk?"

We sit down with cups of coffee. I open my mouth to speak and end up crying instead. I say, "You couldn't have done anything to hurt me more."

He is cool and detached. He says, "I think you need to re-examine your prejudices."

I think, but I have! I've done nothing else for three days! But I don't say that because we aren't really talking to each other. These are rehearsed lines, clever insults flung across the dispatch box. (This is what comes of not exploding in anger in the heat of the moment.)

I say, "Why couldn't you have waited until you'd left home? Why now when you're living here half the year?"

"It's something I've been thinking about for a long time. There didn't seem any reason to wait."

Which makes it worse.

"I'm an adult," he says. "I paid for it with my own money. Money I earned."

But we're supporting you as well, I think. As far as I know, you don't have separate bank accounts for your various income streams. So who knows? Maybe we paid for it. "If you don't want to see it, that's fine," he says. "When I'm at home, I'll cover it up. Your house, your rules."

In my head, I think, I thought it was your house, too.

He says, "I'm upset that you're upset. But I'm not going to apologise."

"I don't want you to apologise," I say. (A lie. Grovelling self-abasement might help.)

He says, "I'm still the same person."

I look at him, sitting there, my 21-year-old son. I feel I'm being interviewed for a job I don't even want. I say, "But you're not. You're different. I will never look at you in the same way again. It's a visceral feeling. Maybe because I'm your mother. All those years of looking after your body – taking you to the dentist and making you drink milk and worrying about green leafy vegetables and sunscreen and cancer from mobile phones. And then you let some stranger inject ink under your skin. To me, it seems like self-mutilation. If you'd lost your arm in a car accident, I would have understood. I would have done everything to make you feel better. But this – this is desecration. And I hate it."

We look at each other. There seems nothing left to say.

Over the next few days, my son – always covered up – talks to me as if the row had never happened. I talk to him, too, but warily. Because I'm no longer sure I know him.

And this is when I realise that all my endless self-examination was completely pointless. What I think, or don't think, about tattoos is irrelevant. Because this is the point. Tattoos are fashionable. They may even be beautiful. (Just because I hate them doesn't mean I'm right.) But by deciding to have a tattoo, my son took a meat cleaver to my apron strings. He may not have wanted to hurt me. I hope he didn't. But my feelings, as he made his decision, were completely unimportant.

The stars are not wanted now: put out every one; pack up the moon and dismantle the sun.

I am redundant. And that's a legitimate cause for grief, I think.

Tess Morgan is a pseudonym
The Guardian, 11 August 2012 © Guardian News & Media 2012

NOTHING "STEP" ABOUT THIS FATHER, HE'S EVERY BIT A DAD

BY LAUREN CONAWAY

SOME ISSUES:

What do you think makes a good parent?

Is the role of a step parent very different?

Lauren writes about the difference between her attitude at age 15 and her attitude later. What would have caused those changes?

How can people manage to keep relationships working well in step families?

Step. Step. Step. Step. I am fifteen years old and am jogging down the tree lined sidewalk of my street, raggedly breathing in the crisp, cool morning air as I doggedly, rhythmically put one foot in front of the other.

Each step is an admonition as I trot behind my stepfather, Dave. It is 6:00 am, and this run is not an idyllic bonding opportunity for us, but a punishment. I have mouthed off (again), and gotten caught smoking (again), and we're trying something new. Rather than another grounding, I am being forced to clear some of the cobwebs from the lungs I so frequently abuse by going on one of Dave's morning constitutionals with him. I would much rather be sleeping, or feeding on the nightmares of small children, or whatever it is angry teenagers do at 6:00 am on a Wednesday, and I serve my sentence resentfully.

My mother and Dave married when I was nine years old and were together for several years before that. I can't actually remember a time when he wasn't around. On their wedding day, Dave and I also said vows to each other as part of the ceremony. In these vows, Dave promised to love and care for me as his daughter and I promised to respect him as the father figure he was to become. As a nine year old, I'm sure I didn't understand the significance of what we were taking on. I just knew I was excited to be getting a pretty ring and a lot of attention. Now, with the perspective of years, I realise that on that

DAVE HAS BEEN A PHENOMENAL FATHER TO ME, EVEN WHEN I DIDN'T WANT IT, EVEN WHEN I DIDN'T UNDERSTAND IT.

day and every day since, in Dave I have found a quiet tower of strength. He is a man who has always been truly invested in me, and my future.

Very few people understand our dynamic, as stepparents have been mostly relegated to the parental rubbish heap. After all, the "step" relationship is fraught with landmines – how does an often untried, untested interloper act as parent without stepping on a biological parent's toes? How close is too close? What level of discipline is appropriate? What kind of rejoinder does one have to, "You're not my real dad!" I can't even imagine how difficult it must be to integrate into an already formed, albeit often broken family unit.

Amongst my friends who have blended families, I frequently hear phrases like, "Well, that's not my kid, so I'm going to let him deal with it" or "I feel bad asking him to pick them up from school – they're not his kids." As someone who has experienced step-parenting done all in, statements like that break my heart. Dave truly seemed to get (and I suspect that my mom helped him along in this knowledge) that to love my mother for who she was, was to love me completely. He knew that these two women in his life, his wife and the little one she loved

so fiercely came together as a team. I wish that for all of the stepkids out there.

Of course, at the time of this forced exercise, I wilfully ignored his paternal love, choosing instead to be annoyed at Dave's constant involvement (or intrusion, as I saw it) in my life. It certainly didn't help that I got along great with my biological father. Dad was always the "fun" parent and by the time I hit my awkward, pissed off teen years, I had three young siblings. He was often too distracted to discipline much

HE HAD THE COURAGE TO BE UNPOPULAR WITH AN ANGRY TEENAGER BECAUSE IT HELPED HER TO BECOME A BETTER PERSON.

IT'S ONE THANK YOU AMONGST THE MILLIONS HE DESERVES FOR CHOOSING TO LOVE ME

or impose many rules. This was a welcome departure from the laser-like focus I received at my much quieter primary home, populated just by my mother, my Dave, and me. As far as I was concerned, the constant questions about grades, who I was hanging out with, and the smoking were a serious cross to bear.

It all crystallised for me one day when my mom pulled me aside to listen to a voice mail on her cell phone. The message was simple enough, consisting of Dave, growling, "Our stupid kid has been tying up the phone line for the past hour and I wanted to tell you that I'm coming home early tonight. Love you." I looked to my mom sheepishly, assuming that she was going to berate me for being on the phone far past my allotted time but she was smiling with a faint glint of tears in her eyes. I was confused, and exasperated that we still hadn't joined the 21st century and gotten Call Waiting.

Mom explained that she was crying because Dave's use of the phrase "our kid" rather than "your kid" made her so happy. At that moment, I was more wound up at being called stupid – but after fifteen years of reflection, I think I understand why that moment was so meaningful to my mom. (Yes, I also kind of get how tying up the

phone line for hours on end, night after night, might elicit the occasional frustrated jibe from one of the most patient men I have ever met.)

It had never occurred to me that this was something my mother thought about, the hope that Dave viewed me as his child. I certainly didn't, ensconced as I was in the firm belief that in our house, all roads led to me. It had never even crossed my mind that I wasn't Dave's daughter. Then, I could attribute that to the hubris of youth but even now, there has never been a day when I felt "less than" where he was concerned. That probably seemed unremarkable, judging by how easily I blew it off, but today I recognise how truly special that is, and how truly special Dave is.

I always struggle with Father's Day presents, as both of my paternal figures tend to buy the things

they need when they need them. I asked Dave what he wanted this year and he gave me his usual, unhelpful response – that my gift to him should be me not spending money on crap he doesn't need. That's why, this year, in the words of Elton John, my gift is my song (or blog post, if you will). My gift is the acknowledgement that Dave has been a phenomenal father to me, even when I didn't want it, even when I didn't understand it. It's one thank you amongst the millions he deserves for choosing to love me, when he had no stake in the game as far as society was concerned. For having the courage to be unpopular with an angry teenager because it helped her to become a better person.

Perhaps most importantly, this year my gift is the recognition and the admission of the overwhelming gratitude I feel, that he was there for so many of my steps (even the sweaty, forced ones), when there is absolutely nothing "step" about him.

15 June, 2014
originally published on
GoodmenProject.com

MOM EXPLAINED THAT SHE WAS CRYING BECAUSE DAVE'S USE OF THE PHRASE "OUR KID" RATHER THAN "YOUR KID" MADE HER SO HAPPY

How more paternity leave will spell less discrimination against women

Women of child-bearing age are less likely to be employed because companies don't want to risk the extra cost

Caroline Criado-Perez

SOME ISSUES:

Why do you think women are considered to be the main carers of children?

How would men benefit from more paternity leave?

How might society benefit if men take more time to care for their children?

How will women benefit in the workplace from shared maternity and paternity leave?

A few months ago, a friend of mine got married. To do this, she moved to London from Germany, leaving behind her friends, her family – and her job. She wasn't too worried about this: she'd built up more than a decade of experience and achievements. She could speak perfect English. She'd miss her family but financially, she'd be fine.

Unfortunately, London had other ideas. She went to interview after interview. They all ended in rejection.

Finally, she went to an interview where she was asked some odd questions. She was asked which part of London she lived in. She was asked what her husband did. And finally the interviewer just came out with it: "Look, your husband is obviously doing quite well for himself, you've just got married, why do you even want a job?"

Undoubtedly, that question contained the sexist (not to mention economically antiquated) idea that women just work for pin money. But it also hinted at another issue: the issue of babies. The issue of maternity leave. The

The issue is at heart incredibly simple: it's about money.

issue of "why should I hire you when you'll probably just end up costing me thousands of pounds in wasted pay a few months down the line?"

The Equality and Human Rights Commission has just been given £1m by Maria Miller, the minister for women and equalities, to investigate just how bad this situation is. This follows on from a damning Slater & Gordon poll showing that many

"Why should I hire you when you'll probably just end up costing me thousands of pounds in wasted pay a few months down the line?"

women were returning from maternity leave to worse jobs – or sometimes no job at all.

Research into this area is of course welcome. But I can't help but feel that we are ignoring the most obvious reason why women are discriminated against in this way. The issue is at heart incredibly simple: it's about money.

Women from the age of 30 to 45 are viewed with suspicion and seen as a liability. They are a fecund cost waiting to happen. So why, these companies think, should we take the risk on this well-qualified woman, when we can place a safe bet on this man. He might not be as effective at the job, but at least he'll be around in six months' time. And so the cycle continues, with brilliant women floundering in their careers, overtaken by men not as a result of merit, but as a result of a shrewd cost decision. And perhaps the most irritating thing about this cycle is how easy it is to fix.

It is currently enshrined in law that women are the primary care-givers. Women get 26 weeks of ordinary

Until men are seen as equally likely to take time off this kind of discrimination will continue

maternity leave, and 26 weeks of additional maternity leave. Men get one or two weeks of ordinary paternity leave, and 26 weeks of additional paternity leave. There is no reason for this disparity, beyond a traditional notion that women are somehow more innately qualified than men to bring up children.

It's great that the government is finally sitting up and taking notice of this problem. It's great that it is seeing that legislating against discrimination doesn't mean

that it stops. But what we need to see now is some action to change that. And splitting leave equally between the two parents of a child is the obvious and equitable way to do that.

Until men are seen as equally likely to take time off because of the child that they have brought into the world, this kind of covert, wink-wink discrimination will continue – and it will continue to affect women who don't intend to or can't have children, as much as those who do. If a company can't know either way, it is going to take the safer bet. And that bet is going to result in more women like my friend, who is still looking for a job, and still not finding one. I'm starting to wonder if she ever will.

The Guardian, 5 November 2013
© Guardian News & Media 2013

Opening up to:

Online Dating

Having spent the last five years single, blogger Tam Gilbert now feels she wants to look for a new relationship. Here she takes those first hesitant steps.

SOME ISSUES:

Do you think online dating is a good way for people to meet up?

What might be the positives and negatives to online dating?

How can people keep safe when meeting people in real life who they have met online?

Why might dating be more complex for someone with disabilities?

Desperate times call for desperate measures and I have finally laid aside my reservations and joined the mysterious world of online dating, something my friends have been urging me to do for a long time!

I have had many conversations with non-disabled friends and family members about whether,

and what, to write about my disability on my profile. Should I leave mentioning my impairment until I start messaging any potential suitors, or even save it until we meet? Many thought I should be upfront and list all details alongside my personality traits. But I was loath to do this at first. Of course my disability is a big

I have had many conversations with non-disabled friends and family members about whether, and what, to write about my disability on my profile.

part of me, but it does not solely determine who I am and what makes me tick. But I guess we must cater for those unfamiliar with disability. So I have referred to it in passing, without giving away the specifics.

And the type of site to go for – free or subscription? As I'm sceptical when it comes to the internet, I started with a cheapish subscription on match.com, reasoning that I was more likely to find someone who would take the time to get to know me, rather than a freebie surfer who may not want anything 'different'.

Site chosen and with a six month subscription purchased, it was time to sit down, write my profile, hunt for a decent photo and upload it forthwith. Easier said than done.

It is hard for anyone, with or without a disability, to summarise themselves in a few paragraphs without making their profile sound like a CV. What surprised me the most was the amount of drop-down menus relating to physical appearance and characteristics. Would I describe my Style as 'trendy' or 'cool', 'classical' or 'casual'? Or 'other'?

Asked to describe my body shape fairly early on in proceedings flummoxed me a great deal. Many women have issues about their bodies. But as we know, for some disabled people, due to poor diet, medication, limited exercise, weight is, to some extent, taken out of their control. To be asked to choose between 'athletic and toned,' 'slender' or 'curvy' (only some of the options available) could be daunting, and rather than leaving the box blank and open to interpretation, they might choose to shut the window and walk away. In a world where first impressions

are directed by a speedy click of the mouse, image is clearly an issue on Match.

I was keen to compare the importance of image on a disability-specific dating site. What, if anything, would replace 'body shape' in the drop-down menu? I was shocked to find that it was 'Health condition'.

I had thought that disabled people would not want to generalise about their own health condition or the type of impairment they are looking for in their partner. If we have to say anything at all, surely choosing the relevant option in the above mentioned menu is enough initially? Aren't our hobbies and interests more important than the finite details of our disability and care packages?

But it seems that many feel more comfortable looking for someone with a similar disability to their own. While I can see the attraction of not having to explain the effects of my disability to my date, I am still unsure about using a disability-specific site, particularly one with the

uninspiring and segregating name Disabilitymatch.

I have only been part of the online dating community for a few weeks, and already I have been contacted by some strange characters.

All I can say for now is that my friends are right – it is fun, and as addictive as Facebook - something else I swore I'd never join! I am still slightly sceptical of course; but who knows what the future will bring?

Disability Now, July 2013

In a world where first impressions are directed by the speedy click of the mouse, image is clearly an issue.

Financial issues

Keith Gillespie: How I blew £7,215,875

Fame & Fortune: Keith Gillespie was dubbed the new George Best when he broke into Man Utd's first team at age 17, but he says his lifelong gambling habit spiralled into bankruptcy

By Lorraine McBride

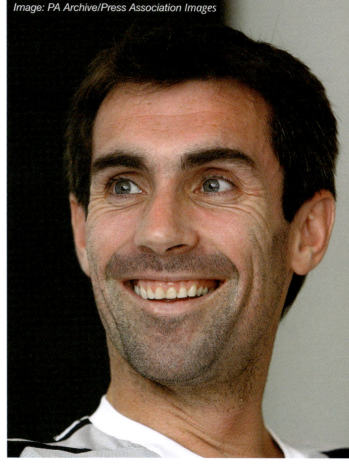
Image: PA Archive/Press Association Images

SOME ISSUES:

Why do you think people can become addicted to gambling?

What can be done to help gambling addicts?

Should financial guidance be offered to people to help them control their spending?

How did your childhood influence your attitude to money?

Growing up, my dad was a prison officer in HM Prison Maze and my mum was a nurse, though she gave up work once she had kids. Without doubt, my parents were hard workers from a working-class background and, at school, they always told us, "You don't get anywhere in life without working hard." We didn't have much, so we were definitely taught to appreciate money, though when I started to make money, I soon started to gamble it.

By 16 you were an apprentice with Manchester United. What did you spend your wages on?

I got involved in gambling pretty much straight away so most of my £46-a-week wages were spent at the bookies. I was probably too young for nightclubs at that stage, but at certain times when I wanted to go out, I couldn't afford it. It was quite tough to manage at that stage. I lived in digs with other apprentices, including a Welsh boy called Robbie Savage. Robbie was my room-mate, which meant every morning waking up to the sound of his hairdryer – he was my alarm clock.

When the apprentices finished training in the afternoon, we swept and mopped the dressing room, and cleaned the players' boots. I cleaned for Lee Sharpe and Russell Beardsmore and, at Christmas, I remember getting a £30 tip from Sharpey.

Has there ever been a time when you worried how you were going to pay the bills?

For an apprentice, £46 wasn't an awful lot to live on every week. Then I signed my first professional contract at 17 in a four-year deal worth an initial £230 a week with a £20,000 signing-on fee, split into five instalments. I felt like a Lotto winner. I paid £90 a week for my keep and, after tax, I probably came out with £90 a week in my hand, which doubled what I was earning before.

When Alex Ferguson transferred you to Newcastle, remarkably, he acted as your self-appointed agent for a few hours. What happened?

After an FA Cup game, we thrashed out terms at midnight in a hotel in Sheffield. Back then I was a £250-a-week player.

I remember Alex sitting there with a pen and paper, adding up figures and scribbling away. He told a bit of a white lie to Kevin Keegan: "Keith's on £600 a week at the moment so he'll be looking for an increase on that." He didn't tell me this would happen so I sat there with a poker face, giving nothing away. Newcastle were happy to double my wage and an hour later I shook hands on a deal worth £1,200 a week.

Fergie rang my mum, explained the situation and promised her that he'd look after me in terms of sorting out a deal. My mum trusted him, I trusted him and Fergie was true to his word. I was grateful that he managed to get me that deal; he had my interests at heart and that's the way he was with all the young players. Fergie was a great manager to start out under.

What was your best moment in football?

My debut for Manchester United at 17 was surreal because 18 months earlier I was at school, so to play for one of the biggest clubs in the world – and being a Manchester United fan – felt almost like a dream. We were playing Bury in the FA Cup; obviously I was very nervous, but running out at Old Trafford and hearing the roar from the fans was an incredible feeling.

Your memoir is called How Not to be a Football Millionaire. Surely that's impossible in today's Premiership?

I know that a lot of players suffered around the same time as me. I know the [huge] amount of money players get paid now, but players do get involved in gambling, which is a big

problem when you've got so much free time on your hands. When you're that little bit older, you're usually married, but when I first went to Newcastle, I lived in a hotel for five months. I didn't know anybody so my way of curbing boredom was going to the bookies.

You calculated that you squandered £7,215,875 during your professional career; where did it go?

Basically, I lost an awful lot of money through gambling over the years, but I also lost money on property and got involved in a film scheme like a lot of footballers did. It wasn't the right scheme, but at the time you think it's great. The problem was you start paying the tax towards the end of your career when your earnings are waning. I went bankrupt a few years ago, and a lot of footballers still involved with the same film scheme are finished in football yet are still struggling to pay that money back.

How bad was your addiction?

At Newcastle, I was 19, going home to an empty hotel room and I gradually spent more and more time at the bookies as it spiralled out of control. A low point came at 20 after a 48-hour gambling spree when I lost £47,000 in one day, only to lose £15,000 the next. I blew a total of £62,000 in just two days. When the press got hold of it, it was difficult having to ring my mum and explain I'd blown money that she could only dream of. It was sickening because, as a gambler, you're always trying to chase that next winner. It was also the last race of the day, so it wasn't like I could try to win it back. I had all sorts of feelings going through my head. I was in my second year at Newcastle earning £1,400 a week and I knew I was in big trouble.

Later, the introduction of online and phone accounts was the worst thing that could have happened. In the old days, when I went to a bookie I lost money in my pocket, but now when I rang to put a bet on, I wasn't physically handing over money. At Blackburn when I was on a £14,000-a-week salary, I rang up Ladbrokes so regularly to put on a bet, when the person at the other end heard my voice, they'd say, "Mr Gillespie, account number QT3561439, is it?" It got to the stage that I bet on every single race going.

A low point came at 20 after a 48-hour gambling spree when I lost £47,000 in one day, only to lose £15,000 the next.

Did you ever feel you were losing the sympathy of your family?

No, because once they knew about that story, I tried to give up for a few months, only I went back to it. Because I was living in England and they were back home, in Northern Ireland, they didn't realise that I was back gambling, so it wasn't as if I could lose their sympathy.

You became bankrupt in 2010; what was your worst business move?

My worst move was buying into a film syndicate to make films and TV series. Then my financial adviser, who was a friend, took over my affairs in 2002. There were a lot of good investments sitting there waiting for when I hit 35, which is retirement age for footballers. He took over my affairs and the first thing he did was get me to take all this money out and put it into property. I wasn't aware of what money was coming out of which policies. Basically, there was one 10-year policy that I'd put money into for nine years and one month and you obviously make a lot of money in your last year. I was a little bit naive.

What's been the most difficult lesson you've learnt about money?

I think I was too trusting. It's not a bad trait, but in business you've just got to do everything through the proper channels and friendship shouldn't come into it.

How long have you stayed away from gambling?

If it's Saturday afternoon and I'm in a bar with friends watching the football scores come in, I might have a £20 bet, but I can't even remember the last time that I put a football bet on. I don't worry about going down the same path because horse racing was my biggest downfall and now I've got no interest whatsoever. When you've been through as much as I have, you've got to take some positives out of it, and try to learn lessons. I definitely won't go down that road again.

Would you ever sell your football memorabilia?

I played 86 times for Northern Ireland and I've probably got only two shirts left because I always gave them away to charity.

Who should help Premiership stars to cope with the pressures of money and fame?

When we were growing up, we had media training at Manchester United and it certainly helped us. Maybe footballers should also have financial training, but clubs can't watch over players and look into their bank accounts. If players are going to go out and spend money on stupid things, then that's what they're going to do.

If your young son wants to become a professional footballer in future, what would you say?

Well, I'd make sure that he didn't go down the same path that I did. If it materialised, the fact that I've been through so much would act as a good guide and I'd obviously be able to advise him on what not to do and how to handle it. Football is a short career, so you've got to make as much as you can and manage your money the right way.

Does money make you happy?

Ultimately, it doesn't; I've been there, had it and been through two marriages. People try to earn as much as they can, but you also want health and happiness. The best thing is that it's great to be able to treat your family. I was always quite generous in treating mine and able to pay for them at times, but money didn't last for me.

Keith Gillespie's 'How Not to be a Football Millionaire'
(£16.99, Trinity Mirror Sport Media)
Daily Telegraph, 27 April 2014
© Telegraph Media Group Limited 2014

Clubs can't watch over players and look into their bank accounts. If players are going to go out and spend money on stupid things, then that's what they're going to do.

A win for the homeless as a Hungarian lottery winner gives his money to charity

A man who was once a homeless alcoholic has won £1.7m on the Hungarian lottery and plans to set up a charity to help others in need

SOME ISSUES:

Do you think this man and his partner have done the right thing?

Should he have spent the money on himself?

Do you think people with a lot of money have a social responsibility?

What would you do with the money if you won the lottery?

Which causes would you probably support?

In 2013, László Andraschek was down on his luck. At age 55, he had no job, was at risk of losing his home and was in a lot of debt. He had been struggling with his addiction to alcohol but had managed to give it up completely in 2005. He was at a railway station on his way to a meeting for recovering alcoholics when he decided to use his last few coins to buy a lottery ticket.

Even as he purchased his ticket he had a sense of hopelessness: "I had only picked six numbers and the female shop assistant reminded me that I needed to pick a seventh," he said. "I told her to make it 24 – it doesn't matter, anyway."

But his luck changed in the most dramatic way possible. He won 630 million Hungarian forints – one of the biggest ever lottery wins in the country - amounting to £1.7 million pounds.

At the time of their lottery win, Andraschek and his wife Aniko were a year behind with the rent. They had several bank loans. Their electricity and gas had been cut off more than once because of non-payment. They were trying to live on £293 a month - and failing to meet their bills.

Andraschek told The Guardian newspaper: "As I cycled home, I thought: 'It's over; I don't have to think about where to borrow more money to pay the

Image from YouTube

"It is our duty to take those people who have shared our difficult experiences by the hand"

debts. My life was a constant struggle of plugging holes, and I could only ever do that by creating new ones."

Aniko, said, "When László came home and was dancing around the room, my first thought was maybe he had started drinking again. When I watched him call the lottery company and heard them saying congratulations, I realised that he hadn't lost his marbles after all."

First he did the things you might expect, he paid off his debts to family members and he bought homes for his children to live in and a car. He planned to take his wife on holiday, their first ever trip abroad.

Then the couple did something less predictable. Instead of giving in to the temptation to spend the money on luxuries they had never had before, they decided to devote much of their money to setting up a charitable foundation to help people in need. Aniko told The Guardian: "It is our duty to take those people who have shared our difficult experiences by the hand, which is why we are planning to call the foundation 'Stand By Me!' because it is easier to survive and then move on with someone beside you."

Her husband has already given a large amount to the homeless hostel where he lived for seven years - which is how news of his win first became known early in 2014. He hopes the publicity will help to make the plight of homeless people more of an issue in Hungary - whose situation is made worse by laws which punish them for sleeping rough.

Their 'miracle' win does not mean that the Andrascheks have put their years of struggle behind them. As László says:

"I have become rich but I have not become a different person."

Sources: Various

"It is easier to survive and then move on with someone beside you."

To tackle personal debt we need to tackle inequality first!

An inequality test should be applied to all government policies to assess whether they will increase the gap between the richest and the rest.

Duncan Exley

SOME ISSUES:

What can be done to make sure people receive an adequate wage that they can comfortably live on?

What can be done to tackle the wage gap in the UK?

Should voters have a direct say in how the tax system works?

Today's report on personal debt from the Centre for Social Justice makes for sobering reading. With average household debt at £54,000, nearly twice the level of a decade ago, it is clear just how many are struggling in austerity Britain.

We're told that the causes of this astonishing personal debt are people being forced to use credit to pay bills as the cost of living rises, as well as the legacy of cheap credit before the financial crash. These are clearly significant issues, but the reality is that they are part of a far wider, systemic problem. One that many seem unwilling to recognise. The gap between the rich and the rest has widened alarmingly over the past 30 years, with the UK now experiencing one of the highest levels of income inequality in the developed world. Study after study, in both the UK and internationally, has shown that as inequality rises, so does household debt.

According to research by the Joseph Rowntree Foundation, single people need to earn at least £16,850 a year before tax in 2013 for a minimum acceptable living standard. Couples with two children need to earn at least £19,400 each. But according to the ONS, just under half of people don't get £19,400.

The gap between the rich and the rest has widened, with the UK now experiencing one of the highest levels of income inequality in the developed world.

Pay for FTSE Directors may have increased by 14 per cent in the last year, but for the average employee pay continues to fall behind prices.

About a third don't get £16,850. For years, people have been told that if they work hard, they'll get the rewards, but that simply isn't true anymore. This is partly a result of a greater proportion of UK jobs being low paid. The proportion of jobs classed as low paid by the OECD is now among the highest of developed nations, and around 20 per cent of employees earn below the Living Wage.

Another issue is the increasing amount of insecure work such as temporary work and zero-hours contracts. Being trapped in a low-pay-no-pay cycle understandably plays havoc with budgeting. A further problem is a result of inequality driving up prices. This is most obvious in housing costs, where the average person trying to find a home finds themselves in a market where they are competing with people who are buying second homes, and with investors who are fuelling speculation-driven

property inflation. In fact around 85% of new-build properties in central London and 38% of re-sales are estimated to have been purchased by overseas buyers.

Perhaps the biggest problem is also the simplest. Pay for FTSE Directors may have increased by 14 per cent in the last year, but for the average employee pay continues to fall behind prices. We've now had four years of pay falling in real terms for most people. To tackle the debt crisis, the government needs to focus on reducing the UK's high levels of income inequality. An inequality test should be applied to all government policies to assess whether they will increase the gap between the richest and the rest. Raising the level of National Minimum Wage

and incentivising employers to offer jobs that pay a reliable income is a key way of tackling debt, driving demand in the economy, and reducing social security costs.

We also need a more progressive tax system, including proposals like a property speculation tax to stop the rich pricing the rest of us out of a home, but also a fiscal rebalancing away from consumption taxes like VAT, because they hit average and poor people hardest and hold back spending. Inequality is more than a driver of debt, it supresses our economic recovery and fractures our society. If the government wants to tackle debt, it needs to tackle inequality first.

New Statesman, 20 November 2013

10 things about work, life and money every child should know

Most youngsters leave education knowing little about the grown-up worlds of work and money. Here are the key tips Martin Lewis would give to his younger self

If only I'd known 20 years ago...There are many things those with either just the beginning flecks of grey or full-blown silver wish we could tell our younger selves. Yet Doctor Who is fiction, so the best we can do is try to prevent the next generation making some of the mistakes we have.

Financial education in schools will help. Yet that's just a start. Not only because less than half of our schools must follow the curriculum, but because wider lessons will need to be gained from experience.

Recently I had to rapidly crystallise my own life lessons. I'd been asked to my home town, Chester, for its university graduation ceremony, and hadn't realised I'd be expected to speak until I was on the platform. So I jotted down 10 bullet points about work, life and money and crossed my fingers. Perhaps lesson one should have been "read the briefing better".

1. It's about the skills you gain, more than the jobs you do

When I was without a clue what to do, with my London School of Economics days near closing, I had the chance as student union secretary to speak to the school's director (what the LSE calls its vice-chancellor). I asked him what job I should do. His reply: "It doesn't matter too much yet, just get the best job you can and focus on acquiring as many skills as possible".

Looking back, he was right. While it's a narrower pathway for those heading into law, engineering or medicine, the portfolio approach to work is becoming a modern norm.

Even the early casual jobs I did taught me something. Bar work was a confidence and communication boost. Flogging caravan awnings at 18 brought transferable sales skills and a foundation course in commerce, which a stint in financial PR after graduation took up a notch – teaching me techniques I now try to reverse: to work for the shopper, not the shop.

Everything you do, if you give it your all, gives you something, a new skill. Collect them, take them with you. Everything adds up.

2 If you're self-employed, a third of what you earn isn't yours

Those who are salaried receive money via the payroll with the tax automatically taken off, so all the money received is theirs. However, the self-employed and freelance usually get paid before tax.

SOME ISSUES:

Do you think schools should provide more financial and work advice to students?

Are these tips and advice useful?

What advice do you think is most important to young people now?

What advice would you give to your younger self?

Time is a fossil fuel, not a renewable. It's easy to waste it

So for every £100 you earn, around £30 isn't yours, it's the taxman's. Put it straight into a separate bank account, preferably with as high interest as possible. Failure to do this is the cause of many a personal bankruptcy.

3 Don't be afraid to change path

In work years I'm now 18 years old – coming of age. After school or university you're a newborn in the working world. Until you're a few years into a career, it's tough to fully understand what makes you tick.

Hopefully things will go well, you'll be happy, driven and content. If not, don't feel locked in. Make a plan, and if you'll forgive the phrase – ditch and switch.

I left City PR at the age of 25 – a great job to have done, but not right for me. I decided to leave before I was paid too much to risk the uncertainty of change and feel trapped. My family didn't approve of me giving up a secure job to go back to study (a postgrad in broadcast journalism), yet I went for it and thankfully it's worked out. Of course, there's no guarantee, but when it comes to choosing work, don't be afraid to try before you buy.

4 A bank's job is to sell to you

If mass hypnosis were possible, I'd use it so that every time people walked into a bank and saw the word 'adviser', they'd see the word 'salesperson'. Banks sell.

When they offer a product it means it's good for them; it doesn't automatically mean it's good for you. Just look at the various scandals – PPI, Libor, packaged bank account mis-selling and more. Billions wrongly taken from the trusting public through lies, fraud and hard sell.

The one silver lining is that this has increased the degree of scepticism with which the public treat banks. While it's good to communicate with your bank, take its "advice" with a pinch of salt, and do your own reading and research to make your own decisions.

5 Don't repay student loans quicker than you need to

All those who started university between 1999 and 2011 are currently charged 1.5 percent interest on their loans – less than the rate of inflation, so in real terms the debt is shrinking.

Far more important, though, is that many will want mortgages, or commercial loans for further study, in the years after graduation. These are more expensive and, unlike student loans, still need repaying if you lose your income. So using spare cash to pay off debt now, only to borrow back later at a much higher rate, is a poor choice. Far better to dunk it in a high-rate cash ISA, which earns more than the loan costs, so that it's there when you need it. More info at mse.me/studentloanrepay

6 Your time has a value

Time is a fossil fuel, not a renewable. It's easy to waste it. So whether for work or leisure, make the most of it. Your waking hours are a commodity. You sell them to your employer, so when not working, value them at a similar after-tax rate.

This doesn't mean putting your feet up in front of the TV is always wrong; that type of recharging has its place. Yet for those earning little, it may mean spending your time being thrifty, making do and mend, rather than spending long-earned cash. For those who are paid well, it could mean working more and paying someone else to do less lucrative, unrewarding personal chores.

Even I accept that sometimes you don't have the time to save money, but equally it's important to accept that sometimes you don't have the money to save time.

7 Beware borrowing, but ignore "neither a borrower nor a lender be"

Most graduates already have what we call a loan to get a degree. Many more will need a mortgage to buy a home. Thus the

What counts is understanding when, and how, to borrow

Do what you can to improve the lot of you and yours

grandparental wisdom of "neither a borrower nor a lender be" is outdated.

What counts is understanding when and how to borrow. If it's planned, budgeted for expenditure on an asset like a home or a car for work, it can be worth it.

Equally if borrowing leads to a guaranteed net financial gain, such as for a football season ticket rather than costlier individual tickets – or a zero percent card to pay car insurance upfront rather than the extortionate monthly cost, it may be rational.

Yet while the economy is hopefully turning the corner, personal incomes lag behind. Don't be tempted into willy-nilly borrowing to continually fill gaps in income. If you won't or can't avoid it, at least do it cheaply – beware payday loans and high cost credit.

Finally, if you don't know how you'll find the money to repay the borrowing, then admit you can't afford it – no matter how much you feel you need it.

8 You've worked for your degree – be proud of it

Many people knock higher education. Some chant "these days a degree isn't worth it" – certainly it isn't the sole route to success. I know this sounds wet, but the bigger picture is you've worked hard to be members of a special club. Congratulations.

While we often take a dim view of the UK, in relative terms, this is still one of the world's richest and most tolerant societies. Take a step back and count your blessings – you have an opportunity many in this country and more elsewhere in the world will never have. If this privilege works out for you, there comes a responsibility, too. Do what you can to improve the lot of you and yours, but think about the wider world too.

9 Make 'em fight for your business

We live in a competitive consumer economy. Your business is valuable to companies; don't let them take you for granted.

Whether it's haggling to make the AA, Sky TV or your mobile network give you a better deal, making comparisons for the best energy tariff or train ticket, or even choosing where you go for your pint or a sandwich – ensure your custom is valued. If not, ask for better, or tell them you'll go elsewhere.

10 Accept uncertainty – there's not always a right answer

It's very easy when you've been through school, college or university to assume everything must have an answer. Yet it doesn't. We all need to learn to embrace uncertainty.

This is something many people (including me) struggle with both logically and emotionally. It's a great cause of anxiety. Whether the question is...

Should I change my job?

Should I get that car loan?

Should I marry him/her?

Should I save for a bigger deposit to get a better mortgage deal to buy a house?

Without a crystal ball there is no right answer. All you can do is weigh the upside against the downside. Plan for the worst, hope for the best.

And if it does go against you, it doesn't mean you made the wrong decision. You did what you could with the knowledge you had. Don't beat yourself up about it, it's just part of life.

Martin Lewis is a broadcaster and creator of MoneySavingExpert.com. You can join the 8 million who receive his weekly tips emailed at moneysavingexpert.com/tips.

Daily Telegraph, 21 November 2014
© Telegraph Media Group Limited 2014

Without a crystal ball, there is no right answer

I worked hard to get into Cambridge. But I needed benefits too

Poppy Noor

The government's plans to cut welfare for the under-25s will force others in my position to choose between an education and a place to live

*Words in **bold** relate to background information on the third page*

SOME ISSUES:

Do you think students should be offered more financial support to make sure they can complete their studies?

What would happen to students like Poppy if certain benefits were taken away?

What effect would this have?

How else should the government help students through study if they are struggling financially?

I am a Tory dream. If George Osborne heard the Drake lyric "started from the bottom now we here" he might think of someone like me. I was born to a cab-driving father and a mother who was diagnosed with severe mental illness when I was eight. My father was in and out of prison and my home life was unstable, dysfunctional and, in the end, unsafe: I was forced out aged 16. Despite this I made it through sixth form and into Cambridge University, graduating a few years ago.

And yet I still depended on the very benefits for the under-25s that Osborne is planning to axe. As a minor who could not live at home and with no one to take me in, I wouldn't have had a roof over my head without **housing benefit.** Without **income support** I wouldn't have had money to eat.

Was I propped up in a lavish house? No. I was placed in bed and breakfasts and hostels for the mentally unwell where I had to prevent people breaking into my room at night while I worked on my coursework. I rushed between lessons and the Homelessness Advice Centre during my free periods to make sure my benefits were in order. And I was lucky: my brother, aged 16, had to sleep in a telephone box for a week before the council would place him anywhere.

But **Osborne** would have you believe that people like me are making **lifestyle choices,** that we're claiming benefits because it's easier than getting a job. True, I didn't want a job – I wanted an education. That wouldn't have been possible without housing benefit for the under-25s.

It is the very structures that Osborne would scrap that got me where I am today

Photo posed by model

Of course, many of the young people I met in hostels and elsewhere didn't opt for an education. That's not surprising when you consider that if you move out of your borough to go to university you risk being homeless again in the holidays. I was an anomaly: if I hadn't got into such a prestigious university I probably wouldn't have taken that risk, and I was lucky enough to have made friends whose parents loved me and were able to put me up in the summer.

My friends in hostels who had grown up in the care system didn't have those options. Under the new legislation, I wouldn't even have been able to support myself through A-levels – it relies on a **false assumption** that **all under-25s can live at home**, without providing a safety net to help those for whom this is simply impossible.

I represent too small a minority to matter, the government might say. My response is that if you continue to remove the infrastructure that assists those who are not so lucky, you are loading the game in favour of those who are already fortunate: a game of too many snakes and not enough ladders. Axe housing benefit for people under the age of 25 and you will force people like me to choose between education and a place to live, a choice that will only exacerbate the cycle of poverty.

So, perhaps unsurprisingly, I'm not prepared to claim that it was my "hard work" that got me where I am today. I won't be **Boris Johnson's atomistic cornflake** that shakes off the rest to get to the top of the packet; I'm not prepared to kick the proverbial ladder from under the feet of my peers by peddling the myth that it is only the lazy who stay behind.

It is the very structures that Osborne would scrap that got me where I am today, but I suspect that he will continue to claim it is people like me who prove that these welfare cuts make sense. For every benefit that he strips, he will do so singing his song of the hard-working who are unwilling to accept their lot. Well you won't do it in my name, Messrs Osborne and Cameron. You and I are not in this together.

The Guardian, 19 January 2013
© Guardian News & Media 2013

You are loading the game in favour of those who are already fortunate

> *"Today it is still possible to leave school, sign on, find a flat, start claiming housing benefit and opt for a life on benefits."*
>
> *David Cameron*

Benefits

Housing benefit is paid by local councils to help people on low incomes or benefits pay their rent.

Income support is a benefit paid to some people who do not have enough money to live on. You must be one of a group of people who can get benefit without having to look for work. Poppy would have qualified because she was in full time education and was not living with a parent or someone acting as a parent

Lifestyle choices?

In June 2012, the Prime Minister said he was considering removing Housing Benefit for people aged 16-24 and at the Conservative Party Conference 2012 – the Chancellor, George Osborne, asked whether young people who have never worked should have access to independent housing.

He said: "How can we justify giving flats to young people who have never worked, when working people twice their age are still living with their parents because they can't afford their first home?"

At the 2013 Conservative Party Conference the prime minister called for everyone under 25 to be "earning or learning."

"Today it is still possible to leave school, sign on, find a flat, start claiming housing benefit and opt for a life on benefits.

We should ask, if that option should really exist at all.

Instead we should give young people a clear, positive choice: Go to school. Go to college. Do an apprenticeship. Get a job... "

All under-25s can live at home

Housing Benefit for people aged under 25 was around £1.8 billion in each of the three financial years from 2010-11 to 2012-13

According to the homeless charity, Crisis: About 380,000 people aged under 25 are currently supported by housing benefit. Of these, 204,000 are parents (mostly single mothers), at least 66,000 are working, and 28,000 are sick or disabled. Around a quarter (99,000) are looking for work.

There are many reasons some young people cannot live at home. Their parents may have died. There may not be enough space, or indeed they might have moved away to look for or take up work. They may have suffered abuse at home, or have simply been told they are not welcome to stay or move back in.

The number of under-25s sleeping rough in London has more than doubled in the past three years. A full 8% of under-25s say they have been homeless in the last five years.

Cornflakes?

In November 2013 Boris Johnson, the Mayor of London, gave a speech in which he argued that economic equality was impossible and greed and envy were good motivators.

However, he also said that talented people from less wealthy backgrounds need help to "rise to the top". His metaphor for society was a box of cornflakes: "I worry that there are too many cornflakes who aren't being given a good enough chance to rustle and hustle their way to the top."

Sources: various

Food & drink

WHY IS HALAL MEAT IN THE NEWS?

HALAL

"ANIMAL RIGHTS COME BEFORE RELIGION"

SOME ISSUES:

Do you know where the meat you eat comes from?

Why do you think people are concerned about eating halal meat?

Should people be concerned about all animal products?

How much do we want to know about the conditions that the animals we eat live in?

The word 'halal simply means permitted, which, in turn, means that the animal has been slaughtered according to religious rules. Practising Muslims will check whether the meat they are buying or eating is 'halal'.

The majority of people however do not question how the animal they are eating was killed. For this reason, various fast-food outlets, restaurant chains and supermarkets have decided the most economical and efficient option for their business is to sell and use only halal meat. This has caused quite a stir. But why?

The argument comes down to whether religious rules cause the animals more suffering and whether consumers should know about slaughter methods and be able to choose between them.

HOW ARE ANIMALS USUALLY SLAUGHTERED?

Most cattle and sheep are stunned by having a bolt shot into their brain. The unconscious animal is hoisted by one hind leg onto an overhead conveyor and moved to the bleed area. Here the major blood vessels supplying the brain are cut. The animal dies from loss of blood before it can recover from the stun. Pigs are usually gassed to death before being bled. Large abattoirs slaughter poultry using electrical water baths or gas. The birds are hung by both legs onto a moving line, which takes them to a waterbath where they are either stunned or killed outright by an electric current. They are then bled at the neck.

FOR THE MEDIA, HALAL BECAME SHORTHAND FOR ALL RELIGIOUS SLAUGHTER

Photo: ENCIK KOPI O/Shutterstock.com

WHAT IS DIFFERENT ABOUT 'RITUAL SLAUGHTER'?

Ritual slaughter means that animals must be killed in a specific way according to certain religious rules. For halal meat, the animal is killed in the way demanded by Islam. However other religions are also specific about how the animals are slaughtered. For example, kosher meat fits the slaughter rules set by Judaism. Like halal, kosher simply means 'permitted'.

For meat to be halal the animal must be alive and healthy at the time of slaughter, the process must be carried out by a trained Muslim who begins by saying "In the name of Allah". The animal has its throat cut with a very sharp knife so that the death is meant to be as fast and stress-free as possible.

For meat to be kosher the animal has to be killed by a method known as shechita. This must be carried out by a highly trained, devout Jew using a perfectly smooth knife to slice the throat in a continuous motion so

MANY ABATTOIRS FALL BELOW HUMANE STANDARDS

that there is rapid blood loss and the animal loses consciousness. There are some other conditions that must also be met before meat can be counted as kosher.

The main difference between these and the usual methods of slaughter revolves around whether the animals are stunned before they are killed.

WHAT ARE THE FACTS?

Figures from the Food Standards Agency published in 2012 showed that in British slaughterhouses only 3% of cattle, 10% of sheep and goats and 4% of poultry were not stunned before slaughter. Some are stunned afterwards to minimise suffering.

Between 84% and 90% of animals killed for halal meat

in the UK are processed by one of the large number of halal slaughterhouses which do use stunning beforehand. Those killed in kosher abattoirs are not stunned beforehand and most are not stunned afterwards. Since not all parts of the animal are kosher, some meat from these abattoirs will be on general sale.

This means that there is a small possibility that the meat consumers are eating is from a British slaughterhouse that does not stun. However, much of British meat is imported from abroad, and that means we cannot always be clear whether the animals have been pre-stunned or not. We do know that some other countries have lower standards of care for livestock during their lives and in transportation.

THE ANIMAL WELFARE ISSUE WAS BEING HIJACKED BY PEOPLE WITH OTHER PRIORITIES

ANIMALS FEEL PAIN DURING AND AFTER THE THROATCUT WITHOUT STUNNING

WHY IS THIS IN THE NEWS?

In Europe the law says animals must be stunned before they are slaughtered, except in the case of religious rituals. Recently the Danish government decided that all animals must be stunned, saying that "animal rights come before religion". Switzerland, Sweden, Norway and Iceland also ban religious slaughter. The UK however still allows it.

The president-elect of the British Veterinary Association said that Britain too should ban slaughter without stunning because it causes unnecessary suffering.

As the issue became news, it came to light that many food chains and stores always use halal meat as they know it will be acceptable to Muslim customers and that slaughter methods are not normally an issue for other customers.

 The media did not focus attention on kosher meat but used halal as shorthand for all religious slaughter. This drew the attention of some people who were previously uninterested in the method by which their meat arrived on their plate. Their response was a mixture of consumer rights and suspicion of 'foreign' practices.

Other welfare issues, such as battery produced meat, which for many is seen as inhumane and a bigger cause of animal suffering were often not included in the debate.

WOULD LABELS HELP?

There has been some demand for labelling meat as Halal or not. The British Veterinary Association has suggested that labelling meat as 'stunned' or 'not stunned' would be clearer. They were concerned that the animal welfare issue was being hijacked by people with other priorities.

The British Retail Consortium, which includes major supermarkets and many smaller stores among its members, responded: "As the overwhelming majority of meat sold in UK supermarkets is own brand and from animals that have been stunned prior to slaughter so we do not see the requirement to separately label meat based on the method of slaughter."

CRUEL OR NOT?

Supporters of religious methods claim that the way animals are killed under their rules is so swift and skilful that the animal does not feel pain. In contrast, they say, the practices in many non-religious abattoirs fall way below humane standards and methods of stunning are not 100% certain in any case. They also point to the tiny proportion of all animals that are killed in accordance with strict religious rules, (especially true in the case of kosher meat).

Some animal welfare campaigners also feel that how the animals are treated during their lives is being overlooked when we concentrate on how they are killed.

However, a recent European report clearly says: "It can be stated with high probability that animals feel pain during and after the throatcut without prior stunning. This applies even to a good cut performed by a skilled operator".

There, once again, is the dilemma - animal rights or religious rights, which is more important?

Sources: Various including:
Food Standards Agency,
www.food.gov.uk
British Retail Consortium,
www.brc.org.uk
DIALREL project: Report on good and adverse practices - Animal welfare concerns in relation to slaughter practices from the viewpoint of veterinary sciences, February 2010

We don't care how an animal lives, only how it dies

Giles Fraser

SOME ISSUES:

Why do you think people are concerned about halal meat?

What other issues are there within the meat industry?

Do you think that people should be able to know how the animal they eat was raised and killed?

Who is responsible for providing this information?

Yes, I am a hypocrite in eating the very food whose production I morally condemn. But at least I am aware of my hypocrisy

I cannot actually think of a single good reason that I am not a vegetarian. At least, not a single good moral reason. As a matter of taste, however, I love eating meat. The juices, the smell, the texture: none of which can be adequately simulated by vegetarian substitutes. I like my steak so bloody and rare that a damn good vet could probably get the thing back on its feet again and mooing.

And, to make a confession of which I'm not especially proud, I generally harbour an instinctive resistance to the modern-day Puritanism of the self-righteous salad eaters. There is something about tofu that seems to suck all the fun out of life. But this week things have shifted.

It started with the whole halal meat story. Instinctively, it seemed obvious to me that the way in which some

Our food labelling, should tell us that this animal was crowded into filthy pens, physically crippled and then subject to a form of mechanised industrial slaughter

people have been throwing up their arms in horror at the idea some meat is halal-compliant, without being labelled as such, is simply a piece of disguised anti-Muslim racism. The moral alibi that this racism adopts is the assertion that halal slaughter, without stunning, is cruel and painful.

So, as research, I spent an utterly miserable evening watching YouTube videos of the ways in which our meat is slaughtered. They made the whole horror movie slasher genre look very tame fare indeed. Forget halal labelling: if we were going to be fully transparent in our food labelling, it should tell us that this animal was crowded into filthy pens throughout its life, physically crippled by forced growing conditions and then subject to a form of mechanised industrial slaughter that is nothing less than vomit-inducing. Paul McCartney has a point: "If slaughterhouses had glass walls, we would all be vegetarians."

The whole point of halal meat not being stunned before it is slaughtered is that the animal is supposed to be healthy and well before it is killed. The point about slitting its throat with a sharp blade is that we take personal responsibility for what we are doing. I take it that the point about the animal not being killed in the presence of others is that the process is not one of callous mass production. And the need to mention the name of God (by Muslim, Jew or Christian) while doing this is not some creepy religious ritual but a reminder that all creation, humans included, exist under God's care.

Secular atheists may not subscribe to the metaphysics, but the idea that all life – human or otherwise – shares some inherent and fundamental connection is a noble position to take (and, no, you cannot catch Islam from halal food). With the exception of Hinduism, the Islamic scriptures are probably the most diligent in insisting upon animal welfare.

I am not saying that current halal practice necessarily lives up to its theological ideals. For this too has become industrialised. But reading the Qur'an carefully, it is perfectly clear that the sort of disgusting mass industrialised food production that is widely practised ought not to be regarded as halal compliant. Most of our animals arrive at slaughterhouses traumatised after months of ill treatment. The idea that we ignore a whole life of misery and then get morally exercised by what happens in the last few moments of an animal's life is pure moral bullshit.

But, in reality, we don't want too much honest transparency in our food labelling because it would reveal to us the extraordinary cruelty behind so much of the food on our table. Yes, I am a hypocrite in eating the very food whose production I morally condemn. But at least I am aware of my hypocrisy. Loads of us don't even admit this much and prefer to live in denial. We don't actually want the walls to be glass. If you are going to eat it, you ought to be prepared to watch it die.

The Guardian, 9 May 2014
© Guardian News & Media 2014

If slaughterhouses had glass walls, we would all be vegetarians

If you're horrified by a flame-roasted dog, you should be shocked at a hog roast

It is prejudice that allows us to protect certain species, while treating others as mere commodities

Mimi Bekhechi

It's been dubbed the world's most gruesome market. Pictures of dogs crammed together in tiny cages waiting for their turn to be flame-roasted in front of one another and the charred bodies of rats, cats and monkeys lying lifeless on the market floor.

With extreme stories concerning animals, the pictures are usually very upsetting, and anger and xenophobia directed toward the host country almost always follows. But, as the saying goes, people in glass houses shouldn't throw stones. It's time we took an honest and hard look at our own abhorrent treatment of animals.

You don't have to travel halfway around the world to see cruelty similar to that in the Tomohon Market in Indonesia on display: crates and cages jam-packed with live animals, limp and lifeless bodies blow-torched in preparation for eating, whole carcasses on display by meat vendors – it all goes on here, too. The only difference is the species of animal that is being served up.

The thought of tucking in to Spot or Fluffy quite rightly repulses most animal-loving Brits. In fact, if the British meat industry did to dogs and cats what it does to pigs, chickens and cows, it would be prosecuted for cruelty to animals. There is no rational justification for this arbitrary double standard.

It is prejudice and prejudice alone that allows us to protect certain species, to take them into our homes and make them part of our families while treating others as mere commodities. All animals are some one, not some thing to put on a plate. When it comes to suffering, there is no difference between a dog or a cat and a pig or a chicken – we all have the same capacity to feel fear and pain and share the same desire to live, have families and do what is natural and important to us. Irrespective of the species, every living being with a will to live should have a right to live free from unnecessary pain and suffering.

Like many vegetarian or vegan commentators this week, I welcomed JBS Family Butchers' decision to return its display of dead animals to its window – at least it's being honest about where its meat comes from. Why should society be censored from the reality of the bloody violence

SOME ISSUES:

If you are a meat eater, what difference does it make what meat you eat?

Why are people more shocked and concerned about dogs being eaten than other animals?

Does this make you consider becoming a vegetarian?

Can meat eating ever be made less cruel or kinder to animals?

that's behind every slab of steak or bucket of chicken wings?

Don't misunderstand me – I'm outraged by the photos of dogs as they await their executioner and of dead animals with pained expressions etched into their burnt faces. But my anger extends beyond them, to the way we in the UK incarcerate, mutilate, terrify and kill smart and sensitive animals by the hundreds of millions every year – the unseen, unheard victims of our greed and indifference.

I often think of the words of Isaac Bashevis Singer, that "in their behaviour toward creatures, all men are Nazis." It's an uncomfortable notion, but who could argue with it? Like Paul McCartney said, "If slaughterhouses had glass walls, everyone would be vegetarian". If the thought of eating one of the tortured dogs from Tomohon Market disgusts you, stop clinging to a double standard. In today's world of virtually unlimited choices, it's never been easier to make the compassionate choice to leave all animals off our plates.

The Independent, 4 March 2014

I'm outraged by the photos of dogs as they await their executioner... But my anger extends beyond them ... we in the UK terrify and kill smart and sensitive animals by the hundreds of millions every year

The only difference is the species of animal being served up!

Image: djempol

The social supermarket is a step forward for tackling food poverty

Britain's first 'social supermarket', enabling local people on low incomes to buy food at knock-down prices, is a welcome addition to food banks, says **Caspar Van Vark,** though more needs to be done to tackle the roots of food poverty

A new supermarket opened in Goldthorpe, South Yorkshire, in December last year. Nothing exciting about that, you'd think. But this is no ordinary supermarket. Instead, it's a rather exclusive, members-only store.

The Community Shop caters specifically to people who are in receipt of benefits, such as income support, and who live in a catchment area around the store. The first of its kind in Britain, it's known as a 'social supermarket' and sells surplus food drawn from major retailers, stocking many of the same items and brands you'd find in a high street supermarket, except the prices are up to 70% lower. A social enterprise, it's been launched as a subsidiary of Company Shop, a longstanding commercial redistributor of surplus food.

The store will also offer access to other services such as CV-writing skills, debt advice and cookery classes. Goldthorpe is a former coalmining village, and still has high levels of social deprivation; with this pilot, and its additional services, Company Shop hopes that customers in the catchment area will be able to get "on the road back to becoming mainstream consumers."

Food poverty is clearly an issue in the UK, as the rapid spread of foodbanks has shown. According to the Resolution Foundation's Low Pay Britain 2013 report, 4.8 million Britons were earning below the living wage last year – an increase of 1.4 million since 2009. Many people, even those in work, struggle to afford decent food. And food is also a more 'elastic' type of expenditure. It's hard to argue with the rent and utilities, but you can always squeeze the food budget just a little more.

The social supermarket is good news because we desperately need models to complement what foodbanks do. The Trussell Trust, the UK foodbank network, says it is launching three new ones a week, up to a current

SOME ISSUES:

Do you think these shops are a good idea?

Who do you think should be allowed to shop at these stores?

How can people who are not struggling for money assist those who are?

Whose responsibility is it to make sure everybody can afford good food and drink?

The store will also offer access to other services such as CV-writing skills, debt advice and cookery classes

It sells surplus food drawn from major retailers... except the prices are up to 70% lower

total of 345. Is that because foodbanks are exactly what we need everywhere, or because there haven't really been many other options around to address food poverty?

They are a catchy idea, but even The Trussell Trust itself doesn't position them as being a complete solution to the issue of people not being able to afford enough food. For example, to use a foodbank, you have to be referred by a social agency and you then receive vouchers for just three visits (though there is some discretion in this). They may also be less accessible for some people (such as the elderly), and the nature of the scheme means that you get what you are given, so there's little room for choosing the foods you need or which might best address your nutritional gaps. There's also an element of social stigma. Some people might choose to go without, rather than accept perceived charity. There is certainly a place for foodbanks, but they are a sticking plaster.

The social supermarket is therefore a useful additional way of addressing food poverty. It's not 'better' than foodbanks as such – many

people will continue to need emergency help if they are temporarily penniless – but as an intervention, it is more suited to addressing longer-term food poverty, and there was a gap in the market for that kind of service. Once you qualify and register to become a member of the Community Shop, you're free to use it as a supermarket. It's just a much cheaper one.

More Community Shops are expected to launch in other parts of the country this year, so even more people will be able to shop for good food at knock-down prices. And with their supplementary services, they may help people find a job if they're unemployed, and then maybe they won't need the shop any longer.

But as the Low Pay Britain 2013 report shows, even being in employment is no

guarantee of being able to put enough food on the table. So yes, the social supermarket is good news because it brings a much-needed new response to food poverty, but it shouldn't distract us from asking why so many people can't afford to eat in the first place.

17 February 2014, Positive News
© Positivenews.co.uk

More Community Shops are expected to launch... so even more people will be able to shop for good food at knock-down prices

WHY SUGAR IS OUR ENEMY

And what Action on Sugar wants to do about it

What is the problem?

In December 2013, a survey of 57,000 adults showed that what mattered most to them was health, followed by a happy family environment. Yet 60% of UK adults and one in three children are overweight or obese. Are people really choosing to be overweight, with all the health risks that brings?

The food industry is making handsome profits from our human instinct to want things NOW. It does this by making cheap junk food available to anyone, anywhere, at any time. This food is often loaded with sugar, but so is food we don't normally think of as 'junk', such as salad dressings and even "low fat" or "healthy" cereals.

Evidence shows that sugar is the main culprit in our obesity problem. Fat and protein do give us some benefits, but refined sugars offer nothing of value. The body does not require any carbohydrate from added sugar for energy, no matter what the food industry claims. Sugar is just a source of completely unnecessary calories.

SOME ISSUES:

Do you know how much sugar is in the food you eat?

Do you know how much sugar you should have each day?

Why do you think more is not done to tackle the amount of sugar companies put into food?

What should be done to tackle this?

And whose responsibility is it?

Action on Sugar

A group of UK and international experts have launched Action on Sugar – despite some headlines stating "sugar is toxic". Their aim is to pressure the food industry to reduce added sugar in foods, by 40% over four years. That would mean 100 fewer calories per person per day, which, according to the UK Department of Health, would put the obesity epidemic into reverse.

How much is too much?

The UK and Europe guideline daily amounts for sugar have not been updated since 2003 and suggest it is ok to consume a staggering 22 teaspoons of sugar daily.

The World Health Organisation has recently advised a maximum of six teaspoons a day for an adult – and that includes sugars from fruit juice and honey.

Sugars are added to the majority of processed foods in the UK and many products have as much or more than the recommended amount in a single portion. No wonder many of us don't know how much is in our food. This issue can't be left to each person to make a choice. We need rules to protect consumers, especially children.

Where is the extra sugar coming from?

Some sugar occurs naturally in food, but sugars are also added to food in processing, (including to fruit juice and smoothies).

The reason that even sugar in a 'good' product like fruit juice can be bad for you is because it is easy to have too much. Fruit juice doesn't have the fibre of whole fruit which slows the speed that sugar goes into the blood stream. It also makes you feel full more easily. You can easily drink a glass of juice made up from six apples and still feel hungry, but try eating more than three whole apples and you'll struggle.

The added sugar in food is put there to improve the taste and it is used very widely, particularly in 'low fat' foods. Research for the Daily Telegraph newspaper found:

- One "low fat" meal contained almost six times the sugar levels of its "full fat" equivalent dish

- A "fat-free" drinking yoghurt was found to contain almost as much sugar as a Mars Bar

- A single portion of a "healthy living" apple and blackberry crumble contained five-and-a-half teaspoons of sugar

Many products have as much or more than the recommended daily amount of sugar in a single portion

- A one litre carton of a "low fat" chocolate milk drink contained more than 30 teaspoons of sugar, around two thirds of which is estimated to be added.

What is the response of the food industry?

The food industry's usual response to criticism is to say that the ingredients are listed on the label knowing that many people buy food based upon how it's promoted, not on the ingredients. The misleading labelling and health claims on "low fat" foods that actually have shocking levels of sugar added are a scandal.

The industry pretends it is not part of the problem. Barbara Gallani, director of regulation at the Food and Drink Federation, denies that sugar has a role in increasing obesity, despite the large numbers of scientific studies showing this. On BBC Newsnight recently, the president of Coca-Cola Europe said his company's drink, which contains as much as nine sugar lumps, had the same number of calories as half a croissant or a cappuccino. Coca-Cola says that it's OK to consume its

It took 50 years between the first scientific studies linking smoking and lung cancer and effective laws to control smoking

"happy" calories as long as you exercise, but this does not fit with independent scientific evidence. It matters where the calories are coming from.

Stalling for time

We mustn't forget that it took 50 years between the first scientific studies linking smoking and lung cancer and effective laws to control smoking. Why? Because the tobacco industry was very successful in denying the facts. They managed to plant doubt and confusion in the public, bribing political allies and even buying the loyalty of rogue scientists.

In the same way, Big Food continues to sell bad health without worrying about any comeback. They spend billions targeting children with junk food advertisements and even "respected" scientific bodies such as the UK's Scientific Advisory Committee on nutrition, receive large amounts in research funding from Coca-Cola and Mars.

Can I stay a healthy weight through exercise and dieting?

The food industry spends billions in junk food and sugary drink advertising. It targets the most vulnerable members of society including children. Worse, the industry links fitness and sport with junk food and sugary drinks - Mars is one of the official sponsors of the England football team. Yet one regular sized bar contains eight teaspoons of sugar, almost triple the recommended limit for a four- to eight-year-old child by the US Department of Health and Human Services' dietary guidelines.

Although regular physical activity has many health benefits, it often does not result in weight loss. We have similar activity levels to 30 years ago but obesity has rocketed.

This has been like a lottery win for diet companies. A mistaken message has pushed people into reducing calories from fat rather than encouraging good nutrition leading to huge profits for the weight-loss industry. Yet long-term studies show that most people regain virtually all of the weight they lose through diets, and the sort of dieting that encourages rapid weight loss is bad for our health.

Where is the proof?

Most scientists agree that added sugar gives us extra calories that we don't need as well as having other negative effects on our bodies. A recent study showed that those who got more than 25% of their calories from added sugar increased their risk of death from heart disease by three times, compared with those who got less than 10%. This was true even for people who were not obese. We are all at risk, because you don't have to be overweight to be affected by diet-related disease.

What is more, the commonest cause of chronic pain in children is tooth decay and sugar is the number one reason.

Why is the government not doing anything?

Like the tobacco industry, the food industry is a big business with plenty of influence. How does sugar compare to tobacco? A teaspoon of sugar or one cigarette will not harm you. But over time, the habit can be fatal. Unlike Big Tobacco, Big Sugar deliberately targets children. And added sugar has become so widespread in our food that we can't avoid it even if we wanted to. Unlike choosing to smoke, many of us are accidentally consuming sugar in our foods. So it is not simply a matter of personal choice.

But perhaps most disturbing of all the similarities is the way both industries have used the power of their money and their political influence to try to protect their profits, at the expense of our health.

In Parliament, Andrew Lansley MP tried to rubbish the statement of a respected public health expert comparing the harm done by sugar to tobacco. He also claimed, wrongly, that "sugar is essential to food". It is not. He would have been more accurate to say "sugar is essential to food industry profits". Lansley was a paid director of a marketing company whose clients have included Pepsi, Mars, Pizza Hut and Diageo's Guinness.

When he was Health Secretary (May 2010 to September 2012) Lansley created the Responsibility Deal. He invited fast-food

A mistaken message has pushed people into reducing calories from fat rather than encouraging good nutrition

companies to discuss how to tackle obesity. This gave the impression of progress, but only resulted in weak and meaningless voluntary promises to reduce calories in food products.

Recently the current health secretary, Jeremy Hunt said he wanted a plan of action to tackle the obesity epidemic. But he already has one. It's been just over a year since Britain's doctors submitted a 10-point plan to tackle the obesity epidemic. The plan included a tax on sugary drinks, banning junk food advertising to children, restrictions on fast food outlets near schools and compulsory nutritional standards in hospitals.

Not a single proposal has been implemented. Political beliefs are preferred to scientific evidence and the interests of Big Food remain more important than our children's health.

What now?

It's time to wind back the harm of too much sugar, reverse the obesity and diabetes epidemic and the unspeakable suffering it causes. According to Britain's chief medical officer, if we don't act to curb overweight and obesity we may see the first generation in which parents live longer than their children. That is a truly chilling prospect that can no longer be ignored.

It's time for Action On Sugar.

This article has been adapted from several articles by Dr Aseem Malhotra, a cardiologist and science director of Action on Sugar

www.actiononsugar.org

Gender

'I'd hear three rape jokes a day' - one teenager on the epidemic of sexual harassment in schools

17-year-old blogger and activist Yas Necati recounts her experiences of sexism in the classroom, and urges us all - teenagers, parents and teachers - to act.

When I was in school, boys would buy The Sun for Page 3. They'd crowd around the paper in one corner of the classroom and scoff to themselves. It sounds like something from the 70s, but I only finished my GCSEs a few months ago.

I once asked a boy to stop looking at Page 3 whilst sitting next to me in class. He called me a "jealous dyke" and an "ugly shit". We were 12. But we could've been any age; it was a recurring incident throughout our school years. After a while, us girls simply gave up saying anything for fear of being told that we just wanted "better tits"... and truth is, most of us did. Who could really blame us?

Sexism is alive and well in schools. 70% of girls report experiences of sexual harassment at school or college, and school is the most common setting for sexual harassment and coercion. 16% of 15-17-year-olds have avoided going to school because they felt bad about their appearance – hardly surprising when you consider that a quarter of girls are bullied because of the way that they look. 40% of girls feel self-conscious about their bodies during PE and 87% of girls think sexism affects most areas of their lives. The statistics are staggering, and behind each of these

SOME ISSUES:

Have you experienced sexism in school?

Do you think a lot of sexist things go unnoticed in school?

Why do you think sexism has a negative impact on people?

Why does it matter if we treat boys and girls differently?

What can be done to tackle sexism within schools and colleges?

Who should take responsibility for this?

Boys had been watching pornography on their phones in the back of her English class. The teacher did nothing and the girls were too intimidated to react.

numbers are real people with real stories. Looking at my own experience of sexism, it's frustrating to see how commonplace it is. I've spoken to my sister, my friends and reached out to other young women via Facebook to share theirs. We – teenagers, parents, teachers - need to start listening to these stories.

One evening over dinner my younger sister recited her day to me, recalling the still life she'd painted and a joke she'd heard. She paused for a second, grimacing before describing how boys had been watching pornography on their phones in the back of her English class. The teacher did nothing and the girls were too intimidated to react. For my 14-year-old sister, and many girls her age, this is just another day at school.

My sister's revelation of her everyday experience prompted me to think further about sexism I'd experienced at school – and the way in which gender biases and expectations start so young, for boys and girls.

When I was 11, a girl in my class punched a boy of the same age in the face. His cheek had swollen and with a quiet voice he told the teacher that she'd hit him. Mrs. Cedar chuckled and chimed, "Aww, Liam, did you get hit by a girl?" Immediately others began to laugh. Liam's inflamed cheek turned an even

Mrs. Cedar chuckled and chimed, "Aww, Liam, did you get hit by a girl?" Immediately others began to laugh. Needless to say he probably never made the same "mistake" again.

deeper shade of cherry-red. Needless to say he probably never made the same "mistake" again. Can you imagine how the teacher would've reacted if the genders were reversed? We're contradicting ourselves - encouraging children to ask for help, but basing our reactions on gender biases and expectations. This instance may have been subtle, but it's the small actions, and everyday socialisation, that shapes people's minds for the future. This boy's masculinity was checked before he could even ponder it. The culture that we're taught we later put into practice.

In secondary school, Year 7, I remember a rumour going around that a girl in our year had lost her virginity to a boy in Year 9. Everybody called her a slut for the remainder of her time at school. There was no shame

We're contradicting ourselves - encouraging children to ask for help, but basing our reactions on gender biases and expectations.

placed on him, despite him being two years older and having had sex a lot more times than her. "What's the boy word for slut?" my younger friend once asked me after she'd been the victim of sexual bullying for wearing "suggestive eye-liner." "Respected," I said, although I couldn't possibly explain to her why...

Fast-forward a few years to the biggest decision of our lives to that date: GCSE options. I remember my friend telling me he fancied becoming a paediatrician so naturally was thinking of taking Child Development. But there was a problem - Child Development is a "girl's subject," right? He decided to opt out and a few months later switched career path. Only one boy, Jim, took Child Development, though managed to "hide" it from the other students during enrolment. When the term started and the boys found out, he was subject to severe harassment and bullying. A few weeks into the course, Jim dropped out. He continued to be teased for the remainder of his time at school.

Starting college a few months back I decided I should act. I set up a feminist society with a girl in the year above, and welcomed everyone along.

In my final GCSE year, a boy kept calling me "hairy gorilla" for choosing not to remove my leg or underarm hair. When holidaying in Cuba that year, despite the heat, and the fact that I love swimming, I completely avoided the pool (the exposure!). After a whole week of hiding, I decided I'd finally 'take the plunge' on our final day away. For the rest of the academic year, a boy followed me around pointing at his underarms every time he saw me.

In my final year of school I became a little despondent. Years of experiencing sexism and watching others experience sexism was starting to profoundly affect my happiness and well-being. I began counting rape jokes. I realised that I'd be lucky, walking through the corridors, not to hear three a day. I became a feminist, not because I felt it was important, but because I felt it was essential. When I told my teacher she said I should "just give up" as I was "wasting my time."

Starting college a few months back I decided I should act. I set up a feminist society with a girl in the year above, and welcomed everyone along. The response, though mainly positive, didn't compensate for the years of sexism and discrimination we'd all suffered. We felt comforted that others had similar stories to our own. Yet these are stories of assault, bullying and shame; why should we have to experience this?

We're currently working on a local project - similar to Everyday Sexism - collecting experiences of sexual bullying and harassment within the college. After only a few months we found most young women had a story to share. One girl was the constant target of rape jokes and sexual threats because of her sexual orientation; another was told by a boy that he would "make her straight." I know so many young women who've been forced into doing things against their consent. I know young women who've been raped.

Sexism is alive in schools. The teenage years are an uncertain and difficult time for many as they grapple with their identities and try to sculpt themselves into the adults they will become. The culture in schools has a huge impact on this development. Although changes are happening, we've got a long way to go before achieving equality in the classroom. We need a massive shift in the way we educate our daughters and sons, both on the curriculum and off it. Sexism in schools has a negative effect for everybody, and it's time we made a change.

Source: www.mumsnet.com

Sexism in schools has a negative effect for everybody, and it's time we made a change.

Why I Wear Nail Polish

Culture jamming a society that doesn't want me to be myself

Jonathon Reed

A teenage girl sat across from me on the tram today. "Excuse me," she asked, "are you a boy or a girl?" "Boy," I replied. She leaned back and said, "So why are you wearing nail polish?" I stared at her, taken aback by the venom in her voice. "No reason," I eventually responded. She and her friend shared an ugly look. "Honestly," I heard as they got up to leave, "a boy who wears nail polish what a f***ing queer."

What I didn't tell her

"Hey," I didn't stand up and call after her, "you really want to know why I'm wearing nail polish?"

"The first time I wore red nail polish it was smeared on my fingers by a group of laughing kids in a small village in the Andean mountains. I paint it on when I'm feeling sad or lost as a visual reminder of a time that I was happy and fulfilled. It's a piece of self-identity, and it gets me through hard days."

"How dare you try to take that away from me," I didn't snarl.

Break rules and challenge power

She didn't have a problem with nail polish itself. It was only after I had affirmed my identification as a boy that she verbally punched me to the periphery of acceptable society. By painting my nails red, I had broken a normative rule; I had asked her to recognize my subjectivity and distinct gender expression.

She said no.

Of course she did. Our society is built on an imbalance of power that makes it far easier to reject the other than to adapt to unfamiliar realities.

Add in a bit of feminism

Femininity in boys blurs the black-and-white boundaries of the social order, which is why a 2011 clothing ad featuring a young boy wearing pink nail polish was called blatant transgender child propaganda. It's seen as a danger to good and proper binarism—a challenge to traditional power structures.

It also clashes with patriarchal values, which associate femininity with weakness and inferiority. By displaying a typically feminine trait, I was seen as abandoning a superior position as a man. As Lori Duron* asked: "How come when girls play with gender it's a sign of strength and when boys play with gender it's a sign of weakness?"

Effeminate boys are viewed as having given up power, because masculine concepts of physical and emotional toughness have largely remained unquestioned as a boyhood ideal. Somewhere along the line, feminine qualities have become "weaker". For the girl on the tram, being queer meant being less.

SOME ISSUES:

Why do you think the girl on the train responded in the way she did?

Does what you wear reflect the person you are?

Why is it important to wear what feels right for you?

Where do traditions and stereotypes of what boys and girls 'should' wear come from?

Is it important to challenge those stereotypes?

age © Jonathon Reed

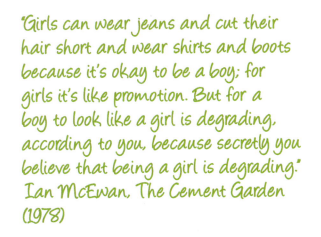

"Girls can wear jeans and cut their hair short and wear shirts and boots because it's okay to be a boy; for girls it's like promotion. But for a boy to look like a girl is degrading, according to you, because secretly you believe that being a girl is degrading."
Ian McEwan, The Cement Garden (1978)

"At stake here is nothing less than how we measure the well-being of our fellow citizens, and how much that wellness hinges on genders that coincide with normative expectations."
Ken Corbett, Boyhoods: Rethinking Masculinities (2009)

My red nail polish really didn't have anything to do with my gender identity, but so what if it did? Why are we so afraid of those who don't conform to rigid binaries? Why do we consider boys who are effeminate to be "lesser than"?

Fight the good fight

And, at the end of the day, should any of this really matter?

Quite honestly, it's up to you. The world is a cruel place; there's brutality and intolerance everywhere you turn. And you know what that means? All we've got is each other. The very least we can do is treat each other with respect and acceptance.

When I wear nail polish, you know who asks me about it most often? Kids. Most of them already have some inkling that I shouldn't be doing it and they are curious as hell. That's how societal change begins—by breaking a few rules, teaching a few people that it's okay to be different. Stand up for those who can't. Defend equality and all that.

Most importantly, be your queer self.

It's all you can do.

medium.com/gender-justice-feminism
* Lori Duron is the author of Raising My Rainbow: Adventures in Raising a Fabulous, Gender Creative Son (Random House, September 2013). The first parenting memoir to chronicle the journey of raising a gender nonconforming child

The power of play

Do your childhood toys dictate your future career?

What were your favourite toys as a child? Lego, a toy oven, superhero models, dolls, Action Man? A survey would probably result in very different lists for boys and girls. But is this division based on an inborn difference or does society dictate what is right for either sex?

SOME ISSUES:

Have toys become more gender specific since you were younger?

What sort of toys do you think both boys and girls would like to play with?

What influences children to choose certain toys?

Might more neutral toys be a good thing?

Are girls naturally always going to choose dolls to play with?

The power of pink

Look at most toy displays and you can instantly spot which toys are aimed at which sex. It isn't only that boys' toys are often things to build, explore or experiment with, while girls' toys are things to look after, to imagine fantasy worlds or (oh dear) to clean or cook with.

The toys for girls are almost always pink. It doesn't matter what colour the items are in real life, in the world of toy manufacturers ALL girl things are pink - pink prams, pink horses, pink cookers, fridges, games. In the boys' aisles you will find toys in every colour - except pink. The message couldn't be clearer - these are for you - but not for YOU. However, just in case, retailers often label the aisles as boys and girls - as if the two were not just separate genders but separate species with very few interests in common.

But why should it matter what young children play with?

They're not just toys - they're messages

Education minister Elizabeth Truss recently voiced her concern that choices of toys affected career choices later. Girls were not being given an early interest in science and maths and engineering because they weren't given toys that stimulated that interest.

Becky Francis, professor of education at Roehampton University, would agree. She told the BBC News Magazine, "Different types of toys give different messages about what's appropriate for boys and girls to do, and have different educational content." She found that boys tended to be given toys that involved action, construction and machinery, while girls were steered towards dolls and perceived "feminine" interests, such as hairdressing. The message seemed to be that boys should be making things and problem solving, and girls should be caring and nurturing, Professor Francis told the BBC.

While no one is suggesting that early play prepares children directly for the world of work, it may influence how they see themselves and what they think they are capable of doing. It can make children familiar and confident with certain skills related to work. Playing with Lego might not turn you into a house-builder but might help develop your belief that you could be one. Children, mainly girls, who are given the impression that certain activities were not for them, might not feel comfortable and confident to develop the skills in later life.

Fighting in the aisles

The movement against gender-specific toys has had some success. The campaigning group Let Toys Be Toys has persuaded major retailers such as the famous London toy store Hamleys, Marks and Spencer, Debenhams and Boots to stop dividing their toys by gender. The campaign has now moved on to persuade publishers to Let Books Be Books, rather than labelling certain ones for boys and others for girls.

Some of the most heartfelt and effective protests have come from children themselves. Seven year old Charlotte Benjamin wrote to Lego asking it to change because there are "more Lego boy people and barely any Lego girls" and "all the girls did was sit at home, go to the beach, and shop, and they

© *Let Toys Be Toys*

Toys may influence how children see themselves and what they think they are capable of doing.

had no jobs, but the boys went on adventures, worked, saved people … even swam with sharks".

In 2012 an angry Irish six year old write to Hasbro about their "Guess Who" game:

"I think it's not fair to only have 5 girls in Guess Who and 19 boys. It is not only boys who are important, girls are important too."

In a YouTube video that has had an astonishing 4.5 million views, five year old American toddler Riley Barry complains about the gender division in a toy shop: "Girls want superheroes and boys want superheroes." In a follow up video she complains about the lack of a female action figure and says, "Every kid in my school gets the message the toy stores are telling us".

At age 13, McKenna Pope was angry that her four year

old brother, who loved to cook, was put off by the girls-only pictures and 'girly' colours of Hasbro's Easy Bake oven. He was getting the message that this toy was not for him and that cooking was not for him - only girls cooked. Using YouTube videos and the petition site Change.org (she managed to get 46,000 signatures in 3 weeks), she persuaded Hasbro to produce a version of the oven in black and silver and include boys on the packaging. And, here's a revolutionary thought, maybe girls would even prefer the black and silver design? After all they are not born liking pink.

Why pink persists

Why and how does the gender division in toys continue? It wasn't always the case. Toy catalogues from the 1970s show items such as bikes in bright colours, such as red, with no gender divide.

© @Seany85

Parents used to be able to save by handing toys down. That can't be the case if that sibling is a different sex, and KNOWS that pink is for girls and blue is for boys!

One reason is pure profit. Parents used to be able to save by giving toys their older children have grown out of to younger siblings! That can't be the case if that sibling is a different sex, and KNOWS that pink is for girls and blue is for boys! If toy manufacturers couldn't sell products exclusively for boys or for girls they would stop producing them - so there must be a demand for them. Some people would argue that this shows an in-built appeal of certain toys to each gender. Do parents decide or do they respond to what their children ask for?

Of course a demand can be created. If there is a strong enough message to parents about what is 'right' for their child, few of them will risk going against it. In our society we will assume that a toddler dressed in blue and clutching a plastic spanner is a boy - and we will comment if it turns out to be a girl. Once the 'rules' are firmly established, they will be reinforced on many occasions. Even small children will correct others for behaviour that doesn't 'fit' including choosing the wrong colour playthings.

Boys will be boys

Writer James Delingpole responded very strongly in The Daily Express to the idea that parents should make an effort to give their children a variety of toys: "If girl toddlers want to spend their time playing with dollies – and they do – and if small boys want to spend their time constructing things out of Lego where exactly is the social benefit in frustrating their natural urges?

"Give a girl a doll and she will cuddle it and nurture it. Give a boy a doll and he will either torture and dismember it or use it as a hand grenade."

In a statement that seems to make the strongest connection between toys and the future of their owners he writes:

"If little girls didn't have those dollyhugging instincts we would all be in a pickle because who in the future would do the mothering and who would work in all those vital caring professions from midwifery to primary school teaching and nursing?

And if little boys weren't hardwired into being obsessive, aggressive show-offs and risk-takers, who would spend hours in the lab before making great scientific breakthroughs or drilling for oil or defending the nation?"

You can't be what you can't see

It's certainly true that more than three quarters of the workers in "science, research, engineering and technology professionals" are men, while 82% of workers in "caring, leisure and other services" are women. But can this be attributed to their different early learning experiences? There must be many other factors that influence career choice. But is there any reason why we can't give all children access to all types of toys and to all the possibilities they suggest?

Sources: www.bbc.co.uk
www.lettoysbetoys.org.uk
www.ted.com
www.express.co.uk

Alternative Princesses

Catriona Stewart

NOW That's What I Call Music, the compulsory soundtrack of 1990s teenagehood, has produced its latest double album – Now That's What I Call Disney Princess...

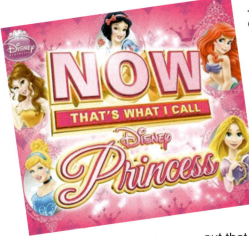

... It's pink, obviously, and it has some sweet-looking, long-haired, doe-eyed lassies peeking out from round that familiar, blocky font.

That Disney princesses are still entertainment for modern young girls, now that's what I struggle to understand.

The troupe of 11 princesses in the franchise are the Disney version of nightclub PRs: slender, made up and employed to sell an aspiration. The gaggle of sweet young husband-hunters was hastily hauled together in a purposeful palette of spangly colours to entice small people to force their parents into buying Disney merchandise.

Andy Mooney, Disney chairman of consumer products, told the New York Times that, waiting to see a Disney on Ice show, he spotted a slew of little girls in princess frocks and worked out that he could monetise their dreams. "I was surrounded by little girls dressed head to toe as princesses ...They weren't even Disney products.

"They were generic princess products they'd appended to a Hallowe'en costume. And the light bulb went off. Clearly there was latent demand here."

A writer in The Telegraph earlier this week said she'd happily blow the brains out of a Disney princess. I wouldn't go that far; that's a lot of a multi-coloured pixels to clean up. But I would tweak them. Sleeping Beauty starring Princess Hear-me-Auroara. She clocks that Prince Charming has already been around the block with Snow White and Cinderella, calls him out as a cad and a chancer and wakes the kingdom up her own sweet self.

Princess Take-no-crapunzel pins her locks to the inside of the tower window, abseils down the wall alone and takes herself to Toni and Guy for a directional haircut.

Princess Twerksnot fancies a career in the music industry but decided to keep her clothes on and let her voice do the, erm, talking. She slays a few dragon-like executives who pressure her to lose two stone and appear naked in a music video.

Princess Nobel wins all the awards - science, literature, peace. She's just one neatly packaged role model. In trousers.

Princess Merida. Sword-wielding, arrow-slinging, anti-marriage ...actually, she'll do nicely.

Herald Scotland, 15 November 2013
Reproduced with permission of Herald & Times Group

SOME ISSUES:

Do you think Disney has a responsibility to create positive role models for young children?

What is positive about the traditional Disney princesses?

Why might the Disney princesses be considered negative role models?

Health

Jab could reduce heart attacks by up to 90%

Scientists believe a single injection which reduces the chances of heart attacks in mice could be used on humans in 10 years.

Dr Kiran Musunuru, from the Harvard Stem Cell Institute, where the research is being done, said: "Heart attack is the leading natural killer worldwide." He explained this new development as a form of vaccination which could reduce heart attacks by between 30% and 90% in humans.

Cholesterol is produced in the liver to help your body build new cells, insulate nerves, and produce hormones. However too much cholesterol in your body puts you at risk of heart disease because it thickens the walls of arteries and so slows down the flow of blood.

We know that some foods can increase the amount of cholesterol in your body but there is also a genetic element to cholesterol levels. A gene in the liver regulates levels of cholesterol. Some people have a variety of the gene that leads them to have high levels and therefore a higher risk of heart attack. A lucky 3% have a mutation of the gene which keeps their cholesterol levels very low. The scientists 'edited' the normal gene to copy this mutation and placed it in the liver of the laboratory mice.

The new jab reduced blood concentrations of cholesterol in the mice by 35% to 40% within days. This rapid, dramatic effect raises the hope of a treatment for humans which could be more effective and more permanent than anything we have at the moment.

Dr Musunuru said although the research was at a very early stage, the first trial patients could be offered the treatment within a decade. The single injection would be a permanent solution, in contrast to the current best option, statins, which have to be taken every day.

Sources: various

SOME ISSUES:

If you were able to speak to the researchers, what questions would you want to ask them?

Is the use of mice in this experiment justified by the results?

Do you think this treatment should be offered equally to people who have a genetic problem and to people who have caused their problem through poor diet?

three people a day die while waiting for an organ transplant – can money solve the problem?

opinion polls show the vast majority of the uk population is in favour of organ donation and would consider donating some or all of their organs, yet 10,000 people are still on the waiting list

SOME ISSUES:

Why do you think more people do not donate their organs?

What can be done to encourage people to donate?

Why is it important that more people donate their organs?

What do you think would be the positives to paying for organs?

And what might be the negatives?

How can enough people be encouraged to donate to meet the demand for organs?

There are 20,333,750 people on the NHS Organ Donor Register but this is not enough. Despite their good intentions, many people fail to discuss their wishes with their family and forget to sign up to the Donor Register. Families, who have the final say, hesitate if they don't know their loved one's wishes.

Each potential donor is precious as fewer than 5,000 people each year in the UK die in circumstances where they can donate organs. Right now more than 10,000 people in the UK need an organ transplant that could save or dramatically improve their lives and each year around 1,000 people die while

waiting for a transplant - that's about three people per day.

The NHS Blood and Transplant service wants to match the best countries in the world for organ donation and transplantation by increasing the family consent rate to over 80%, currently it remains at 55-60%. The service aims to deliver "a revolution in public behaviour in relation to organ donation" through a range of strategies for engaging and informing the public.

One option is to change the donation system. Currently we have an opt-in system. The donor must have expressed a willingness

everyone is paid but the donor; the surgeons and medical team are paid for their work, and the recipient receives an important benefit in kind.

to donate, ideally via the Organ Donor Register, and, at a time of terrible distress and pain, the family must make a rapid decision to agree.

Other countries use an opt-out system. In that case everyone is assumed to have agreed to become a donor unless they specifically say they do not wish to do so. There are variations within this. Such a system can be 'hard' where the views of close relatives are not sought or 'soft' as in Spain, where their views are still taken into account.

Doctors and charities dealing with those waiting for transplants are in favour of an opt-out system. Critics, however, point to the need for a carefully maintained register and to the possibility that doctors could be put in a difficult position if relatives dispute their decision.

Others have a more radical suggestion - why wait for dead donors? Let's get more living donors by paying them for their services.

John Harris, Professor of Bioethics at The University of Manchester wrote in The Times in 2013 "We know that live donations are much more successful than transplants from the dead, but how do we increase the supply of healthy adults willing to donate a kidney? The obvious solution is to give donors an incentive — we should pay them."

He pointed out, "Everyone is paid but the donor; the surgeons and medical team are paid for their work, and

the recipient receives an important benefit in kind. Only the heroic donor is supposed to put up with the insult of no reward."

Canadian researchers have calculated that if donors were paid $10,000 per kidney and this resulted in a 5% increase in donations the health care system would save $340 per patient. If there was a 10% or 20% increase, the savings per patient could reach $1,640 and $4,030 respectively, because the cost of 2 or 3 years of dialysis during the wait is usually higher than $10,000. This study, led by Dr. Braden Manns, a professor at the University of Calgary, also surveyed 3,000 Canadians and found that about 70% of the general public thought that some compensation for organ donation would be acceptable. However only 25% of transplant doctors agreed. The same survey found that about half of people who said they wouldn't be likely to donate an organ changed their minds if the deal included a $10,000 payment.

The objections to such payments are strong. People thinking about selling their organs for money might be in a vulnerable position. If their need for money is strong they may put themselves at risk by ignoring any worries they have about the process. Even if there is the safeguard in this country of only allowing one purchaser for organs, the NHS, there are still concerns: it may mean

that the poorest people are selling parts of their body to keep richer ones alive. Would the trade in organs be worldwide so the developed world would reap an organ 'harvest' from less wealthy countries? And what if donations don't rise because people who before would give freely now feel tainted by a financial transaction?

According to the NHS Organ Donation website: "Transplants are one of the most miraculous achievements of modern medicine. But they depend entirely on the generosity of donors and their families who are willing to make this life-saving or life-enhancing gift to others." Is that a wasteful and illogical state of affairs - or is it exactly as it should be?

Sources: www.organdonation.nhs.uk
bma.org.uk
www.nbcnews.com
and others

Smoking outside the hospital is a break for patients and staff. Why ban it?

Yes, the NHS should help people quit – but depriving people of the relief of a cigarette in moments of stress isn't the way to go about it

Hannah Jane Parkinson

SOME ISSUES:

Do you think it is ok for patients to smoke outside hospital?

What about hospital staff?

Do you think it is the role of the hospital to ban unhealthy actions? Or are they only there to treat the consequences?

Would you mind if a doctor or nurse treating you smoked?

See also It's not harming anyone, p11

The National Institute for Health and Care Excellence (NICE) has issued guidelines that propose banning NHS workers and patients from smoking on hospital grounds. To which I say: if they think that this is a good idea or even remotely enforceable, they must be smoking something.

I am not advocating smoking and nobody is arguing that if you're an emphysemic hacking up your lungs that reaching for a lighter is a great idea. But if you are a patient at a hospital or a psychiatric institution, by definition your life is not great at present. And if you are a smoker, in times of misery, stress and angst, a cigarette makes your situation that tiny bit more manageable. Why else would every photograph of the first world war show tommies in the trenches puffing away?

When I was an inpatient at a psychiatric hospital, admitted because I was fluctuating between suicidal ideation and mania, my mum piped up in my first meeting with the head psychiatrist and said with eager, optimistic eyes that she hoped that by the end of my stay I would have quit smoking.

My psych gravely replied that my quitting smoking was really not the priority at the moment. Because it really, really wasn't. And actually, I'm sure if my mum had been given the choice of me continuing to smoke 15 cigs a day and getting better or me choosing to live and engage with treatment, she'd be perfectly happy. Which she was.

In America, almost half of all cigarettes are sold to people with mental health difficulties, and trust me, I understand why.

Then there is the fact that one of the greatest impediments to quitting smoking is the social side. Now imagine how much more important that is when you are spending your days bored stiff, shuffling around in a paper dress, pissing into a cardboard container or having to queue up for meds. For a smoker in a hospital or psychiatric ward, chatting and having a fag with other patients is the one time you feel human again, like yourself in the outside world.

Another one of Nice's suggestions was preventing NHS workers from smoking "during work hours or when recognisable as an employee". Now, I can understand patients objecting to being treated by someone who smells like they've just hooked up with Philip Morris* in the hospital canteen, but I am pretty certain that smoking members of NHS staff are careful to avoid this; you can't walk five metres in a hospital without getting to a soap dispenser and being reminded to wash your hands. If I'm in hospital all I want from my nurses and doctors is that they do their jobs well, which the overriding majority do. Patients should focus on their job, which is primarily, getting better, not moralising on the private lives of the people who are there to treat them.

And, to be perfectly honest, if I worked for, say, Barts Health NHS Trust, at a time when 1000 staff members are being asked to compete for their own jobs, and 600 nursing posts are being axed or downgraded, I'd be in need of a fag or five.

Not to mention how this ban would be almost impossible to enforce. Would hospitals have to install a mass of CCTV cameras, or

hire fake smoking Gestapo types? The whole thing would just lead to people puffing out of toilet windows. And what about visitors smoking? Do you really want to be the person to have to go up to a distraught mother who has just found out their child has died, or a man who has just found out his wife has had a stroke, and ask them to politely stub out?

It's fine that the NHS is doing all it can to help smokers quit, disseminating information on how best to kick the habit, how smoking impacts on illness and mental health. But making life stuck in a hospital or institution even more depressing than it already is is not fine.

A few years ago the band Editors released a song with the lyrics: "Smokers outside the hospital doors / the saddest thing that I ever saw", which means they probably never watched Marley & Me, or the News at 10. Smokers outside hospital doors are not the saddest thing. The saddest thing is people being in hospital or institutions in the first place, and the way this government is systematically dismantling the NHS. Gimmicks like these are just a smokescreen.

Philip Morris is a global cigarette company. It owns 7 of the top 15 brands in the world

The Guardian, 27 November 2013
© Guardian News & Media 2013

Making life stuck in a hospital or institution even more depressing than it already is, is not fine.

How to cheat death ...

Starting with a skeleton-eating infection when he was four, Robert Glancy's life has been punctuated by a series of near misses

SOME ISSUES:

Have you ever had any major accidents or illnesses?

Why do you think accidents and illnesses might make you think about your life more deeply?

Has the writer of this article been very lucky, or unlucky?

I was four when I nearly died the first time.
Death came in the form of an infection with a long Latin name that crept inside a hairline fracture in my right collarbone. When it started to rot the rest of my skeleton I was rushed to a Zambian hospital for surgery.

But when they opened me up in the wrong place I went from bad to worse. The botched Zambian surgery left a scar the shape of a crazed asterisk, like a teacher marking an incorrect answer with a cross. I was flown to Bristol for an emergency operation and the Bristol scar is a neat tick, a tidy celebration of successful surgery.

Removing two inches of rotten collarbone left me alive, if a touch lopsided. That was my first second-chance. Because I was four, the experience left no existential mark. But it was the first time I came close to being around for the last time.

There were some physical effects, though. My scars – the cross and tick – grew big and ugly as I grew big and ugly. And my right arm compensated for the lack of collarbone by building extra muscle. When my right side grew bigger than my left side, it left me wonky looking, with Barbie's left arm but Ken's right arm.

The botched Zambian surgery left a scar the shape of a crazed asterisk, like a teacher marking an incorrect answer with a cross

My second second-chance came when I was old enough for my fragile sense of existence to be shaken. On holiday in Brunei I accepted a lift from some guy. I knew he'd been drinking but I was in the middle of nowhere and I was 20, so I got in the car.

Everything in Brunei is about oil – even the roads run in long straight lines following the oil pipes that form a grid over the land. Which meant that my drunk driver misjudged a rare turn, throwing the car into a wild spin down an embankment, where it eventually stopped in a crushed smoking mess.

There were five of us in the car. Four of us walked away. The fifth fell to the ground in agony, clutching his back. Alcohol and adrenalin seeped away and, with raw clarity, I saw the situation: on a pitch-black night in the middle of a jungle, a boy lay screaming on the side of a road.

After an eternity an ambulance came and he was taken to hospital. He was very lucky. It was only muscle swelling and

...at least twice

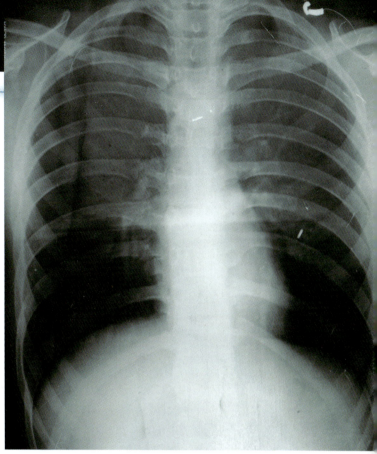

after a few days in a wheelchair he recovered fully.

For days afterwards I felt the world was so fragile that everything was about to fall apart. But once the fear passed I was left with a sense of elation – a second-chance high – that I'd survived a near miss, and for a long time afterwards day-to-day living glowed a little brighter.

Once the fear passed I was left with a sense of elation – a second-chance high – that I'd survived a near miss

My third second-chance was psychological but it still delivered a punch. As part of the health checks on applicants for New Zealand citizenship, they X-ray your lungs to ensure you're cancer-free.

Waiting for my results, I fretted and panicked. I used to smoke. I quit in my late twenties but I knew there was a chance that the damage was already done. But after a few days I forgot all about it. Until a nurse called and said, "Mr Glancy, could you come to the surgery? There's an incident on your X-ray."

"An incident?" I said, "What sort of incident?"

When I arrived the doctor looked very serious, pointing at my X-ray, saying, "The incident is in this area." I searched for a blooming shadow of death but said,

"I can't see it."

"This dark patch here," he said solemnly. He pointed again and added, "You appear to be missing a collarbone. Did you know that?"

The world snapped back and I took a deep breath, filling my cancer-free lungs, and said, "Of course I know that!"

"Oh," he said, sounding disappointed, as if he had hoped that he was revealing some incredible fact to me.

Humans have a talent for taking things for granted. Sometimes we need to have something almost snatched away before we can really appreciate it. All three experiences left me with a pure but hard-to-define notion, an idea so obvious that close explanation causes it to crumble a bit: no matter how bleak or complicated a tangle I'm in, I'm still here, alive, still full of that precious thing that is such an everything that all too often it's taken for granted.

Daily Telegraph, 10 February 2014
© Telegraph Media Group Limited 2014

"Terms & Conditions" novel by Robert Glancy,
published by Bloomsbury

Humans have a talent for taking things for granted. Sometimes we need to have something almost snatched away before we can really appreciate it

Photo: © John Cassidy

Attacking cancer like a business: 'Why I'm crowdfunding my recovery'

Hannah Foxley has just been diagnosed with cancer for the third time in three years. She tells Radhika Sanghani her story and why she has taken the unusual step of trying to crowdfund her latest batch of treatment

SOME ISSUES:

Why do you think so many people have donated money to Hannah?

What would you do to fight a terminal disease?

Do you think people should fund treatments that are not scientifically proven to work?

What do you think about her method of fund raising?

Hannah Foxley has just been diagnosed with cancer for the third time in three years. She is only 36 years old and has already had breast cancer twice, a mastectomy and gone through years of chemotherapy and treatments. Until two weeks ago, she thought she was finally in the clear.

"I thought that episode of my life was over," she says. "But I'm in a lot of trouble. That's a huge shock. I'm a very pragmatic person so I was just like… how can I be in so much trouble and look so fit and healthy – people always tell me how well I look. How on earth has this happened?"

Hannah, from London, was first diagnosed with breast cancer in 2011. She was only 33 years old and immediately began treatment. "The first time I was diagnosed I didn't have the support network I have now; I wasn't in a happy place," says Hannah. "I went through it all on my own. I was really low and depressed; I really struggled through chemotherapy the full time. I had to work full-time through my treatment."

But she did manage to avoid having a mastectomy and was a week away from ending her treatment when she was told the cancer had returned. "When it came back that was the catalyst for me to change and pull myself out of the rut I'd been in for such a long time," she says.

She began to learn about nutrition and exercise, and began an entirely plant-based diet. Then she was told she had to have a mastectomy. "It was really hard," she says. "It's a vital part of your femininity and how you feel as a woman. Being single as well, men don't react that well to this kind of stuff, until I met my partner now."

Hannah had to endure another five weeks of radiotherapy, and in July 2012 she was finally told that the cancer was gone. But, only two weeks ago, Hannah was rushed to hospital after collapsing in agony. Doctors told her that her cancer was back for the third time, and had spread to her liver and lungs, where it was in an advanced stage.

She wants to go for homeopathic remedies – she is willing to try anything.

Hannah has been having regular check-ups every three months since she stopped having treatment in 2012, but the doctors missed the signs her cancer was back. She had no idea she would find herself in this position again – especially with such an advanced form of cancer.

It has spread so far that doctors are unable to operate, and so the only treatment available to her is chemotherapy, which will simply stop the cancer from getting worse. "I realised things were pretty bad," says Hannah, who quit her job as a chartered

Hannah created a page on website 'gofundme', in just over a week she raised £14,000

financial planner two years ago, and now runs a small business giving financial advice to women.

She wanted to explore other natural options, but when her doctor told her she did not have "the luxury of time", she began chemotherapy. But now Hannah has decided she wants to try treatment in an American clinic, and go for homeopathic remedies (there's no scientific evidence that homeopathy works, but she is willing to try anything). The only issue is she doesn't have the funds necessary, and so in an unusual move, she has taken to crowdfunding her new batch of treatments online.

"I'm running a fledgling business and I don't have the money, so I set up [an online] page," she says. "Being like, 'I actually don't have any money', was a really hard thing to do but the response has been incredible. People really want to help me so I thought what I really need help with is money. I don't want to be stressing about how I'm paying my rent because that's a cause of cancer. I thought I have got nothing to lose, so I'm going to just swallow my ego and ask the question."

Hannah created a page on website 'gofundme', with the title 'Let's kick this s**'. It is a change from people using charity-style websites such as Just Giving, which are traditionally where people make pleas for these sorts of donations, but Hannah says it allows her to be more involved with donors by commenting on their posts to her, and linking them to her regular social media updates.

In just over a week she has raised more than £14,000, but will need much more if she is going to fulfil her plan of getting alternative treatments. "People have been so supportive," she says. "I was overwhelmed by the responses. Sadly, I do need a lot more." Her initial goal is £25,000.

She says she has been surprised by how many of the donations have come from complete strangers. One donation, of £120, has been from an American financial expert who has never met her but writes: "After browsing your website it appears we have much in common. Please stay strong (both physically and mentally) and please let me know if I can help in any way."

She doesn't know how bad her cancer is at the moment, because her doctor told her he couldn't "un-tell her" once she knew, but she knows her situation is serious. "[My boyfriend] said I know this might end in a lot of heartbreak for me," she says. "I was like, I can't promise you it won't."

However, she still believes that her new spiritual attitude and move towards natural remedies will help her. "I was in warrior mode before," she says, talking about when she previously battled cancer. "But my body doesn't have the resources to fight. Now it's about being really feminine and a gentler healing energy. If I survive this I want to be a mother."

Daily Telegraph, 27 February 2014
© Telegraph Media Group Limited 2014

STOP PRESS:

Hannah's GoFundMe page shows £29,480 raised by donations from 717 people in 4 months. Her last entry appeals for £10,000 to keep her in India but a month after she wrote it a friend posted the news of her death.

Dr Kate Granger

A better way of death?

Have you thought about dying? Have you made plans for your funeral and talked about them with your relatives? If you have, you are the exception. Most of us are like Woody Allen who joked: "I'm not afraid of death; I just don't want to be there when it happens."

While we think of ourselves as more frank and open than previous generations about a whole host of matters, death remains a difficult topic to approach with our nearest and dearest. Asking people about their dying wishes seems tactless. How could you even start the conversation?

In 2014 the Dying Matters Coalition, an alliance of care groups, conducted a survey about people's plans for the end of their life. Only 21% of people had discussed their wishes at all. Only a third had written a will. The chief executive of the coalition said; "Dying is one of life's few certainties, but many of us appear to be avoiding discussing it or in denial altogether."

But perhaps this is changing. As with so many different subjects, social media may be allowing us to talk about the subject more freely and the influence of some high-profile cases may mean that we understand and plan more.

While most of us live our lives without thinking about the inevitable end, there are those who are forced to confront that knowledge. We now see people faced with a terminal illness, whose final days are played out in public via Facebook and Twitter. These are strangers whose dilemma provokes a response and forces us to consider our own lives, our own characters and our own final departure.

One such person is Dr Kate Granger. She has a rare form of cancer. She is documenting the progress of her incurable disease (as well as many other aspects of her life) to 24,000 followers on Twitter and her YouTube video "Kate's Story" gathered 10,000 views in a month. As she says, she uses her blog to "muse about current issues especially

SOME ISSUES:

Do you admire the people written about in this article?

If you knew when you were going to die, would you do anything different with your life?

Is it really necessary for most of us to think about preparations for death?

Cancer "I don't mean to be rude but you didn't bloody keep your side of the bargain did you?!"

relating to end of life care, communication and patient centredness. I also write about my experiences as I approach the end of my life."

In March 2014 she wrote her third 'letter' to her cancer in which she mentioned one of the most difficult decisions for terminally ill people: "How does one choose between probable rapid death or a toxic treatment in the full knowledge of how horrible the experience of undergoing that treatment will be?" With grim humour she rebukes the cancer "I don't mean to be rude but you didn't bloody keep your side of the bargain did you?! I asked you really politely to let the chemotherapy subdue you and help me to feel less pain." Although she admits she is getting weaker and may have to give up the medical work she loves, she ends on a defiant note: "I would like to finish by reminding you when I die so do you and then where will you be?"

In fact, like many of those who are given a definite time warning about their own death, Kate is determined to leave a legacy. She has raised thousands of pounds for the Yorkshire Cancer Centre and her campaign to make care more personal through the simple method of having doctors introduce themselves has already borne massive results. Her campaign #hellomynameis has been taken up by many other medical professionals.

If Kate Granger, at 32, is too young to have to consider her end of life care, how bitter must that experience have been for 12-year-old Reece Puddington and his family? He was originally diagnosed with cancer when he was only five years old. After treatment the cancer went into remission,

but when he fell ill again aged ten it was discovered that cancer had spread throughout his body. His condition was terminal.

Reece drew up a bucket list of things that he wanted to do and he began a Facebook page recording his life, which attracted 38,000 followers. With their help he achieved many of the items on his list but in February 2014 he made a momentous decision. He decided to refuse any further treatment. At age 11 he had decided to die.

This is how he announced his decision on Facebook:
"As you know after the latest scan results I was sent home to rest and think over the 2 possible options...

I could opt for another trial, but this would mean travelling a lot to the hospital and coping with the side effects, but could also hopefully extend my life, or....

I could simply do nothing, stay at home and let nature take its course which would lead to me losing my life slightly earlier than if I'd had more treatment.

My mum had always hoped over the last 5-6 years that she would have the courage to know when enough was enough.

After careful consideration, my mum thought that if she was doing it for herself she would keep sending me for treatment as she wouldn't want to let me go, but if she was doing it for me she'd let me go.

Well, she's letting me go....."

Reece drew up a bucket list of things that he wanted to do

Reece Puddington
Photo: Courier Media Group Ltd

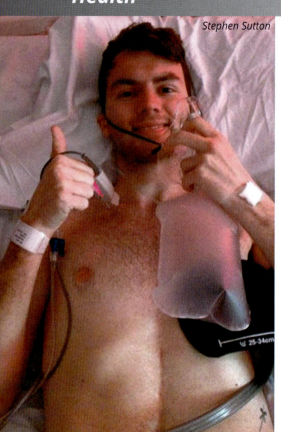

Stephen Sutton

The photograph of his cheerful smile and thumbs up sign, when he had been told he was about to die, went viral

His story was carried by national newspapers, struck with the awful situation and his courage in facing it. Followers on Facebook told him how brave and inspirational they found him.

In May 2014, Reece announced that he was too ill and tired to continue his Facebook entries and later that month his mother broke the news of his death, writing: "Reece Puddington 6th December 2002 at 12.11am - 20th May 2014 at 12.11pm. Hobbit, Pirate & all round inspiration!"

One legacy from his bucket list is still being completed; Reece's Retreat, which is a beach hut in his native Whitstable which will enable seriously ill children to enjoy a day by the sea.

And then there is the phenomenon of Stephen Sutton. Diagnosed with bowel cancer at age 15, he lived by his own motto "I don't see the point in measuring life in terms of time any more. I'd rather measure life in terms of making a difference."

And what a difference he made. He set out to raise £10,000 for the Teenage Cancer Trust. The photograph of his cheerful smile and thumbs up sign from his hospital bed, when he had been told he was about to die, went viral. Celebrities such as comedian Jason Manford took up his campaign and Stephen found himself with a million friends on Facebook and 200,000 followers on Twitter. Stephen died on 14th May 2014. By the time of his funeral, 330,000 people had donated and he had raised £4.5m for his charity, their biggest ever donation.

His funeral was a testimony to his emotional impact. His coffin lay in state in Lichfield Cathedral and 10,000 people took part in a vigil. The public part of his funeral reflected his cheerful spirit - it featured drummers, balloons, a wreath with a smiley face symbol and his family were given a round of applause. The Dean of Lichfield said Stephen had taught us "how to make the unacceptable, beautiful".

The media, particularly social media, give us a new, very public, way to engage with death, something that has been increasingly made private and purely medical. They allow us to share the hopes and pains of strangers in a way that appears quite intimate. We find it encouraging that a hopeless situation can be transformed into something positive, that the victims of a fatal illness can regain some control.

A cynic might say that supporters are ghoulish spectators, enjoying sickly sentiment and manufactured tears and celebrities involve themselves because it is good publicity.

Yet surely it must be a good thing that we empathise with someone facing this final challenge. When we do that, we are bound to consider our own ultimate end. We are bound to wonder what characteristics we would show in such a crisis. Would I be as resilient and cheerful? Would I be able to think of others even while facing the end of my own life? Would I be admirable or abject? Miserable or magnificent?

Jason Manford said of Stephen Sutton: "The reason we took to him so passionately was because he was better than us. He did something none of us could even imagine doing."

Because of the examples of these people perhaps we can now imagine our own end of life, even if we can't emulate their spirit. Because of them we can start to think and talk about how people should approach their final weeks, what we consider to be a good death and a good pathway to it. That could be a lasting legacy.

Sources: various

Internet & media

Do you know where your children go online?

Sexting, bullying and getting round security settings... young people tell Olivia Gordon what really happens on the internet

SOME ISSUES:

When did you first use the internet?

What dangers do you think there are online?

Is the internet a positive or a negative thing in your life?

Why might parents be worried about what their child does online?

What can be done to encourage internet safety?

See also Mums, I spy on my kids, p64

Thirty years ago, children were taught never to accept sweets from strangers, but the equivalent modern message, about staying safe online, doesn't seem to be getting through. For all its positives, the online world is full of potential hazards to young people. Sexting, bullying and sexual approaches from strangers are online dangers modern teenagers routinely face. And adults' knowledge of what young people are doing online is often vague and complacent.

Nearly half of British children now have online access in their bedrooms, while a quarter of 12- to 15-year-olds owns a tablet of their own. The number of this age group using smartphones to send, receive and post photos online has risen significantly in the past year, and Ofcom points out that children's online safety skills have failed to rise at the same rate, with particular risks coming from the lack of privacy on social networking sites. Most parents of five- to 15-year-olds believe they know enough about the internet to keep their children safe, but, according to research by internet security system McAfee in 2012, four-fifths of teenagers say they know how to hide their online behaviour from parents.

Some parents feel their only recourse is to restrict internet access, but James Diamond, of parenting and technology website Quib.ly, says: "A big reason that children don't tell parents about abuse is that the default reaction of parents is to take the internet away from them."

Internet safety needs to be taught, with specific ground rules and open communication between generations. Parents need to know that the dark side of the online world can't be avoided – if they have teenage children, it is almost certainly already in their lives.

Cal Davis: 16
From: Kenilworth, Warwickshire
Hours online a day: Six
Online devices: Smartphone, tablet,
two laptops, desktop, Raspberry Pi,
e-reader, feature phone
Age when first went online: Nine

My internet access was monitored and controlled by my parents until I was 14 or so. But teenagers like to have a private life away from their parents, and parents don't necessarily know that they're on websites like ask.fm – and if they do, they're not entirely sure what goes on on them.

If anyone has a child with a moderate level of online popularity who has joined ask.fm, you can almost guarantee that they will have received an abusive message. Questions are posted publicly on your profile page, and you can reply to them, but the senders are anonymous. Most of my friends who have had Ask have received a question saying, "Why are you so ugly?" or, "When are you going to kill yourself?"

I've received some over time, too. They are pretty common, but I don't go on it much because I'm not a fan. People get abused for being, appearing, seeming, acting anything that's not "norm". Stuff like being gay. But there are also more intellectual questions, which I enjoy answering. Like: "Why in your opinion do some people move when they are nervous?"

If people get a lot of abuse, for some reason they seem to get even more. People go on their page, see they're getting abuse and join in. I've spoken to people my age who have admitted doing this. They say, "Oh, I was just being an idiot. I was just not very happy with myself, so I did it to other people." They think if somebody else is more miserable than them, then they're not as miserable.

I know people who have been hospitalised by Ask. People already suffering from depression go on Ask and get questions saying, "Why don't you kill yourself, cut yourself?" It's affected them and they have actually ended up cutting themselves. In some cases, their parents found out; in others, they didn't. With one person, even when they went to hospital, their parents didn't know what had happened until a few weeks later.

I know people who have been hospitalised by ask.fm. People already suffering from depression get questions saying, "Why don't you kill yourself, cut yourself?"

Katie*: 16
From: London
Hours online a day: One to three
Online devices: Smartphone, laptop
Age when first went online: 12

Last year my stepsister – who was 14 at the time – put on Facebook that I'd slept with someone I hadn't. Everyone was asking me about it, and I just told them it wasn't true, and luckily it didn't spread too much. You can post stuff denying the rumours yourself, but not many people want to. They'd rather try to ignore it.

It happens every day on Facebook. There are lies about people constantly. You can see people saying stuff about people's family history, or that people cut themselves, or tried to kill themselves when they didn't. If it's stuff like sleeping with people, a lot of people feel like they can't talk to their parents about that. I told my mum, and she told me to just ignore it.

My stepsister once sent a naked picture of herself to her boyfriend, and when they broke up, he printed it off and made a poster saying, "Look at me, I'm a slag" that had her phone number and her BBM pin [her "address" on the BlackBerry Instant Messenger service] on it. The posters were put up round his school. She started getting messages five minutes later. She ended up changing her number and getting Mum to buy her a new phone – she told her it was broken. The boy probably got told off for putting the posters up, but no one ever contacted my stepsister. Our mum still doesn't know.

A whole school can turn on one person. They look down on the girl whose boyfriend sent the picture. The girl gets called a slag, a slut, a whore. It happens to boys, but not often. It's not going to sound very nice, but if a boy's big down there, they get left alone. If it's small, the girls will send the picture around and take the mick.

Older men, people I've never spoken to, are always adding me on Facebook, Twitter and Instagram. I've had a message saying, "I hope you're a real ginger – I want to taste you." It has become normality. The technology can't be taken away. On Facebook people can message you even if you don't have them as a friend. I am very careful with the small number of social network sites I do use, but there is only so much you can do and most people will not bother to do as much as me. Going round schools and warning kids from a young age will help. That's why I work with a project [run by Arc Theatre] that does this. I've been to 10 schools in east London. Some children as young as 11 had already been sexting. Kids at that age are really naive. If they haven't got anyone telling them about the consequences, they won't know.

Some children as young as 11 had already been sexting. Kids at that age are really naive. If they haven't got anyone telling them about the consequences, they won't know.

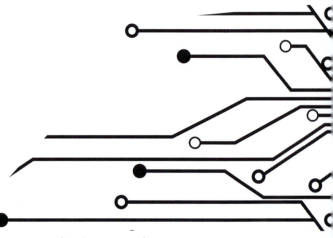

Tom*: 15
From: London
Hours online a day:
Seven
Online devices:
Smartphone, iPod
Touch, laptop
Age when first went
online: Seven

The sort of stuff we do, boys my age, is go on pornographic websites. Most are massive collections of all types of free content. I could watch from two minutes to an hour a day. Does it affect the way I look at women? Massively.

When I first got my laptop, Mum put on a free filtering system that didn't do its job. Now we've got this expensive one and I have to resort to using phones or iPods. But Mum's taken away my iPod Touch. She'll have a good go at trying to stop me, but I'm going to do it. It's natural.

Mum was quite surprised when she found out what I do online. She went through my messages on Facebook and stuff. On Facebook I was flirting with girls. Sometimes it was explicit. The common slang for it is sexting, but I wouldn't call it that. It's just talking. The fact it's through the internet makes it slightly different from saying it to a girl's face, which would quickly end up being quite awkward. At school the next day, we'd talk like normal. Quite a lot of them have been real relationships. I tend to avoid things that are completely online.

I found out about Snapchat when a girl offered me a picture of herself. You take a picture, write something and then when the message is opened, the receiver has 10 seconds to see it before it deletes itself. I think, though they don't say it, it's designed for children my age to send inappropriate pictures. I haven't sent any, but I have received topless pictures from girls I know, generally from my class at school. It's unlikely the girls' parents know. They're probably better at hiding it than I am. Half the time I just look at the pictures and don't reply. When you don't reply, they can see that you've opened it, which normally makes them send a couple more messages, saying, "Reply to me, goddammit."

What would I advise a parent? Never, ever buy your son or daughter anything electrical. Fifty years ago, people my age were more innocent, doing stuff like bike rides down the canal. Now, you're stuck in your room. The real you is your second life; life on the internet is your first life.

> # When I first got my laptop, Mum put on a free filtering system that didn't do its job. Now we've got this expensive one and I have to resort to using phones or iPods.

* Names changed

The Guardian, 9 November 2013
© Guardian News & Media 2013

For more information on Arc Theatre visit:
www.arctheatre.com

I was an internet troll

Anonymous

'Every time I criticised her, she would post screenshots and get more support which would make me even angrier...'

Grace was a girl at my school. She had an Ask.fm account and would answer questions sent in to her, which would then appear on her Twitter and Tumblr accounts. She was in a dark place. She used to post pictures of her self-harm, using Instagram filters to make it look artistic.

She would write about how she was very depressed and people would send messages of support, like, "Don't worry, Grace, we're all here for you." But it wound me up: the way I saw it, she was doing it for attention.

At school, she had a lot of friends who would give her support. We weren't friends, but we had mutual friends. She was very outspoken and she used to give her opinion on things that I felt had nothing to do with her. It would annoy me when she'd talk about things in the news, things I didn't think she understood.

Then, at 2am one morning when I couldn't sleep, I anonymously sent her questions on Ask.fm. I asked if her family were proud of her and the stuff she was posting. I told her her parents must be ashamed, that she was attention-seeking –

At 2am one morning when I couldn't sleep, I anonymously sent her questions on Ask.fm

SOME ISSUES:

Why do you think people troll other people on the internet?

What are the dangers of trolling?

How could this writer have stopped herself from becoming a troll?

What can be done to keep people safe from trolls on the internet?

I was sick and tired of her getting all of this attention. And yet I would go on asking her all these questions that would generate even more

that no normal person wanted to see pictures of self-harm. I don't know why I took it upon myself. I knew it was cruel.

I was sick and tired of her getting all of this attention. And yet I would go on asking her all these questions that would generate even more, so I was fuelling my own hate. I kept on for about two months. Every time I criticised her, she would post screenshots and get more support, which would make me even angrier.

I'd only do this anonymously. I ran a proxy on my laptop so it would appear to come from another IP address. I didn't want to be associated with cyberbullying, but at the same time I couldn't stop. I didn't feel guilty at the time. I'd post something and then I'd go on to her Twitter feed and I'd wait, refreshing the screen until she answered. It was a rush, like watching the last five minutes of a football match. It's 1-1, your team's attacking and you feel the goal's going to come at any point, only the goal was a new tweet from her, replying to my messages. It was a visceral thing.

There were a couple of times when I was about to post and realised I'd logged in as myself and I'd get this sick feeling. I'd have no excuse if people knew it was me. My family would be ashamed of me, and rightly so. When I saw her at school, I didn't say anything to her.

Then around the time I was sending the messages, I noticed that she became very withdrawn and started missing school. One day, on the way home, a mutual friend told me Grace was posting suicidal thoughts, which she hadn't done before. I hadn't sent her a message for about a week, but I still had this thought in my head: you have contributed to this. I kept refreshing her Tumblr page, and when she stopped posting, I felt sick. The

Around the time I was sending the messages, I noticed that she became very withdrawn and started missing school.

whole night, I didn't sleep. That was the point of realisation – I couldn't believe what I thought I had done. I went to school the next morning and she was there. I've never been so relieved. When I saw her, I knew it had to end. I'd learned my lesson at the expense of a teenage girl.

I closed the computer down and thought: I am never, ever doing that again.

I have seen her only once since leaving school, in a photo on Facebook. She looked the same as before only with cleaner arms. The caption said something about the fact that she hadn't self-harmed in six months. I was happy to see it as things seemed to be looking up for her.

It never occurred to me to send a message saying sorry. I just felt that it had happened and I had to leave it alone, which I know makes me sound selfish. I closed the computer down and thought: I am never, ever doing that again.

• *Names have been changed*

The Guardian, 6 June 2014 © Guardian News & Media 2014

Why all this selfie obsession?
We take these snaps without irony, sans shame, fishing for feedback

Even Pope Francis couldn't say no when he was asked to pose for a "selfie" soon after he became the Bishop of Rome

Grace Dent

Selfie – snapping a picture of yourself, largely for egotistical purposes – is the Word of the Year for Oxford Dictionaries editors. The frequency of its usage has increased by 17,000 per cent over the past 12 months.

Frankly, I'm not wholly trusting in Oxford Dictionaries' scientific methodology as they also shortlisted "schmeat". You know? Schmeat? The slang term for man-made, in vitro meat? No, of course you don't. Schmeat isn't "a thing" this year, but "selfies" definitely are. In fact, historians will look back at 2013 and note that in the UK, during a time of financial woe, youth unemployment and mass disenchantment, the buzzword of the year described the cheap, pocket-friendly pastime of staging a picture to look like a fantasy version of oneself. Cheeks sucked inwards. Zoolander pout. Biceps flexed. Boobs spilling from frock. Tits and teeth. Maybe with one arm round a minor celeb whom you just accosted and who couldn't swat you away #goodfriends #soblessed.

In 1993, if you went to Woolworths three times a week to sit in the Foto-Me booth

snapping pictures of yourself pulling "The Fonz is Cool" poses, your ego would have been the stuff of local legend. Now, a selfie-a-day is unremarkable. I sat in a bar recently while one friend took a dozen separate pictures of themselves in the toilet as "it was such amazing light". We take selfies without irony, sans shame, posting the results online as bait in the great murky cyber-sea. We fish never-endingly for compliments, comments… indeed any feedback at all. Maybe just a Facebook like? A little Instagram regram and a new surge of followers. Anything – please God, anything – which indicates we were bathing, remotely, momentarily in another human being's gaze.

We're living through an age where a crucial aspect of public socialising is a little private party with oneself – staring at one's phone – editing, colour-filtering, posting. Also, interestingly, we're living through an age where people see harvesting celebrity-selfies as some sort of human right.

Because how dare anyone refuse such a request? I watched Cher walk through a room recently and she had to

SOME ISSUES:

Why do you think people take selfies?

Do you agree that phones distract people from their own thoughts?

What might be the negative side-effects of taking so many pictures on your phone?

By and large, though, the snapping and posting of selfies is a way to avoid our own thoughts.

The happiest people will live several days a week away from their phones. And they won't need selfies to prove that they are happy.

wrestle-off determined fans – frothy-mouthed, enveloped in red-mist – to have their "Look at me with Cher" selfie. I'm sure X Factor's Rylan in Superdrug would have the same effect. "Let me gather all these people in my famous-person-selfie stamp collection!" we pant, groping the stars and making them grin.

Nowadays the selfie-with-starring-role – not just celebs, but anyone deemed good for social climbing – is an optimum tool for repositioning one's brand on Planet Earth. Many perfectly mediocre people elevate their careers via a campaign of hustled selfies masquerading as #myclosefriends. Of course, the opposite of the social ladder selfie is the antagonistic selfie, aimed not to impress but to infuriate. "Yes, I am out with your rival!" it says, "And look! We're cheek to cheek in selfiepose and we're laughing like larks!"

By and large, though, the snapping and posting of selfies is a way to avoid our own thoughts. One reason that we sit with smartphones glued to our hands is so that, each time a difficult thought enters our brains, the distraction is literally at our fingertips. Thoughts like, "I need to load the dishwasher" or "How will I feel when my mother dies?" or "Why am I alone at Christmas?" or "Can I afford to replace the grubby stair carpet". With a new selfie to post, and feedback to monitor, the pain is averted. Selfies are a mindless act available every time we need to be mindful.

Being mindful of difficult emotions, sitting with them, letting them torment you for a bit, and then working out solutions, used to be how human beings got stuff done. In the 21st century, organisations like Headspace*, or David Lynch** and his transcendental meditation chums, work hard to convince us that 10 minutes a day of just thinking, eyes shut, without laptop, without phone, is doable. Just a short time without thinking: "Guys! How do I look? Do I look better today than yesterday? When you notice me what do you think? I'll take any feedback, stay tuned for another selfie."

In 2023, I can't help thinking, the happiest people will live several days a week away from their phones. And they won't need selfies to prove that they are happy.

Headspace is a website that promotes meditation

**Surrealist film director*

The Independent, 19 November 2013

Photo posed by model

Humanity is better than the media suggests

The media can acquaint us with the shared values of many cultures and promote a sense of deepening relationship, argues Simon Marlow

But we need unfiltered, unbiased reporting to help cultivate this sense of relationship

We are living in a time when major changes desperately need to be made to the way human beings live and relate to each other and to the wider biosphere, of which we are an integral part. But we are responding to this need, and one of the signs is that everywhere, there are demands for freedoms that have long been repressed.

Apart from the basic freedoms connected with ongoing events in North Africa and the Middle East other, psychological freedoms are also being upheld. One example is the freedom to know the truth. This has been brought into focus by the News of the World phone hacking scandal.

A serious side effect of using gossip and sensationalism to boost newspaper circulation figures is that the crucially important issues of our present time can become marginalised in the popular press. The pity of this is that a deep human characteristic — the desire to enquire, to understand and to know — is misused and wasted. Given the right information, people can and do respond in imaginative and creative ways and with the necessary depth and compassion that are needed to transform our values and social structures.

Power

The media is incredibly powerful in moulding public opinion and influencing the political process. So much so that wealthy business magnates are keen to own vast swathes of it. But if the media can direct public opinion in order to support the self interest of its owners, then equally the media can be a wonderful instrument to support the expansion of human consciousness and deepen our sense of relationship with the world and one another.

Used well, the media can bring us into contact with the lives of people in every part of the world. It can acquaint us with the shared values of the many cultures that weave the colourfully varied tapestry of human life on our planet. In this way it highlights the rich diversity of our species and promotes a sense of deepening

SOME ISSUES:

Do you think the media has a responsibility to encourage positive change?

Who should decide what the newspapers and news programmes report?

Should the news be more positive?

What sort of stories would you like to see on the news?

relationship by showing that the same emotions and sensitivities run through all people. The natural outcome of this is huge amounts of empathy and goodwill and a constructive interaction between different nations and cultures.

Unbiased

But we need unfiltered, unbiased reporting to help cultivate this sense of relationship. And we need to remember that when there is manipulation and distortion of the truth by the media, it can divide, fragment and debase on a similarly large scale. This poses a real and insidious threat to the psychological freedom of humanity.

Perhaps our default view in the west is that what we read in the papers or on

Given the right information, people can and do respond in imaginative and creative ways

news websites, see on TV or hear on the radio is near enough true. But people who have been involved in something reported in the media are sometimes surprised to find that the reports don't exactly match their personal experience of the event. And when we remember that many professionals in the media appear to believe that good news is not newsworthy, we might indeed become suspicious about the daily diet of news that we are being fed.

Discrimination

But perhaps this can encourage us to discriminate and not to accept at face value what the media presents. If so, here, paraphrased from an ancient spiritual teaching,

is a useful rule of thumb: Diminish by a factor of ten all the bad we know, and increase by a factor of ten all the good we know – perhaps this might help us to gain a truer picture of the reality?

It might also help us realise that the gloom that many feel about the future for humanity and the planet need not be a self-fulfilling prophecy. Humanity is better than we are led to believe. Goodwill can, does and will transform communities. There is much to be practical and hopeful about, and good news is the best news there is.

Positive News, 10 October 2011 © positivenews.org.uk

Law & order

Clive Chilvers / Shutterstock.com

Sorry for mugging you!

Man apologises via Facebook 35 years after the crime

Michael Goodman

Claude Soffel

The apology was late but it was sincere - and if it wasn't for Facebook it could never have happened at all.

Michael Goodman, now 53, was a teenager when he held up another young man in an attempt to impress his tough friends. In fact he was immediately arrested and had to be collected by his father. He was eventually sentenced to three weeks of community service: cleaning up graffiti on the subway. But guilt over the incident stayed with him.

Decades later, he read a Facebook post about a bagel shop closing and recognised the name of the person he had robbed all those years ago - Claude Soffel. He knew this was his chance to apologise. He posted:
"You may not remember this (about '76 or '77) but a long long time ago I walked up the steps of The Museum of Natural History one afternoon, trying to look like a tough guy to [*name omitted*] & saw you standing there at the top of the steps, I walked up to you & mugged you for your bus pass... Finally I can say - I'M VERY SORRY that you had to go through that crap that day long ago, I wish it had never happened but it did ... forgive me & thanks for reading this "strange" & very long message! Peace & love to you my brother...!!!"

There was a delay of about 11 hours before his victim replied:
"Clearly you're a "bigger man" today. Wow. Memory is a funny thing, I recognize your name now, as well. So, apology accepted... Any man who draws a line for himself, "Today I step forward for myself, my family, and humanity" is a hero to me. So let us now, jointly, put this in its proper place, behind us."

The public apology and forgiveness delighted other Facebook users - but no-one was more pleased than Goodman, "A very large weight has been lifted off my shoulder," he said. "I feel peace and dare I say joy. I'm even happier this is bringing joy to other people."

Sources: Various

SOME ISSUES:

Why was saying sorry so important to this man?

Was the victim right to accept the apology?

If the victim had not been so forgiving would that have changed how Michael Goodman felt?

Should criminals always be given a chance to apologise?

"Clearly you're a 'bigger man' today. Wow... Apology accepted!"

Finders Keepers?

What would you do if you found a huge sum of money?

Imagine this - you are out walking your dog in the open land around the small town of Spalding in Lincolnshire. It's a flat area, crossed by waterways and drainage ditches. In one of these, the South Drove Drain, you spot something in the water - it's a bank note. In fact not one but hundreds of bank notes, floating on the surface of the water. What do you do?

This is exactly what happened to a dog walker in October 2013. The finder, who remains anonymous, called the police. They retrieved the money and their first count revealed that there was actually about £60,000 in the drainage ditch. Some of it had been damaged by the water but a fair amount was in good condition.

But whose money was it and how did it get there?

The short answer is, no one knows.

The investigating officer, DC Steve Hull, of Spalding CID, said, 'It isn't everyday that an amount of money like this is found and somebody must have information that will help the Police trace

SOME ISSUES:

What would you have done in these circumstances?

Where do you think the money came from and how did it get into the water?

Do you think that taking the money people gain from crime is effective?

What should be done with that money?

Essential Articles 2015 • www.completeissues.co.uk

the lawful owner. I would be grateful to hear from people who have genuine information to pass on to me'.

The police are allowed to hold on to money if they suspect that crime might be involved, while they carry out investigations. In this case they needed a forensic examination of the money and contact with the Bank of England to help find out where the money came from.

By April 2014, several people had made a claim on the money but no one had proved that they were the owner. The money remains with the Police until the investigation is complete.

What does the law say?

If you discover money in the street, you must either hand it in or report it to the police.

If you report it but don't hand it in, and the owner reports the loss, you must hand it over.

If you choose to hand it in you will be given a form that allows you to collect it after 28 days.

If you don't report it to the Police, you are guilty of 'theft by finding' and can be charged.

However, police cannot let finders keep unclaimed mobile phones or objects that may contain personal data, such as laptops or iPads.

However, the police can 'seize' money that they suspect might be the proceeds of crime. If the money has been obtained by criminal means it can be 'forfeit' - not given back.

If you don't report it to the Police, you are guilty of 'theft by finding' and can be charged.

Sources: Various
Images courtesy of Lincolnshire Police

What counting dead women tells us that Clare's Law cannot

Drawing connections between the murders of women by men is surprisingly rare. Attempting to accurately calculate women who died because of a sexist culture is even harder.

Holly Baxter

One day, Karen Ingala Smith started counting dead women and couldn't stop. It was January 2012, and the year had begun with seven horrific incidents of domestic violence in its first three days: all women killed, in various ways, by their male partners. After a couple of months, Smith stopped restricting her attention to murders purely involving domestic violence. Instead, she focused on clear incidences of misogyny - serial killers who only targeted women, for

SOME ISSUES:

What do you think about Clare's Law?

Do you think news reports and crime statistics can really make people aware of the issue?

Do you think that naming women who have been killed is a more effective way of raising awareness?

What should be done to tackle and prevent domestic violence?

instance, or men who killed the sisters or female friends of their girlfriends or wives.

Smith's reason for counting dead women is simple: to humanise and draw attention to the problem. Her argument for change is that the government should start recording and researching femicide in a way it never has done before. Most murders of women by men are not random, she believes; these murders should be seen in the context of a sexist society, where violence against women is endemic. "I want to see the connections between the different forms of fatal male violence against women," she writes. "The statistic 'on average two women a week [are] killed through domestic violence in England and Wales' is well known. People seem to be able to repeat this without getting outraged or upset... through connecting and naming the women killed, I'm trying to make the horror and unacceptability of what is happening feel more real."

Drawing connections between the murders of women by men is surprisingly rare; attempting

to accurately calculate the numbers of women who died because of a sexist culture is even harder. One woman on the @CountDeadWomen Twitter illustrates this best by her description of the suicide of a 15-year-old schoolfriend, who had been raped by her boyfriend and then jumped out of a window after fearing that her father would murder her for dishonouring the family. "She wasn't killed by the hand of a man," @marstrina conceded - but she was still the victim of a society that routinely blames the victim in cases of rape and still often sees women as the property of their male relatives. Deaths like these are not as far removed from domestic violence murders as conventional crime statistics might lead one to believe.

Smith's tactic of naming women and documenting the way in which they were killed undoubtedly hits a nerve, and perhaps the most disturbing part of the entire project is the frequency with which she tweets the details of new victims. As she has pointed out, quoting statistics can only get anyone so far. But there are statistics worth bearing in mind

Naming women and documenting the way in which they were killed undoubtedly hits a nerve, and perhaps the most disturbing part of the entire project is the frequency with which she tweets the details of new victims.

beyond the oft-quoted 'two women per week killed by former or current partners' – for instance, the Women's Aid data stating that in the case of domestic violence, an average of 35 assaults happen before the police are called. Or the fact that rates of domestic violence have increased by 17% during the recession, but the government has responded by cutting funding to violence against women programmes. In London alone, services for women seeking help from abusive relationships have been cut by £1.9 million since 2009. These numbers build a picture of serial political failures - meanwhile, Counting Dead Women continues to put a face to the effects of such policies.

So how should we respond? It was announced today that Clare's Law, which allows people to check the police records of their partners and has been piloted in Greater Manchester, Wiltshire, Nottingham and Gwent since 2012, will now be expanded to cover all of England and Wales. The law's namesake is Clare Wood, a young woman murdered in 2009 by a boyfriend with an extensive history of violence against women – but it's unclear

whether Clare's Law would have actually saved her life. Domestic violence charity Refuge has raised issues with the law in the past and continues to do so, arguing that most abusers aren't known to police and more deaths could be avoided by focusing on the police response to violence against women.

Clare's Law allows people to check the police records of their partners

Sandra Horley, chief executive of Refuge, stated at the disclosure scheme's inception that "it is another way for the government to sound tough on domestic violence while actually doing very little." I can't help but agree. Rhetoric and emotively named laws are easy; identifying and changing a culture that trivialises misogyny is much more difficult. Telling women that they can visit their police force after a few dates with a new boyfriend and check that he hasn't been convicted of GBH in the past is one thing. Questioning why

violence against women is all too often treated flippantly by the police, on the other hand, involves a forbidding amount of self-examination. As Horley also pointed out, police already had the power to disclose the crimes of Clare Wood's partner to her - but for a number of reasons, they didn't use it.

Only when we start to acknowledge the links between violent acts against women can we tackle one of the most stubbornly persistent problems in the UK. Until then, we have no option but to continue counting dead women, all the while working towards a future when there will be no more victims to count.

New Statesman, 25 November 2013

Rates of domestic violence have increased by 17% during the recession, but the government has responded by cutting funding to violence against women programmes.

Kids need hugs, not paranoia and fear

Vicky Allan

SOME ISSUES:

Why do you think people are paranoid about the way they treat children and young people?

Is this a positive thing?

What might be the negatives?

Can a lack of hugs affect a person and how they develop?

Now and again, when I've comforted a weeping child who is not my own, kissed a cheek or ruffled some hair, a fleeting thought has passed through my mind that, if I were a man, this might be considered inappropriate. This thing that is most natural and right - to hug a crying infant, or offer a cuddle as warmth and affection - would somehow be tinged with badness.

Of course, you don't have to be a man for that to be so. Our culture is suspicious of any adult-child physical contact. And that attitude appears to be snowballing. In recent years we have heard of nurseries that ban hugging and kissing; of a teacher in England being sacked for hugging his pupils; of another teacher, in Scotland, not putting sun lotion on a child for fear of accusations.

That this train needs to be halted was brought to the attention of Members of the Scottish Parliament by Sir Harry Burns last week. At a meeting of the Scottish Parliament's health committee, Sir Harry - now professor of public health at Strathclyde University - called for the retraction of bans on "physically comforting children". The current rules and regulations, he said, are getting in the way of us acting like human beings.

I hugged my own son this morning (I have hugged him many times, of course, but this one was memorable). Immediately beforehand, the air had been thick with irritation, wails, anger, hate - he didn't want me to be his mum any more. Afterwards, there was calm and peace. Scientists now know the biology of this - the oxytocin that is released and the role it has in regulating stress. They also know it is an important element in how we learn physiologically to self-regulate and deal with stress - an element of development. Yet we have become a culture that would deprive children of this magic, in the name of shielding them from some other ugly abuse.

Of course, we are doing this for the sake of the kids. Of course, we all want the utmost to be done to protect children and in this era of Operation Yewtree, Jimmy Savile, Rochdale and countless tales of institutional abuse, it's no surprise that we are anxious. But in our attempt to shield, we may in fact be neglecting. It may be that there are children growing up today who will have cause to complain in future years that their abuse was lack of hugs. One wonders particularly about those looked-after children in homes, described by Burns, where, if someone "walked past a child's room one night and heard the child sobbing, they would not be allowed to do anything about it".

Burns sees the current climate as dehumanising - and it is, indeed, a contrast to one school he describes in Spain where pupils line up and give teachers a kiss in the morning. Scotland's Children's Commissioner Tam Baillie last year raised a similar concern when he declared that "touching children shouldn't be taboo, it should be an expectation".

Burns is flagging up the fact that we may have gone too far in our desire to protect. "Damaging a child in any way is a really, really serious crime against humanity," he says, "but we're damaging children by not showing them that

key empathy as well." We need to cultivate more empathy, and, as he notes, this is "not something that's exclusively the province of the parents - it's the province of other people who show affection for the child".

Some within the child protection field agree. At the same health committee meeting, leading child protection expert Alyson Leslie of Dundee University said that she felt society had gone "completely bonkers in the culture and ethos that have grown up around child protection". It seems to Leslie ridiculous that people could not "hug or reach out to a child, particularly when the child is in distress". For her it is imperative that we change the message.

Yet it's hard to see how to shift the culture. After all, for the most part it's not necessarily about legislation or actual bans but about countering a general pervading fear, a paranoia that reigns everywhere from the play park to the nursery, which makes men, in particular, police their language when talking about children and the warmth, affection and responsibility they feel towards them. One man I talked to on this subject (who isn't a father) uttered the words "show kids love", then retracted them as if they were somehow inappropriate.

One thing we can do, says Leslie, is change our language, stop talking about child protection and instead talk about child nurturing. "The more

we talk about child protection," she adds, "the more we create the sense that we have to take children and put them some place safe, away from everyone." As she notes: "Child protection is not about restricting nurturing affectionate contact but encouraging it - with safeguards."

Though she is "hawkish" in her approach to assessing risk to children, she believes that where risk is minimal, common sense should prevail.

"As a species," she says, "we are programmed for affectionate contact: that should be the norm."

A few years ago, Burns says, he made comments such as this to the Association of Directors of Social Work and "there were gasps of horror in the room - there was a view that this man was a raving lunatic who wanted to hug children". Little has really changed since then. We are a long way away from creating a culture that delivers the "affectionate contact" that should be every child's right. Arguably the fear of contact has heightened.

And it is the children who do not get it from their parents, who are in care homes, or who are taught in schools where teachers don't dare touch them, who are being failed. They are the biggest victims of the paranoia and regulations.

What of those children who never get a hug?

The Herald, 18 May 2014
Reproduced with permission of Herald & Times Group

But in our attempt to shield, we may in fact be neglecting. It may be that there are children growing up today who will have cause to complain in future years that their abuse was lack of hugs.

Mental health

The search for the stranger who saved a life

Jonny's story

Jonny Benjamin was only 20 when he decided to commit suicide. He had been diagnosed with a mental illness, schizoaffective disorder, and he was convinced that his life would never return to normal. About one in 20 people suffer from the same illness. It produces very high or very low moods and sometimes causes a person to lose touch with reality. Jonny was receiving treatment but he could see no future for himself.

On 14th January 2008, at about ten in the morning, he went to Waterloo Bridge and climbed onto a ledge, intending to throw himself into the River Thames. Just at this point, a stranger spoke to him.

The man was in his early twenties and was on his way to work. Seeing clearly what Jonny was about to do, he approached him and spoke calmly. He simply said: 'Please don't do this... you can get better. Let's have a coffee and we can talk about this,' Jonny would later explain. "The pivotal moment for me was when he said 'You can get through this, you can get better' because up until that point no-one had said it would get better."

Jonny climbed back down from the railings and the police took him to safety. So the coffee and talk never happened and, in his distressed state, he never had a chance to thank the stranger or even to learn his name.

Jonny later became a mental health worker and campaigner. He made YouTube videos and a documentary showing that recovery was possible.

SOME ISSUES:

What would you do if you saw someone in need of help?

Do you know who to talk to if you have problems you need to discuss?

How can people support those suffering from issues such as Jonny's?

What does this story tell you about the importance of raising awareness of mental illness?

Rethink Mental Illness.

We've #foundmike

"The pivotal moment for me was when he said 'You can get through this, you can get better'

Six years after that desperate day, in January 2014, Jonny launched a campaign to find and thank the stranger who he decided to call 'Mike'. He wrote: "His act of kindness changed my outlook on life and I have thought about him ever since. I want to find this man so I can thank him for what he did. If it wasn't for him, I probably wouldn't be here today."

His campaign, on Facebook and Twitter, used the hashtag #findmike. It immediately caught people's attention and was soon trending in the UK, Canada, South Africa and Australia. There were TV and radio interviews. As well as thanking the stranger, Jonny wanted to spread his message of hope and recovery and he ran his campaign in collaboration with the charity Rethink Mental Illness.

Neil's story

Of course the stranger had not forgotten the encounter either. When Neil Laybourn, a fitness instructor, was shown the story by his fiancée, he knew immediately that he was the passer-by involved and got in touch.

He recalls, "She saw it on her phone a couple of days after it had gone viral, and straightaway she called me up and as soon as I looked at it I saw how big it was, so I just got in touch as soon as I could really."

Remembering the event, he said, "It was a very cold day, a very windy day, and Jonny just had a T-shirt on and was sitting over the edge of the bridge and it was glaringly obvious why he was there.

"I walked up around him and just calmly approached him and I said: 'Hi mate, can you tell me why you're sitting on the bridge?' and he told me that he was going to take his life that day.

"We just went from there, I just kept asking him questions and wanted to engage him and that if he wanted to talk I was there."

We #foundmike

When Neil Laybourn came forward, Rethink Mental Illness tweeted: "We #foundmike! *Huge* thank you to everyone who shared the #findmike campaign, you made THIS happen"

Naturally, the meeting between the two men was emotional.

Jonny: "I feel like I've won the lottery – I'm totally elated. It means the world to me to finally have the opportunity to say thank you. It's as though I've come full circle and that chapter of my life has now closed. He's such a warm, genuine person – everyone should have a friend like Neil."

Neil: "I was so pleased to see how well Jonny was doing, I had thought about him over the years and had always hoped he was OK ... Hand on heart that Jonny is one of the nicest people I have ever met, it's brilliant to see him smiling again."

The act of listening

Paul Jenkins, CEO of Rethink Mental Illness commented: "The overwhelming public support for Jonny and his search has been incredible. Every single person who shared his appeal has not only helped find 'Mike', but has also helped to open up millions of conversations about mental health."

Both men know that what happened that day to save a young man's life was based on something basic, human and possible for everyone, "It really shows how the simple act of listening can be a huge support to someone who is struggling with their mental health and we can all learn from that," says Jonny Benjamin.

And there is something very admirable and encouraging about Neil Laybourn's comment on what he did that day:

"I didn't feel it was that big a deal, I did what anyone would do. I wasn't trying to fix his problems that day, I just listened."

Sources: various and www.rethink.org

"I feel like I've won the lottery – I'm totally elated. It means the world to me to finally have the opportunity to say thank you"

"Black dog's" return doesn't scare me as much as it did

Denise Welch

As I write this I'm coming out of the other side of one of my depressive episodes. They come so infrequently now it really has caught me on the hop.

I have suffered depression for 25 years now so I know all the signs and I'm aware when the "black dog" is nipping at my heels.

I used to be terrified of flying but, as my desire to escape our bleak mid winter is so strong, I battled to cure myself of this a few years ago.

However, at Malaga Airport last week I could feel the panic rising when boarding the plane as we were first told we were facing an 80mph tailwind but were hit by a 70mph headwind instead and the turbulence was so strong the cabin crew could not be released.

My poor husband Lincoln didn't know what had hit him as I started shaking and crying like a baby. He held me tight, told me there was nothing to worry about and how much he loved me.

Depression is such a cruel, isolating condition.

Of course we landed safely, but I knew my over-reaction was the start of a bumpy ride of a completely different nature. I slept badly and when I woke the next morning my "thing," as I call it, was there.

Depression is such a cruel, isolating condition.

No one can see it. I look the same to most people, but those who love me can see what they call the deadness in my eyes.

My mum used to say that she could look across a crowded room, see me talking to a group of people and know that I was ill.

SOME ISSUES:

Why do you think admitting to mental health issues is so difficult?

Are there misconceptions in our society about people who have mental illness?

What can be done to remove the stigma surrounding mental health issues?

What could schools and colleges do to support students suffering with mental health issues?

I've not got anything to be "depressed about" but clinical depression is a condition not a mood

Being an actress has come in very handy as I'm very good at covering it when I'm in work and social situations.

Depression robs you of your feelings. It takes away your ability to properly love those closest to you. You have no energy for anything.

The simplest tasks seem almost impossible and so dishes that need washing can reduce the depressed person to tears and become an almost insurmountable chore.

I called my first book Pulling Myself Together because that's the sort of comment that the depressed hear all the time. "Come on snap out of it. What have you got to be depressed about," is another unhelpful comment.

That's the cruelty of mental illness. I have not got anything to be "depressed about" but clinical depression is an illness not a mood.

The advantage of having lived with this illness for so long is that as awful as it is I'm not frightened of it in the way I used to be. I know now that it will lift and I will return to my old self.

I want to thank my Lincoln for being such an amazing husband and friend. He had never been around anyone with clinical depression and partners and family play an integral part to recovery.

The reason I have written about this today is because as a spokesperson for the charity Mind it's part of my role to break down the stigma of mental illness.

If you have a doctor who is unsympathetic to your depression change them. Mine is wonderful so this is to you Rob Hendry for always being at the end of the phone.

I'm supposed to be flying to America this weekend to see my son Matt playing in LA and I also have three meetings... at my age.

So I hope I'm well enough to go. I've been so excited so fingers crossed.

Manchester Evening News, 1 November 2013

I'm not frightened of it in the way I used to be.

SPEAKING OUT ON SCHIZOPHRENIA

Of all mental health conditions, it remains the one on which a hostile media out to shock is most likely to pounce. John Pallister says we should listen to those with direct experience, not the scaremongers.

JOHN PALLISTER

The media habitually portrays mental health conditions, and schizophrenia in particular, as frightening and to be spoken of only with difficulty. I have schizophrenia myself and I think, by contrast, that it's vital that experiences like mine should be spoken about openly and not sensationalised or hushed up.

The common notion of schizophrenics as having split personalities is a dangerous misconception. Schizophrenia does indeed mean "split mind" but the condition has varying degrees and symptoms. Schizophrenics can have good insight into their condition and along with good medication and support can manage their illness and day-to-day life.

With any illness, mental or physical, it's important to remember that with determination, guidance and a willingness to succeed, a person can maximise their capabilities within the limits of the severity of their disability.

What I've found, across different areas of society, is that prejudice can be harder to manage than the illness itself. I have a strong work ethic and desire to succeed, but I've struggled with being misunderstood or not supported in the various jobs that I've taken.

I've also been surprised by the gap within the health service itself between non-mental health doctors and nurses who were very much cut off from the mental health side. Patients with mental health difficulties may find that treatment for non-mental health problems is more difficult than for the rest of the population. Lots of people needing mental health services are reluctant to mention their mental health, which causes further problems where it has a bearing on non-mental health problems. What holds them back is fear of discrimination or lack of treatment.

SOME ISSUES:

Why do you think there is a stigma surrounding some mental illness?

What can be done to encourage people with mental health issues to speak out about their experience?

How can society become more understanding and accepting of people who suffer with mental health issues?

WITH DETERMINATION, GUIDANCE AND A WILLINGNESS TO SUCCEED, A PERSON CAN MAXIMISE THEIR CAPABILITIES.

It is therefore important that people feel comfortable talking about their mental health, especially at job interviews or in discussions about their health and welfare or housing.

I have been out of hospital for over five years now and although not working at the moment I have carried on trying to keep occupied. I am an active campaigner, working and writing for the local paper, appearing on radio and talking to psychology students about my recovery.

These experiences have made me realise the huge steps still to be taken to overcome this stigma.

The growing willingness of some celebrities to talk about their mental health problems has been an eye-opener and shows how much we have moved on as a society. I'd like to see even more openness from society's role models.

My own symptoms began when I was 20 (I'm 31 now). The underlying causes are not clear but seem to have been stress related. I experienced paranoia, hallucinations (hearing voices) and delusions, along with an acute phase of psychosis. The episodes were intense; thankfully they were also short.

Other symptoms of schizophrenia can include mood swings, depression, manic behaviour and what I would call a flat feeling.

Medication can control all these symptoms but I found that the best medical response was support. Too often, people are over-medicated or forced back into society where they can't achieve anything valuable or enjoy an active and meaningful life. Helping someone gain insight into their condition is often the most powerful way of preventing or managing mental health problems.

There are lots of support groups that can help people in this respect, but unless you have an illness or an interest in mental health they can be hard to find, leaving sufferers struggling and undiagnosed. I'm sure that if I'd known 12 years ago what I know now, I could have sought help from the relevant sources and prevented or managed my symptoms much earlier and more actively.

I'd urge support groups not only to reach out much more to the diagnosed but to make themselves better known to the public. People need to be encouraged to talk about their concerns and come forward if they start to be aware that they might have an early onset of an illness. That's what I'm committed to doing in my own work.

Disability Now, August 2013

THE WILLINGNESS OF SOME CELEBRITIES TO TALK ABOUT THEIR MENTAL HEALTH PROBLEMS HAS BEEN AN EYE-OPENER.

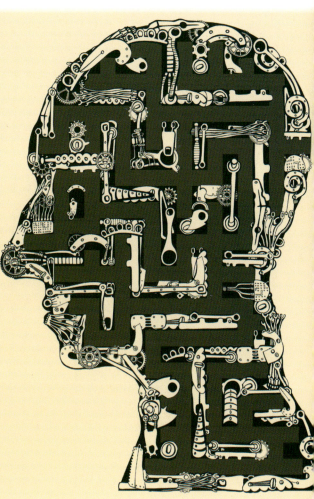

Could I have Alzheimer's, like my friend Mavis?

My short-term memory is failing me – but I'm just a bit forgetful, because I've got too much on my plate. Aren't I?

Michele Hanson

Alzheimer's seems to be everywhere lately. Last week, my friend Mavis rang to tell me she has Alzheimer's. Help! She sounded all right to me. My own short-term memory is shot to hell. What's the difference? How does Mavis know she's got it?

Because her children were worried and took her for a test. She has drugs to slow it down, says she, and scientists are working on something to stop it properly. Hopefully, they'll find it in time to save her. How brave and positive. I'd be weeping in a darkened room if it were me.

Then on Sunday the Radio 4 appeal was for the Alzheimer's society. There are 800,000 people with it in the UK, there will be twice as many by 2050, and they called it "the slow death of the brain". Terrifying. This is the last thing I fancy. But how can we be sure we're not just a bit forgetful, because we've got too much on our plates?

Yesterday, Rosemary trekked all the way to town to buy tickets for a show, booked some balcony seats, was almost home on the bus and realised how foolish she had been. She didn't want balcony seats. How would she and her chum totter up all those stairs? So she went all the way back, and there was the same chap in the booking office. "You bought seats in the stalls," said he. "You decided you didn't want the balcony, because of the stairs." Blast.

On Sunday, I emptied my hot water bottle to fill it, but the kettle was empty. Why? Because I'd already filled the bottle, only seconds before. No wonder the water I poured from the bottle looked rather hot and steamy. Had to do it all over again.

SOME ISSUES:

Do you know how to recognise if somebody is suffering from Alzheimer's?

What can be done to help people suffering from Alzheimer's?

Why do you think ageing affects our memory?

How can we help maintain our memories as we get older?

Then forgot the dandelions for Daughter's tortoise, which I had especially searched for, picked, brought home, forgot to take out of my bag, forgot they existed, visited Daughter without them, which meant another dandelion delivery next day. Rosemary and I are exhausted by it, and ergonomically hopeless. But do we have Alzheimer's? I don't want to know.

Anyway, what was that last question?

The Guardian, 13 January 2014
© Guardian News & Media 2014

> On Sunday, I emptied my hot water bottle to fill it, but the kettle was empty. Why? Because I'd already filled the bottle, only seconds before.

Religion

Is Britain a Christian country?

David Cameron thinks so...

On 9th April 2014 he held a reception for prominent Christians. This is something he also does for other faiths at times of the year which are significant for them – for example for Eid and Diwali - but this Easter gathering became controversial. The Prime Minister chose to emphasise a particular message, saying:
"I am proud of the fact we're a Christian country and we shouldn't be ashamed to say so."

He went on to compare the role of government with that of the religion:
"...what we both need more of is evangelism. More belief that we can get out there and actually change people's lives and make a difference."

Some prominent figures disagreed:
50 well-known people - authors, TV and radio presenters, scientists and comedians - sent a letter sent to the papers arguing that calling Britain a Christian country "fosters alienation and division in our society".

They wrote:
"Britain has been shaped for the better by many pre-Christian, non-Christian, and post-Christian forces. We are a plural society with citizens with a range of perspectives, and we are a largely non-religious society."

So can we call Britain today a Christian country?

SOME ISSUES:

Should our society be defined by religion at all?

To be a practising Christian do you need to go to church?

Should religion be involved with politics, or should it be a personal matter?

Do you care what religion the Prime Minister practises?

Should the country represent the most popular religion, or no religion at all?

Yes

The figures prove it!

The Daily Telegraph conducted a poll in April 2014 after this speech. It asked, "Do you think Britain is a Christian country?" 56% of people said yes. 52% in that poll said they were Christian. So the majority think that it is.

In the 2011 census 59% of the people in England and Wales, 54% in Scotland and 83% in Northern Ireland said they were Christian.

No

The figures prove it!

That same Daily Telegraph poll showed that although 52% of people said they were Christian only 14% of them were practising their faith. The other 38% were Christian in name but didn't go to church or pray.

The 2011 census also showed that the number of people who said they were Christian had fallen by 4 million in ten years.

Yes

Yet people think of themselves as Christian people, even if they do not all practise their faith. It is part of their heritage and culture and that makes us a Christian nation. Even with the fall in numbers, that is still a majority.

No

But 41% of people in that Daily Telegraph poll said they were non-religious and another 5% belonged to another faith. The same pattern shows up in the Census, the number of people with no religion has almost doubled since 2001 and there were increases in the numbers of Muslims, Hindus and Jews. Not to mention the people who thought it was funny to give their religion as Jedi. That can't make us a Christian nation – we're a mixed bunch.

Yes

All our traditions, laws, major holidays, school terms, even the way we organise our working week point to us being basically Christian. Organisations like Scouts and Guides started as Christian groups. Our social services have come out of Christian belief in fairness and protection of the weak.

Many of our most beautiful buildings are churches and cathedrals. In many districts the church is at the centre of community life.

Christianity is part of being British.

The head of our country, the Queen, is the supreme governor of the Church of England and has the title of Defender of the Faith.

No

Many Christian holidays took over older pagan festivals from even longer ago. Anyway, that is the past. It is true that Christianity is part of our history but now we are a society of people who have many faiths and people who have no faith. Even the Scouts' promise has different versions for different religions. This is going to be the pattern for the future.

Christianity doesn't have a monopoly of good behaviour or care for others, it seems to be the basis of most religions. There will be plenty of varied and beautiful buildings still built – they don't have to be churches.

There are many new laws that make life better for many people that were actually opposed by the Christian church and its representatives. There have been changes in laws on abortion, homosexuality, marriage, divorce and adoption which were supported by most people yet the church fought against them.

Yes

But people still turn to the church when they want to mark the most important occasions in their lives. You can get married in lots of places but there are 1,000 weddings every week conducted by the Church of England. People still want to have their children christened and to have god-parents for them.

No

People will get married anywhere that provides good photos. The church wedding is just a traditional hangover, an empty ceremony before the party. Getting married in church is just using the church, the same way as people suddenly get converted to religion just in order to get their kids into a good school.

Even with the people who go just to gain a school place, there are only about 800,000 people who go to Church of England services on a Sunday. That is half the number that used to attend in 1968.

Yes

The Church of England conducts 3,000 funerals a week. When it comes to these huge personal events people turn to their families and to the church. That's where they find the right rituals and the right words to fit with something bigger than themselves.

No

And they forget about it during the rest of their lives.

Can Britain be both a multi-faith society and a Christian society? Perhaps it can. Perhaps people who think of themselves as Christian but are not fervent in their belief are able to accept and reach out to other faiths. Perhaps our multi-faith future is secure because tolerance and inclusiveness are the most useful Christian virtues.

Sources: various

Why I ditched God for good

My Give Just One Thing campaign was born out of the desire for my daughter to grow up a good person in a kinder world

Ariane Sherine

SOME ISSUES:

Do you think religion promotes kindness in people?

Without religion why would people choose to be kind?

Do you think having no religion could allow a person to be more free with their thoughts and choices?

Is kindness more important than any religion?

What would help us all get along better as people?

Five years after my atheist bus campaign went global, I'm launching a very different kind of campaign. One night this year, as my two-year-old daughter was curled up next to me, I looked at her and thought: "I don't mind what you do when you grow up, or what you look like, or who you choose to love. I don't mind if you become a bin lady, or sext your boyfriends during assembly, or get a tattoo of Michael Gove. I only hope I can teach you to be kind."

I knew I had changed when I realised that I didn't mind whether Lily grew up to believe in God or not. Instead, I worried about the world she was growing up in. I wanted it to be a kinder place – but what did that mean in practice?

If I didn't know what kindness was, I couldn't contribute to this vision of the world, and, if I wasn't kind, what hope did my daughter have of contributing, either?

It is hard to define kindness. I see it as acting for the benefit of humanity, animals or the environment. It doesn't invalidate the act if people know about it, nor if the giver feels good as a result – as a Harvard study* shows, this effect is a happy by-product of giving. Unfortunately, the coalition government's cuts are the exact opposite of kindness. I wonder if the uncaring example it has set is partly why research published today** suggests that nine out of 10 Britons rarely perform a simple act of kindness.

As an atheist without a rule book on how to act, I looked to my friends for inspiration. There was Graham, who had given blood 50 times and had been vegan for 12 years; Nick, who had signed up without remuneration to an NHS medical trial; and another Nick, a charity worker and former VSO volunteer, who had organised a sponsored cycling trip in aid of disabled children in Tanzania. I was surrounded by people doing good things, and I'd barely been aware of it.

I resolved to become a better person. I spent six months training and qualifying as a

"I don't mind if you become a bin lady, or sext your boyfriends during assembly, or get a tattoo of Michael Gove. I only hope I can teach you to be kind."

I resolved to become a better person... I went to donate blood for the first time, signed the organ donor register and became vegan.

massage therapist, then gave massages for 40% of the going rate to charity workers, nurses, students, the unemployed and people on low incomes. I went to donate blood for the first time, signed the organ donor register and became vegan. I recycled as though my life depended on it, switched my electricity to Good Energy, and signed up with Age UK to volunteer to visit an elderly person for two hours a week. I also decided to sell 50% of my possessions in eBay charity auctions (which started last night), aiming to raise more than £3,000 for Médecins Sans Frontières. And, unexpectedly, I

found that every new thing I did made me happier.

It is impossible to talk about your own acts of kindness without looking as though you're after praise and yet, if you don't, you can't reasonably encourage others to give. As a single mum on a low income, I'm unable to give much to charity or spend much on ethical companies – so I've decided to write and campaign about philanthropy instead, in the hope that it will encourage others to do so. I asked my altruistic friends for help, and together we created a campaign advert and wrote

an ebook, Give: How to Be Happy. The campaign, as explained in the book, is called Give Just One Thing, and the idea is to encourage everyone to make a commitment to one of the 10 actions outlined in each chapter, from giving blood to voting in every election.

I will always be an atheist. However, I think that encouraging people to change their actions is more essential than trying to change their beliefs. If everyone in the world became an atheist, it wouldn't solve all the world's problems; if everyone became kind and good, it would.

*'Feeling good about giving'. One of the conclusions of the study was: "that happier people give more, that giving indeed increases happiness,"

** Research was part of a campaign by Friends of the Elderly

The Guardian, 3 December 2013
© Guardian News & Media 2013

Ariane Sherine, creator of the Atheist Bus campaign, now thinks kindness is what matters most.
Image: PA Archive/Press Association Images

Allah vs atheism: 'Leaving Islam was the hardest thing I've done'

A growing number of Muslims are speaking out about losing their faith, but it can mean being shunned by their families, or even threatened with death. Sarah Morrison meets the atheists

Amal Farah, a 32-year-old banking executive, is laughing about a contestant singing off-key in the last series of The X Factor. For a woman who was not allowed to listen to music when she was growing up, this is a delight. After years of turmoil, she is in control of her own life.

On the face of it, she is a product of modern Britain. Born in Somalia to Muslim parents, she grew up in Yemen and came to the UK in her late teens. After questioning her faith, she became an atheist and married a Jewish lawyer. But this has come at a cost. When she turned her back on her religion, she was disowned by her family and received death threats. She has not seen her mother or her siblings for eight years. None of them have met her husband or daughter.

SOME ISSUES:

Why do you think that leaving behind a religion can be so difficult?

Is religion a personal thing?

Should your family be affected if you change your religion?

Can you understand the feelings of the people in this article?

Does religion play a big part in your life?

"It was the hardest thing I've ever done – telling my observant family that I was having doubts. My mum was shocked; she began to cry. It was very painful for her. When she realised I actually meant it, she cut communication with me," said Ms Farah. "She was suspicious of me being in contact with my brothers and sisters. She didn't want me to poison their heads in any way. I felt like a leper and I lived in fear. As long as they knew where I was, I wasn't safe."

This is the first time Ms Farah has spoken publicly about her experience of leaving her faith, after realising that she did not want to keep a low profile for ever. She is an extreme case – her mother, now back in Somalia, has become increasingly radical in her religious views. But Ms Farah is not alone in wanting to speak out.

It can be difficult to leave any religion, and those that do can face stigma and even threats of violence. But there is a growing movement, led by former Muslims, to recognise their existence. Last week, an Afghan man is believed to have become the first atheist to have received asylum in Britain on religious grounds. He was brought up as a Muslim but became an atheist, according to his lawyers, who said he would face persecution and possibly death if he returned to Afghanistan.

Image posed by model

"It was the hardest thing I've ever done – telling my observant family that I was having doubts. My mum was shocked; she began to cry"

In more than a dozen countries people who espouse atheism or reject the official state religion of Islam can be executed under the law, according to a recent report by the International Humanist and Ethical Union. But there is an ongoing debate about the "Islamic" way to deal with apostates. Broadcaster Mohammed Ansar says the idea that apostates should be put to death is "not applicable" in Islam today because the act was traditionally conflated with state treason.

Some scholars point out that it is against the teachings of Islam to force anyone to stay within the faith. "The position of many a scholar I have discussed the issue with is if people want to leave, they can leave," said Shaykh Ibrahim Mogra, the assistant secretary general of the Muslim Council of Britain. "I don't believe they should be discriminated against or harmed in any way whatsoever. There is no compulsion in religion."

Baroness Warsi, the Minister of State for Faith and Communities, agreed. "One of the things I've done is put freedom of religion and belief as top priority at the Foreign Office," she said. "I've been vocal that it's about the freedom to manifest your faith, practise your faith and change your faith. We couldn't be any clearer. Mutual respect and tolerance are what is required for people to live alongside each other."

Yet, even in Britain, where the freedom to change faiths is recognised, there is a growing number of people who choose to define themselves by the religion they left behind. The Ex-Muslim Forum, a group of former Muslims, was set up seven years ago. Then, about 15 people were involved; now they have more than 3,000 members around the world. Membership has reportedly doubled in the past two years. Another branch, the Ex-Muslims of North America, was launched last year.

In more than a dozen countries people who espouse atheism or reject the official state religion of Islam can be executed under the law

Their increasing visibility is controversial. There are those who question why anyone needs to define themselves as an "ex-Muslim"; others accuse the group of having an anti-Muslim agenda (a claim that the group denies).

Maryam Namazie, a spokeswoman for the forum – which is affiliated with the Council of Ex-Muslims of Britain (CEMB) – said: "The idea behind coming out in public is to show we exist and that we're not going anywhere. A lot of people feel crazy [when they leave their faith]; they think they're not normal. The forum is a place to meet like-minded people; to feel safe and secure."

Sulaiman (who does not want to reveal his surname), a Kenyan-born 32-year-old software engineer living in East Northamptonshire, lost his faith six years ago. His family disowned him. "I knew they would have to shun me," he said. "They are a religious family from a [close] community in Leicester. If anyone [finds out] their son is not a Muslim, it looks bad for them." He added that people "find it strange" that he meets up with ex-Muslims, but he said it is important to know "there is a community out there who care about you and understand your issues".

Another former Muslim in her late twenties, who does not want to be named, said the "ex-Muslim" identity was particularly important to her. "Within Islam, leaving [the religion] is inconceivable. [The term] atheist doesn't capture my struggle," she said, adding that her family does not know the truth about how she feels.

Pakistani-born Sayed (not his real name), 51, who lives in Leeds, lost his faith decades ago. He left home at 23 and moved between bedsits to avoid family members who were looking for him. He told his family about his atheism only two years ago. "I was brought up a strict Muslim, but one day, I realised there

"Whenever I tell my sister or my mum that I am depressed, stressed or paranoid, they say it's because I don't pray or read the Koran enough"

was no God," he said. He told his mother and sister by letter that he was an atheist but they found it difficult to comprehend.

"Whenever I tell my sister or my mum that I am depressed, stressed or paranoid, they say it's because I don't pray or read the Koran enough," he said, adding that he will not go to his mother's funeral when she dies. "I won't be able to cope with the stress or the religious prayers. There's quite a lot of stigma around."

Iranian-born Maryam Namazie, 47, said that it does not have to be this way. Her religious parents supported her decision to leave their faith in her late teens. "After I left, they still used to whisper verses in my ear for safety, but then I asked them not to. There was no pressure involved and they never threatened me," she said. "If we want to belong to a political party, or religious group, we should be able to make such choices."

Zaheer Rayasat, 26, from London, has not yet told his parents that he is an atheist. Born into a traditional Pakistani family, he said he knew he didn't believe in God from the age of 15.

"Most people transition out of faith, but I would say I crashed out. It was sudden and it left a big black hole. I found it hard to reconcile hell with the idea that God was beneficent and merciful.

"I'm sort of worried what will happen when [my parents] find out. For a lot of older Muslims, to be a Muslim is an identity, whereas, for me, it's a theological, philosophical position. They might feel they have failed as parents; some malicious people might call them up, gloating about it. Some would see it as an act of betrayal. My hope is that they will eventually forgive me for it."

The Independent, 19 January 2014

They might feel they have failed as parents; some malicious people might call them up, gloating about it. Some would see it as an act of betrayal.

Fully veiled women hinder progressive Islam

Toleration is good but not when it prevents fair interrogation and robust argument

YASMIN ALIBHAI BROWN

SOME ISSUES:

Do you think religious belief should be more important than the law?

Do you agree with the writer about the negative representation of the hijab?

Should people be free to wear whatever they choose?

At Blackfriars Crown Court, Judge Peter Murphy ordered a 21-year-old, veiled defendant to show her face. The accused had been charged with witness intimidation and pleaded not guilty. Whatever the results of that case, she and her supporters certainly intimidated the judge, who backed down so the trial could proceed.

Birmingham Metropolitan College was similarly cowed and had to reverse a directive forbidding students from covering their faces. One hooded lady crowdsourced a protest against the college. Some overexcited student union members, Muslim objectors and online petitioners have forced a U-turn. Shabana Mahmood, MP for Ladywood, Birmingham, welcomed the capitulation. Happy days. Muslim women can now to go to courts and college in shrouds.

That all-covering gown, that headscarf, that face mask – all affirm and reinforce the belief that women are a hazard to men and society. These are unacceptable, iniquitous values, enforced violently by Taliban, Saudi and Iranian oppressors. They have no place in our country. So why are so many British females sending out those messages about themselves?

Culture

Some think they are outsmarting anxious Western institutions by covering up, winning dispiriting culture wars which will give them no advantage in our fast moving world. Young women in niqabs are either testing the state as teenagers do their parents or think their garb is political action – but for what? Many women, mothers in particular,

That all-covering gown, that headscarf, that face mask – all affirm and reinforce the belief that women are a hazard to men and society

have been brainwashed by proselytisers who want to spread conservative Islamic worship across Europe and North America. They are well funded by sources based in Saudi Arabia and the Gulf states.

And then there are those vacuous females who argue that it is their right to be objectified, that they must be allowed to live as invisible creatures. I don't know which of these dubious forces prevailed in the examples above. But I do know that this trend is growing fast and cannot just be "tolerated" as a minority tendency, just one of many choices people make.

Toleration

Toleration is good but not when it prevents fair interrogation and robust argument. I have written hundreds of times about the prejudices and discrimination experienced by Muslims, and other minorities. It isn't easy being a Muslim anywhere in the world – not in Muslim lands or the West. But when Muslims wilfully create problems and build barriers, anti-racists and egalitarians have an absolute duty to engage with them critically and in good faith. I know frank engagement is avoided because it gives succour to the EDL, BNP, neocons and manic anti-Muslim atheists. I, too, have to think hard before penning columns like this one. In the end though, I don't think we should abdicate these grave responsibilities because so much is at stake.

The woman before the judge must know that she or others like her will never be judges or barristers. Will she make her daughters do the same? The system wasn't picking on her – a defendant in a micro mini would have caused as much disquiet. And the aggrieved college student, what future does she imagine? She denies herself jobs for the sake of

None of the sacred texts command us to cover our faces

what? They keep apart from fellow Britons by withholding proper human interactions. It's not right or fair.

None of our sacred texts command us to cover our faces. Some branches of Islam do not even require head coverings. These are manmade injunctions followed by unquestioning women. We are directed always to accept the rules of the countries we live in and their institutions, as long as they are reasonable. For security, justice, travel, education and health, identification is vital. Why should these women be exempt? We Muslims are already unfairly thought of as the enemy within. Niqabs make us appear more alien, more dangerous and suspicious. If it is a provocation for Ku Klux Klan to cover up so they can't be recognised, it is for Muslims too.

Struggle

This is a struggle between the light of the faith and dark forces here and also in Islamic countries. The clothes symbolise an attempted takeover of the religion just when believers are looking for liberty, autonomy, democracy and gender equality. Malala Yousafzai doesn't hide her determined face. Nor do our female Muslim MPs and peers or civil rights lawyers.

Some of the bravest human rights activists are Muslim women. Take Tamsila Tauquir awarded an MBE for her charitable work with Muslims and Tehmina Kazi, director of British Muslims for Secular Democracy, which I co-founded seven years ago. The two of them, with other idealists, have embarked on an "inclusive mosque" initiative, with pop-up prayers in various venues, where men and women, gays and straights, humanists and modernists can pray together. Many others are trying to promote progressive Islam, which fits our times and needs.

Islamic zealots must fear these developments and want to crush them. Whether they know it or not, fully veiled women are part of this reactionary mission. Our state must not aid and abet them. The judge and the college should not have retreated and handed them this victory.

The Independent, 15 September 2013

Some think they are outsmarting anxious Western institutions by covering up

Bikeworldtravel / Shutterstock.com

Sexual issues

A 12-year-old mother is a case not for the midwife but the police

The story of Britain's youngest mother and father shows us how parenting in this country has gone seriously wrong

Allison Pearson

SOME ISSUES:

Why do you think there is a legal age of consent?

Why are people concerned when others have children at such a young age?

Whose responsibility is it to prevent teenage pregnancy?

What should be done to help the child in this situation?

A girl aged 12 years and three months became Britain's youngest mother over the weekend. She was still at primary school when the baby girl was conceived. The baby's father is more mature. He is 13.

That puts him in the same school year as my Small Boy. Now, the Small Boy has many nice qualities, but the ability to be a responsible father is not among them. An adolescent male, whose voice cracks and creaks like a ship in a gale and who cannot locate his own underpants on the floor of his lair, is to fatherhood what skateboarding is to space travel.

And so the cycle of wasted human potential repeats itself. Amazingly, this fact seems to be lost on the baby's maternal grandmother,

a sprightly veteran of 27. According to The Sun, the 12-year-old's mother is being very supportive: "Her mum is sticking behind her. She was a teenage mum as well, so she isn't being judgmental."

God forbid that you should be judgmental when your 11-year-old child starts having sex with her 12-year-old boyfriend! An activity which, and I'm sorry to be picky, is actually illegal. Technically, the 13-year-old boy is guilty of rape. (What kind of consent is an 11-year-old girl capable of giving?) Following an outcry over a number of horrible sexual assaults by children, the Sex Offences Act 1993 abolished the presumption that boys aged 10 to 13 were not considered capable of committing rape. Add to that the clear evidence that both

Photo posed by model

sets of parents in this case (I mean the adult parents, not the kiddy parents) have been staggeringly negligent in allowing their vulnerable youngsters to have a sexual relationship, and you have to ask: Is there not a crime here? And, if so, where is the punishment?

What would once have been a source of shame and stigma has mutated over three generations into a kind of gleeful boast. "The baby's mum and dad have been in a relationship for more than a year, so this isn't a fleeting romance," chirrups one family source proudly. "They intend to stick together and bring their daughter up together."

A relationship? Oh, Lady Bracknell, thou shouldst be living at this hour. Adults have relationships. Twelve-year-olds have Nintendos and nits.

As the baby's grandmother doesn't want to be "judgmental" – or, as it used to be called, teaching your child right from wrong – let me help her out here. By allowing her daughter to have a baby that young, she has wrecked what remains of her childhood, and most probably doomed her adulthood as well. Having had a baby herself at the age of 15, she should have tried to protect her daughter from the same fate.

Instead, she made it acceptable to bring a child into the world before you are capable, emotionally and certainly financially, of taking care of it. This has created another burden for the taxpayer, which is particularly unfair on those couples who are saving hard to be able to afford a baby. Instead of a role model, we get a role muddle.

God forbid that you should be judgmental when your 11-year-old child starts having sex with her 12-year-old boyfriend! An activity which is actually illegal.

Photo posed by model

By allowing her daughter to have a baby so young, she has wrecked what is left of her childhood

One solution is for the social services to take the baby away and put it up for adoption!

Call me judgmental, but if your daughter and grand-daughter can play with the same toys at Christmas, then something has gone terribly wrong.

One solution, and it is undoubtedly the most draconian, is for social services to take the baby away and put it up for adoption. We may wince at such a cruel thought until we look at the statistics. According to a landmark American study, "the offspring of teenage parents are at high risk of medical problems, emotional difficulties, school failure, child abuse and pregnancy". Is that really a kinder option than letting baby be adopted by loving grown-ups who can give her a hope in hell of a good life?

There is a much bigger issue here. As a parent who is trying (though not always succeeding) to bring up

her children to be decent, responsible individuals, I am fed up of the way that so much government time and money is devoted to making up for the deficiencies of an aggressively anti-social minority. People like those parents on Channel 4 the other night who applauded their kids for opening up water hydrants in the street, because "we paid for it".

No wonder a report this week by Prof Terry Haydn found that poor pupil behaviour has been seriously underestimated in our schools, and unsupportive or indifferent parents are partly to blame. "Teachers in England," says Professor

Haydn delicately, "are often working in more challenging contexts than those in other countries where parental support for schools and teachers was more positive".

In other words, the parents who don't give a damn what their 11-year-old is doing in her bedroom with her "boyfriend" are the same feckless fools who could not care less that their child is swearing at teachers and making education nigh-on impossible for kids who really want to learn.

Unto us a child is born – to another child. The poor baby of Britain's youngest parents gives little cause for rejoicing. Instead of calling the midwife, we should call the police.

Daily Telegraph, 16 April 2014
© Telegraph Media Group Limited 2014

Sex education is key if the teenage pregnancy rate is to continue to fall

Whoever you credit for this welcome news, one policy remains vital

Jane Merrick

SOME ISSUES:

What do you think about the amount of sex education students are given in schools?

What do you think sex education within schools should cover?

Why is it important to try to continue to reduce the teenage pregnancy rate?

What more can be done to improve sex education?

There was rare good news yesterday, with figures showing that teenage pregnancies are at their lowest rate for 45 years. As with the revelation earlier this year that crime has fallen to its lowest rate in more than 30 years, it shows that, when we are so often told everything is getting worse, and that the country is going to hell in a handcart, things can get better.

In 2012, the rate of pregnancies among under-18s was 27.9 per 1,000, compared to 42.9 a decade earlier. Conceptions were down 10 per cent on 2011. These figures are good news for children, women, indeed society as a whole. Post-natal depression affects teenagers more than older mothers; teenage mothers suffer damage to their long-term job and education prospects, with a fifth of them more likely to have no qualifications by the age of 30, and 22 per cent of them more likely to be living in poverty by that age. There are greater health risks for children, with infant mortality 60 per cent higher among babies born to teenage mothers, and they are more likely to grow up in child poverty.

Aside from the benefits to women and children, there is a huge saving for the state – for every £1 the NHS spends on contraception, £11 is saved on the cost of abortion, ante-natal and maternity care, with savings on welfare too.

With the celebration of the figures comes a debate about why this fall has happened, and which government can take the credit. The Coalition would argue that, while teenage pregnancy fell gradually under the last Labour administration, the number of conceptions went from 46,000 in 1998 to 40,000 in 2008 – hardly a significant drop. The target of halving teen pregnancies by 2010 was never met. It was only after 2008, towards the end of the Labour

Despite repeated attempts, the government has blocked making sex and relationship education in schools compulsory

government, that the rate began to drop more sharply, and by 2012 it was down to 27,000.

In 2010, the Coalition axed the national Teenage Pregnancy Strategy, which cost £280m over a decade, money spent on contraception and education of young people. Critics of this strategy – and of the Labour government's social policies more generally – would match the two, arguing that all that money made no difference to teenage pregnancy rates and that it was only when the spending was axed did conception rates actually fall. Those who put this side of the argument claim that exposing young teens to sex education and contraception makes it more likely they will have sex.

Former Labour ministers would argue differently, insisting that changing social behaviour takes time, particularly in the education of young people, who are more likely to be swayed by their peers – and by whether their classmates are having sex – than they will be by teachers, by a brightly coloured leaflet, or the offer of a free pack of condoms. And yes, they would argue, while the rate fell slowly at first, the sharp drop after 2008 shows the Teenage Pregnancy Strategy was gaining momentum.

It is undoubtedly true that pregnancy rates are a lagging indicator of policy and investment. It would be difficult for ministers to claim that the figures, which are from just two years into the Coalition and are in line with a general downward trend, are the result of their policy to axe the Teenage Pregnancy Strategy funding.

Surely education is the answer to reducing Britain's teen pregnancy problem, which remains one of the highest in Western Europe. But despite repeated attempts by Labour in the Commons and the Lords, the government has blocked making sex and relationship education in schools compulsory, saying only that there is an "expectation" that schools should teach it.

This gives schools an easy opt-out, and leaves pupils to find out about sex from unreliable sources – online or from their friends. Just because the rate of teenage pregnancies is falling, the sex education of young people shouldn't be left to chance.

The Independent, 26 February 2014

Just because the rate of teenage pregnancies is falling, the sex education of young people shouldn't be left to chance.

USING THE WORD 'GAY' TO MEAN 'CRAP' IS A FORM OF BULLYING OF GAY PEOPLE

YOUNGSTERS MAY NOT INTEND TO BE HOMOPHOBIC BUT THEY NEED TO LEARN THAT SUCH LANGUAGE CAN BE VERY OFFENSIVE AND UPSETTING

Will Young

SOME ISSUES:

Do you agree that language can be as powerful as he says?

Why should people think about the words they use?

What should be done about language that upsets people?

How can you change the language people use?

I like to think I'm down with youth culture and its slang. Well, a bit anyway. I understand that the word "sick" can mean "cool", and "bare" can mean "a lot". This is pretty much the limit of my knowledge. But I do like to think I can tell the difference between words that have changed their meaning in a quirky but harmless way, and those that have a damaging knock-on effect.

The evolution of the word "gay" is a case in point. Once it meant carefree or merry. Over time it came to be used to describe a sexual orientation. Now – for many at least – it has been appropriated to mean "rubbish" or "crap". So a word that started out meaning "happy" has ended up being used to denigrate. Well, language changes, doesn't it? Many would see no problem with a shift driven by everyday speech.

It is a problem, however, for those of us – a whole swath of society – who are actually gay, and for whom the word forms an important part of our identity and sense of self. It might not be obvious to those who aren't. But the casual, insulting use of the word, in schools and elsewhere, hurts us. In fact, it seeps into the subconscious. It fuels people's perception of gay people as wrong or bad.

If a young person, growing up gay, constantly hears the word being used to refer to something that's disliked, useless or stupid, they are quite naturally going to feel that reflects on them. They are going to feel disliked, useless and stupid. And young gay people have enough to deal with already. Look at the statistics: 23% of gay or bisexual young people have tried to take their own lives and 56% have self-harmed. This isn't inconsequential squabbling over the use of an adjective. No one is looking to fetter freedom of expression. This is about stopping a new generation of gay people from growing up in a climate of persecution and ostracism.

THE CASUAL, INSULTING USE OF THE WORD, IN SCHOOLS AND ELSEWHERE, HURTS US.

THIS IS ABOUT STOPPING A NEW GENERATION OF GAY PEOPLE FROM GROWING UP IN A CLIMATE OF PERSECUTION.

Image: Featureflash / Shutterstock.com

Gay charity Stonewall is leading a campaign against homophobic language. I share its view that the young people using the word gay negatively are not necessarily homophobic. There is a difference between labelling a statement or action homophobic and labelling someone a homophobe. What is needed is better education – of students and teachers alike.

This isn't a question of punishment, but one of enlightenment. Young gay people have told Stonewall that when they hear phrases such as "that is so gay" they feel ashamed; like they are outsiders. Once again, this isn't oversensitivity, or nitpicking over language that may have been used quite innocently. I believe that political correctness for the sake of it can be counterproductive. No, this is a form of bullying – intentional or not – that has obvious consequences.

But are we fighting a losing battle? Can you really stand in the way of a linguistic change, or the way kids choose to behave in their own friendship groups or the playground? I firmly believe that young people's attitudes can rapidly change once they've been educated about something – I've seen it with my own eyes. I have faith in them. Give them the information they need about the harm being done and they will stop using language that hurts and upsets many of their peers.

Most of the time, young people don't want to offend. They want to understand things and, ultimately, behave well towards one another.

The devil is in the detail when it comes to language that is used to ostracise people. It is the detail that we have to get to grips with. People "tolerate" gays and lesbians; Joe Bloggs "admits" to being gay. Double maths is "so gay". These seemingly minor examples can lead to damaging emotional responses. They subtly undermine and erode confidence. The results are bad for society as a whole.

Language is key. Language is everything. After all, what else do we have?

The Guardian, 24 November 2013
© Guardian News & Media 2013

R U coming out?

RUcomingout.com inspires, supports and unites those who are living their lives either completely, or partially in the closet; who have not yet told all their friends and family that they are lesbian, gay, bisexual or transgender.

It invites people to share their coming out story. This is Joe's story

Joe | 20 | Manchester, England | Radio Producer

It's probably important to start all of this by saying that I'm happier now than I've ever been as a result of the events of the past few years.

From a young age, the only time I ever heard about 'gays' was from the bigoted slurs of my uncle (related by marriage, thankfully) whenever there was a reference on TV or in the newspaper. When you're so young, it doesn't occur to you that the adults that you look up to could possibly be wrong about these things, so I suppose I just believed what he said as fact. The way he cursed 'gays' is something that has stuck with me throughout growing up.

We won't dwell on that though, he's been divorced and currently resides somewhere in Llandudno, Wales. If you're ever there and happen to see him, throw glitter at him and chant the chorus of 'Born this way' with an interpretive dance accompaniment. That'll show him.

Something that I also picked up on at a young age was the cliché, stereotypical examples of gay people that were presented to us all in the media. Nothing ever made me think I could be gay because I wasn't anything like these people. I just knew (or thought I knew) that it was bad to be 'gay' and I'd been given the impression that it was something that one would not wish to be.

SOME ISSUES:

Why are websites and forums important for people?

Why do you think it is so difficult for homosexual people to 'come out' to their friends and family?

What can be done to make this a more comfortable and normal experience for people?

It was like something was missing and I couldn't put my finger on it

Something that still bothers me is the fact that a child so young is not to know that the media does what it needs to make a buck, and that not all gay people fit the narrow silhouette that they'd have us believe. All this created a bunch of negative images of gay people in general based on the few I'd actually seen on telly. Children are supposed to be impressionable, how would they learn otherwise?

Life was as wonderfully irritating and frustrating for me as it was for anyone else until I reached the interesting age of around 13 or 14. I did what all teenage boys do. I explored the internet.

Without going into too much detail, the content that I was looking at became boring. As though the novelty of it had 'worn off' and I couldn't explain why. It was like something was missing and I couldn't put my finger on it.

I got to that age in school where people were talking more and more about sex. I can only put this down to me having subconscious doubts and wanting to prove something to myself (which sounds awful when I put it into words like that), but I slept with a girl from my school. I knew she liked me, and I was convinced that I liked her too. I remember afterwards having the lingering feeling of being completely deflated and feeling rubbish, and I didn't know why.

After about a week, it was something to brag to my mates about, and once more, any thoughts that I didn't know how to address were suppressed. A string of 'relationships' continued on and off with the same deflated sensation as the outcome, but I did it just enough to keep myself convinced that I was okay. What I didn't realise was that this was affecting me in ways that I couldn't anticipate.

College started and I never looked back. Off I went into the city centre making a new group of friends, minus a few important pals. It was great! It was a completely different atmosphere from the testosterone driven competition of High School.

There was a friend I'd met there and gotten on famously with. One day when he told me about a girl that he liked and it felt like my stomach had physically dropped to the floor. Quite quickly, I announced that I needed to go home. On top of the fact that I was devastated that he was after this girl, I was now struggling to deal with the racing thoughts as to why I was so bothered about it. The more I thought about it, I got lower and lower. I was desperately trying to deny to myself what I'd always tried hard to disprove. That gut feeling I'd put to the back of my mind - I felt like I was losing.

I quickly went from being a confident young lad, to being quiet and vacant, and people were noticing. I lost weight and I very nearly had to leave college as a result of my lack of focus or motivation.

I quickly went from being a confident young lad, to being quiet and vacant, and people were noticing

Not only could I not find the words to say how I felt, I didn't even want to. I made myself ill with these recurring thoughts that couldn't shake. I started employing little routines and rituals when performing certain tasks. This became a big problem and was later diagnosed as Obsessive Compulsive Disorder.

Just before the half term of my second year, we were given the task to study a soap opera storyline that either 'subverted or enforced a dominant representation of a particular character type' (It sounds fancy but was an excuse to escape and watch telly that I was willing to take). I used this as a green light to innocently explore the portrayal of a young gay lad in Emmerdale. He was 'normal'. This was the first gay character I had found that was a realistic comparison to myself. I was hooked from the word go. Before I knew it, I'd watched the storyline from start until the emotional climax.

After the months of bottling up these feelings that I refused to deal with, something as trivial as a soap opera storyline was enough to crack me.

That was finally enough to make me see that however deep in this I was, I had to tell somebody through fear of what'd happen to me if I let myself carry on. So on November 4th, I spent the whole day playing out scenarios in my head about how I'd say it to my mum. I sat there, white as a sheet with the full intention of telling her for hours, then just as I'd psyched myself up almost enough to tell her, she got up and said, "Right, I'm off to bed".

It was possibly the worst thing that could've happened at that point. All of this energy, stress and heart ache. What would I do now? So, like a scene from a movie, I tried writing a letter but my bin soon became stacked with crumpled up failed drafts. The words simply failed me.

Needless to say, I did not sleep well. I was so lost and I could think of nothing to do but crawl into my mum's bed the next morning, wishing things away, as though I was a child again. When she woke to see me sniffling and rubbing my eyes, she asked what was wrong.

After pausing, I blurted out words before I'd even thought about them – "I just hate the thought of anybody being different around me."

Which was true. It wasn't being gay that bothered me, at all. It was that people might treat me as if I was different because of it. I'd started and there wasn't a way back. Understandably, she asked me what I was talking about. It wasn't my most coherent of moments. I went on to just simply saying it. No letter, no big speech. I just said it. For about 30 seconds, she looked at me puzzled, as though she didn't believe me. I'd had girlfriends and I didn't act any differently to my straight mates. But she could see how torn up I was. So we went and sat in the kitchen and had a very lengthy chat about the whole thing, slowly. Talking about it was as new to me as it was to her. She was fantastic.

I'd always known my mum was very accepting and normal around the whole gay thing. She'd gone out of her way with all of the younger ones in our extended family to make sure we knew that being gay was nobody else's business but your own, and it was completely okay. Whatever she did and said when I was younger, it was obviously good enough for me to muster up the courage to let her be the first person in my life to know, which is something I am proud of her for.

Without pressuring me, it was mum who urged me to talk to somebody about the ways in which I was making myself ill. So after talking to a doctor in depth, about what I was going through, it was decided that I was to start talking to somebody more senior and more specialised in the areas that I needed treatment. The stigma around mental health is something that I'm guilty of enforcing myself but through growing up

It wasn't being gay that bothered me, at all. It was that people might treat me as if I was different because of it

People that know you well aren't going to divorce themselves from you just because you're gay

and facing problems myself, I've learnt that it's not okay to have that attitude. You wouldn't suffer with a chest infection and not go to see a GP, so why would it be any different with mental health?

For a long time after I'd told my mum, I didn't tell anybody else.

I'd started following a few gay people on Twitter who I found funny and easy to relate to. I liked them because they were the type of people that I felt similar to and that made me feel better about myself.

One of the chaps I found as a result was @WayneDavid81. Coincidentally, just days after I began following him, he announced on twitter about a project he was planning to launch called 'RUComingOut'.

The general advice of people on the website was that it was easier to tell others once you'd bitten the bullet and told the first.

I went on to slowly tell my friends, one by one. It was only in university on a night out that (I thought) I got a negative reaction. My housemate had seen me holding a boy's hand and confronted me about it. He marched me outside and I thought I was going to get a lecture. To quote him: "Why would you not tell me?! Did you think I would be upset, My uncle is gay. Now buy me a beer and don't kiss me".

He showed me that the chances are, the people that know you well aren't going to divorce themselves from you just because you're gay.

With this encouragement from some of the important people in my life, there was only one more hurdle: Dad. I think a lot

I met my lovely boyfriend as a result of the website

of young gay men have a big issue telling their dad for a few reasons. A big one for me was that I'm my dad's only child so the grandchild issue (naively) quite upset me whenever I thought about it. It wasn't fair of me to keep it from him. So, once I was confident enough, I asked my mum to tell him. You might think this was a bit of a 'cop out' but my dad has never been one for openly speaking about issues. As anticipated, dad took a little while to adjust. He said he had no clue, which is what threw him the most.

Finally, with everyone who was important in my life aware and accepting, I could look back and smile.

I owe a lot to RUComingOut. Not only did they help me make the transition from being trapped in my own head to being happy and confident about myself, but also, I met my lovely boyfriend as a result of the website!

We are very happy together and owe a lot to Wayne. So for that, I thank you very much!

Follow Joe on Twitter @JoeFlinders
Joe's boyfriend Pete also wrote his coming out story for RUComingOut.com, you can read that and many more on the website

Sport
& leisure

Photo: wavebreakmedia / shutterstock.com

10 things no one tells women before they run a marathon

Photo: Padmayogini / Shutterstock.com

The London Marathon is extremely popular, so here are some essential insights from marathon runner Helen Coffey

SOME ISSUES:

Would you consider running a marathon?

Why do you think people like to put their bodies through such tough challenges?

Does this list make you more or less likely to run a marathon?

Why is sport good for us?

Having completed two marathons in as many years, I finally feel qualified to call myself that most noble of titles, a Lady Runner. (Or Woman Who Runs. Or Running Girl. I haven't decided which I like best yet.)

Those two marathon experiences couldn't have been more different. Paris 2013 dawned a bright, clear day; the crowd was cheering, I had done all the training and set off with a spring in my step, high fiving small children and grinning at my adoring fans as I went. You know, generally behaving like a bit of a tool.

Cut to Rome 2014, and it was sheeting it down. The Italians who had bothered to turn up watched quizzically from the side-lines, uncomprehending as to why anyone would run 26.2 miles by choice (I was struggling with that question myself). By the time I started I was soaked to the skin and shivering, with no confidence in my ability to finish the race after a calf injury the month before had curtailed my training at a crucial stage.

I did manage to finish it (yay!), but only after breaking down in tears, shouting at my mother and almost throwing up some neon orange Gatorade in the street.

After experiencing the full rollercoaster of long-distance running emotions – joy, sorrow, self-loathing – here are some of the things that no one tells women about running a marathon…

You will become an unstable, irrational wreck

You will find yourself blowing kisses to the crowd and high fiving small children.

1. You will think you're Beyoncé

For the first 13 miles – before you start seriously questioning whether what you're doing actually constitutes self-harm – you will feel like a rock star. People are cheering for you! They're chanting your name! You will find yourself blowing kisses to the crowd and high fiving small children, and this will seem like totally normal behaviour. By mile 22, you will remember that girl you once were and hate her.

Photo: Tupungato / Shutterstock com

3. You'll wish you had smaller breasts

The glorious female form, while very good at lots of things – like looking quite nice in an oil painting – is not particularly well designed for, to use the technical term, jiggling. Running involves a great deal of jiggling. In fact, a marathon is pretty much one long jiggle-fest from start to finish. And the more voluptuous you are, the more problematic this is. As no one has as yet found a way to detach their breasts and leave them at home during a run, it really is worth shelling out for a decent sports bra; you are never going to regret investing £40 to get the girls rounded up and under control.

2. You will happily "lube up"

By mile 24 your whole body will hate you regardless, but never underestimate the negative effects chafing can have on one's psyche. The skin on skin/skin on material rubbing dynamic will slowly but surely bring you to your knees like nothing else, unless you take preventative measures. Before you embark, lubricate like it's going out of fashion – Vaseline up every bit of your body that might touch another bit of your body or clothing, including breasts, bum and inner thighs. If it helps, pretend you are doing it in preparation for a misogynistic music video, or a Maxim cover shoot.

4. You might lose your s***

However "together" you are in real life, striding around in an independent, feminist, having it all-type way, after 35km of running you will have become a highly emotional, unstable and irrational wreck. You may break down into inconsolable sobbing when it turns out your mother is 2km further along the course than she had promised. Which may lead to you screaming at her in the street about how she has let you down (sorry again, mum).

A generous length of bog roll tucked in a pocket goes a long way.

Your toenails might fall off. And yes, it does look as disgusting as it sounds.

5. You'll get penis envy

Men have it a lot easier when it comes to long distance running, purely because they can take a whizz just about anywhere. Look around during any marathon, and there will be guys weeing up against trees, parked cars, statues, bollards, dogs – you name it, someone will be relieving themselves on it. Women, on the other hand, have no choice but to queue for 10 minutes to use one of the world's worst portaloos when nature calls. (Picture Glasto and then imagine everyone there has a dodgy tummy from too many energy gels.)

Tip: Be prepared. A generous length of bog roll tucked in a back pocket goes a long way.

6. You will become a running bore

In the weeks leading up to the race, you will undoubtedly find yourself in the pub on a Friday night, talking to a friend with intense zeal about how you "really need to work on speeding up your splits", or you've "been experimenting with a combination of electrolytes and gels". STOP. Take a breath. Go and take a long, hard look in the mirror. And ask yourself why you have turned into a loser.

Running has a tendency to take over your life when training for an event, but try to remember that most people won't be anything more than vaguely interested. This is particularly true when on a first date – just watch their eyes glaze over as you bang on about techniques to avoid "hitting the wall"…

7. You will not look good

Contrary to fitness adverts depicting toned, fresh-faced girls running while looking better than you did on your wedding day, your body simply is not going to look good during or after a marathon. Your skin may be spotty after all that sustained sweating has played merry hell with your pores. If you are anything over an A cup, you may end up with welts or sores from where your sports bra has rubbed. You may have, against all common sense, put on weight.

People will say things like: "You must be losing loads of weight now you're training for a marathon". Don't count on it – those long runs are going to be fuelled by a shed load of carbs so that you avoid burning fat, as converting the latter into energy is a far more tiring process.

8. Your toenails will drop off

As bad as the rest of your body looks, your feet will look even worse. Cracked heels, hard skin, calloused, bulbous toes – and all just in time for sandals season. And, of course, you can look forward to your toenails turning black and dropping off. Yes, you heard me: your toenails might fall off. And yes, it does look as disgusting as it sounds.

9. You will voluntarily enter a wet t-shirt competition

Well, strictly speaking it's not a competition – there are no prizes for a start. But as things hot up, and you see basins of water and people holding out wet sponges stationed in front of you, you will be drawn to them. You will be enticed by the cool, watery goodness. And you will, against all your previously held attitudes, pour water over yourself while making orgasmic noises like you're auditioning for a Herbal Essences ad, because it feels SO GOOD. Just go with it.

10. You will want to do another one

Running a marathon is a bit like childbirth. You will hate parts of it, it will be immensely painful and you will swear to yourself NEVER AGAIN. Six months later, the agony all but forgotten, your brain will trick you into thinking it's a good idea to do another one.

You can protect yourself against this masochism posing as athletic ambition by telling a broad selection of friends immediately after the race that, should you ever enthuse about doing a marathon in future, they are to prohibit such foolhardy optimism and channel it in a safe, healthy way. Like suggesting a karaoke night instead. Or that you buy a sports car. Or go out with a 20 year old.

You will then ignore them and do it anyway.

Daily Telegraph, 11 April 2014
© Telegraph Media Group Limited 2014

Photo posed by model

Why I love swimming

When I'm in the water I'm elementally myself, floating free of any worries. What's your reason for pestering the pool? **JENNY LANDRETH**

SOME ISSUES:

Does this writer make you want to swim too?

What sports do you enjoy?

Are sports good for the mind as well as the body?

What sports would you like to try?

I've written around the subject of swimming without talking much about the doing of it, perhaps because writing is so at odds with what swimming is. But I like a challenge – I swim in cold water, of course I like a challenge – so I'm going to plunge in.

Before that, let's stand at the side of the pool in our swimming costumes; it's as near naked in front of strangers as most of us will ever get. (I've taken advice and am saying no more.) I understand that for some people even putting on a costume is difficult, too revealing. The only thing I have to offer here is my limited and anecdotal experience, and for me it's key to the whole thing. It's this: nobody is judging. Or if they are, they're doing so silently (and then hopefully drowning in their own bile). Pools feel egalitarian. It doesn't seem to matter what your costume is like; it doesn't seem to matter if you're old or young, big or small, if bits hang off oddly, or you don't have all of them. It doesn't matter what the past [flubbles lips] years have done to you. It doesn't matter what you've done or not done during those years. There will be nobody chasing you up and down yelling "but your legs are fat and your head's too small and you look …". Unless you pay them to do so, in which case you probably need help.

So I shove my costume on, stick my chin up and stand there, the same as everyone. And yes, OK, we mostly do all have our arms crossed. But here is my body out in the air, and no one is falling over laughing or turning away in disgust. We are all equal in a swimming cap, as I've been known to say.

I like the "c" word. Community. I'm part of a community defined by this one thing and nothing else. I swim with people I've known for ages, but I don't know much about them outside of this one thing. Identity is irrelevant. That can feel quite liberating. Am I a mother, a partner, a success or failure? Who knows. In the pool, we all just do what we're capable of, whatever that is. And once you're swimming, no one else is counting, no one muttering "she didn't do much" or "she's slow". We're all here, is what counts.

The first bit of a swim is my favourite: the glide. I put my shoulders under and ready myself, lift my feet behind me to connect with the wall and push off, arms arrowed ahead and body … for a few seconds … suspended. Even in the thinking, I can feel the wall under my foot, really trying to get this bit right because it's so satisfying, a good glide. In my mind I'm a line, aerodynamic and forceful. Then engage. Pull the first arm back, kick a foot, start the clockwork, head still down before the first breath is needed. As I do the first length, my body starts to wake up, realising what is required;

my immediate feelings are about how everything is today, the mechanics of me and it. At the start I'm a little slow. If I was a car, I'd still be in first gear.

At the end of the first length I stop, hold on to the bar for a minute and look back to the start. I'm here, I'm in, I'm doing this thing. My breathing has shifted into the right place; any slight cold-water heart-race or panting has calmed down. I'm deciding again what's already decided: shall we swim? Yes, let's. I'm ready. Let's go.

Then I'm conscious swimming. My head engaged, fixed on what my body is doing. Finding the flow, the catch, spearing my arm in. A physical mindfulness, and for a person who still hides behind the bike sheds for most "organised sports", it's a revelation. Whatever I feel about my body, right now it'll do nicely. I can start to stretch out and enjoy how clever I'm being. Imagine being able to do this – how ridiculous! It's like I can fly! How on earth did it happen? I'm in a rhythm, held by the water. I could go and go, swim to Birmingham in this state. I start to really pull back as my catch drops, and give it some power. I roll consciously into each reach, going for the next rung on the ladder. Then I'm in fifth gear.

And I start to notice and enjoy little visuals. Tilting my head as I breathe, getting that view right across the water's

horizontal. The sun, if there is one, glancing off my wet arching arm. The rain, flicking and pinging the surface.

Then comes the real mindful stuff. Maybe "mindless" is a more apt word: when my body's cruising and my head goes elsewhere, solving, chuckling to itself, thinking – or actually not. Nothing. Like dreaming or being nowhere. Suddenly a leaf hitting my goggles wakes me, reminds me to invent windscreen wipers for outdoor swimmers. And then I'm back and I'm done and I get out, water runs off me and I pad to the shower, conscious of my physical self again.

When I'm swimming, I'm in the moment fully, purely experiencing. I float free of all the shit I carry around (I'm tempted to say "literally" at this point, though of course not exactly). I'm entirely, elementally myself. Let the day chuck everything it has at me. I'm right in it, alive. I'll make time to feel alive again tomorrow.

Now how about you? What are the things that pull you back to the pool time and again?

The Guardian, 19 November 2013
© Guardian News & Media 2013

> **The first bit of a swim is my favourite: the glide... arms arrowed ahead and body... for a few seconds... suspended.**

Carl Froch: Why I love boxing

Carl Froch dismisses the challenger for his WBA and IBF super-middleweight titles as a 'kid who claims he's invincible' as he discusses pain, fatherhood and his plans for the future

Donald McRae

SOME ISSUES:

Do you think boxing has a positive or a negative image?

What do you think of it as a career choice?

How important is it in sports to have a positive frame of mind?

Should more be done to promote boxing?

"I feel pain quite a lot," Carl Froch says as he tries to explain the essential difference between himself as a fighter and as an ordinary man outside the ring. He gazes across a small table as if deciding whether or not he should issue an invitation. "You know what? If you were to punch me hard in the nose right now it would f****** sting. But when I get punched much harder in the nose during a fight I don't feel it because I'm full of adrenaline. I'm full of the heat of battle. Your body releases a natural endorphin when you're fighting. You don't feel pain. Now, it's different. Poke me in the ribs? Pinch me? It would hurt. But punch me in the face on fight night and I don't feel it."

"When you're fighting you're in fight or flight mode," Froch says as he prepares to enter the ring in Manchester for the 34th bout of a long and impressive career as he defends his WBA and IBF super-middleweight world title belts against George Groves, his unbeaten challenger from London. "I'm a fighter."

It's almost five years since Froch won his first world title – the WBC super-middleweight bauble being his prize after a brutal contest against Jean Pascal in December 2008.

Froch suffered against Pascal, when he entered the ring with a cracked rib and a perforated eardrum incurred during sparring. "That was a heavy

Poke me in the ribs? Pinch me? It would hurt. But punch me in the face on fight night and I don't feel it."

night," he murmurs. "The perforated eardrum was OK. But the ribs were hard because the pain was so bad I had to do shallow breathing all the way through. I couldn't take deep gulps of air because it put pressure on the rib cage. That was tough and I got cut for the first time in my career against Pascal. I remember the blood going in my eye and clouding my vision.

"I still won but after the fight, when I got back to the pub where I was living, I was not breathing too clever. My rib was hurting. My eye was stinging. My hands were sore. My elbows and my back were f***ed. My neck too – I had a bit of whiplash. For 10 days after that I was, physically, in a bit of a state. But I can feel that after a heavy sparring session. I wake up in the morning and I can't move. It's just the muscles getting used to the punishment."

Froch is an articulate and impassioned supporter of boxing. Leaning forward in a remote corner of the English Institute of Sport in Sheffield, where he trains, Froch gently bangs our table. "There are people who don't like the sport and talk about the brutal injuries. But boxing is not even in the top 10 of dangerous sports. The amount of people that get injured or killed is so few and far between. No sport is more geared to the warrior's code of honour, pride and respect. That's why I love boxing. It's mano a mano. One against one. It's driven by fear and your need to conquer it. I don't think there is anything more proud or glorious than standing in the arena as a fighter – that you've done it in on your own. That's why I love fighting."

I have a brain scan every year and my brain doesn't move!

"I don't see where boxing's not good for you," Froch says.

How about when you're getting punched in the head as hard as Kessler hit you? "I have a brain scan every year and my brain doesn't move. I've never had any bruises or bleeds on the brain. The only boxing injuries I've sustained have been superficial – cuts, bruises, cracked ribs, perforated eardrums. Nothing in any of my brain scans tells me anything is deteriorating neurologically."

The dangers may be unproven to Froch but he is smart enough to be wary of the threat – and it clearly requires a special brand of courage to step inside a ring again and again. "You can get an invisible energy from being positive. Is it a spirit, or the soul? I'm not religious but there is something mysterious inside you that makes you the person you are. I call it my spirit, or personality to put it simply. My personality means I feel better when I'm training hard, eating right, being nice, treating people with respect. That's why I don't like George Groves, because he's arrogant and cocky and rude and cheeky and horrible. He doesn't make you feel good. It's probably part of his game plan. But it's all very negative."

Groves, away from the ring, is actually amiable and interesting. He's also 11 years younger than the champion. Does Froch not see a little of himself, at 25, in Groves? "Only in the air of invincibility that's not backed up by any facts.

© Adam Davy/ PA Wire/Press Association Images

COBR

#ANDSTILL

You can get an invisible energy from being positive. Is it a spirit, or the soul?

That's naivety. But I've never been arrogant. I've never been rude. I've never been disrespectful because I was brought up very well. So I don't see a lot of me in George. He's a 25-year-old kid who claims he is invincible – which is silly. His bravado is fuelled by fear. It's the only ridiculous way he can give himself any mental edge – by trying to minimise my achievements. But the magnitude of the event will be hitting him now. Come the press conference and the weigh-in, reality will kick in and he'll be in serious trouble mentally."

Is it difficult to face an unbeaten fighter? "No. Unbeaten records don't mean anything. I've been beaten myself and I'm at the top of the game. So,

Photo: Featureflash/Shutterstock.com

mindset. Being an atheist, for me to get any faith in the future I look to my kids. That's the reason I'm here – to let them have a good life. It all boils down to procreation in the end. You live, have your kids and you die. Then they live, have their kids and die. That's how it is."

He laughs before suggesting that Groves is also "a selfish kid" in need of an authoritative lesson. "He's going to learn the hard way when I start hitting him. It's man against boy – and the kid is going to get hurt. But Groves might be a little wiser, and nicer, after I'm done with him."

Froch believes this fight will be one of his last bouts before he retires in late 2015 and pursues an interest in Ironman triathlons and property development. "I need to reiterate that I'm not fighting for money. I've invested wisely and I've got a very big property portfolio. I love buildings and I've made a lot of money out of property. So I'll be busy once the fighting stops.

"I've got two more years maximum in boxing. That's four more fights – five counting Groves. But if I don't feel good in the buildup to any of them I'll just stop. I won't care if it's a massive money-fight in America – If my training camp doesn't go well I'm clever enough to pull out because I know that, potentially, I could get hurt. If I'm not at my best I'll chuck the towel in. You can mark my words on that. But we've got a way to go before that happens – as George Groves will soon discover."

The Guardian, 20 November 2013
© Guardian News & Media 2013

rather than the unbeaten record, I look at the quality of opposition. If most top-10 super-middleweights had fought Groves' résumé of fighters they'd all be unbeaten. It means absolutely nothing. He'll find out how to lose when I start hitting him. He'll find himself on the floor."

Groves has cranked up the psychological warfare this week, claiming that Froch "looks grey" and that the champion is "having trouble sleeping". Froch counters by suggesting that he spends more time thinking about his children than fretting over Groves.

The fighter grins slyly before thinking hard again when considering how fatherhood has changed him. "You realise that you're not the most important person any more. Your kids are. You become less selfish. Boxing is a very selfish sport, a very lonely sport, but when you've got kids you change your

Update

In the fight on 23 November 2013, Groves was comfortably ahead on points but in the ninth round the referee, seeing Groves shaken by series of blows from Froch, stepped in and stopped the fight, meaning that Froch retained his title. According to the challenger, and many fans and commentators, the referee was too quick to act and had saved Froch from defeat.

In the rematch on 31st May 2014, Froch knocked Groves out in the eighth round with a mighty right hand punch. He then finished his momentous evening by proposing to his girlfriend in the ring.

I could get hurt. If I'm not at my best I'll chuck the towel in. You can mark my words on that. But we've got a way to go before that happens.

Women on the slow road

Susan Swarbrick

The film, Half The Road, directed by Kathryn Bertine, charts the issues, obstacles and struggles faced by many professional women cyclists around the world as they battle for parity with their male counterparts.

A journalist and former pro triathlete, Bertine fell in love with cycling seven years ago after being involved in an ESPN.com documentary "So You Wanna Be an Olympian?", following her efforts as a rookie road racer trying to make the St Kitts and Nevis team for Beijing in 2008.

Immediately she was struck by how modern day women's professional road cycling appeared to be stuck at the equivalent level of women's professional tennis in the 1970s. "Quietly, I wondered 'why?'" she recalls.

When Bertine, a three-time national champion, realised her ambitions of joining the pro ranks with a berth on US outfit Team Colavita in 2012, that burning question continued to niggle. At races, she began to interview her peers among the peloton about their experiences. The project grew into Half the Road, a powerful documentary.

The key issues tackled include the arguments that women deserve to be given a minimum salary and equal prize money, as well as being allowed to race equivalent distances to men.

Bertine - alongside double Olympic gold medallist Marianne Vos, former world time-trial champion Emma Pooley and triathlete Chrissie Wellington, a four-time holder of the world Ironman title - spearheaded an online petition last year urging Tour de France director Christian Prudhomme to allow women to compete in the world's most famous bike race.

Within three weeks it had garnered 96,000 signatures, the campaign succeeding in the creation of La Course, a one-day race which will see a field of 120 women compete on the hallowed cobbles of the Champs Elysees on July 27.

"It's the first step and I believe that it can and will grow from there," says Bertine. "Some people might say: 'Oh, you only have one day' but that's our foot in the door. I would

SOME ISSUES:

Why do you think women face more obstacles when wanting to pursue a career in sports?

What should be done to support and promote women's cycling?

Do you think if women's cycling was given more priority, more young women would want to take it up as a sport?

What other example of sexism in sport do you see?

rather have one day in 2014 than wait five years for two or three days. It's great we have the progress and can build on it."

Among the vocal supporters of women's cycling is Guy Elliott, a director of SweetSpot, the company behind the successful revival of the Tour of Britain in 2004. Elliott and his team spent a year devising plans for the inaugural edition of the Friends Life Women's Tour which was held last month. His vision was for it to be "the only cycling event in the world where women are not second best".

The five-stage race, won by Vos and attracting a host of world-class riders including Emma Johansson, Ellen van Dijk, Lizzie Armitstead, Laura Trott and Scotland's Katie Archibald, debuted to great acclaim.

Elliott, however, would be the first to admit that getting the event up and running felt like hitting a brick wall at times. "It was very difficult," he says. "There is significant discrimination against women in sport, I would argue, from puberty onwards.

> **"As far as I'm concerned women's racing is equal to, or better than, a large proportion of men's."**

"When I was approaching potential sponsors I heard repeatedly: 'No one is interested in women's cycling', but we have photographs of stage finishes where the crowds are as big as the men's Tour of Britain. I'm going to get one of those printed up and write underneath: 'No one is interested in women's cycling'. It shattered some of the myths."

Elliott hopes the race will continue to grow in years to come, believing it has a crucial role as part of a wider social agenda.

"The rate of drop-out from sport among teenage girls is catastrophic," he says. "Now you can say to 12 or 13-year-old girls, look at Hannah Barnes. Last year she was a part-time waitress working in a hotel in Northamptonshire but on stage one of the Women's Tour, she was third behind Olympic champion Marianne Vos. That is a really strong message."

According to the most recent figures from the Women's Sport and Fitness Foundation, only 7% of the media coverage and 0.4% of the commercial investment is devoted to women's sport.

"Growing up my son had a range of role models encouraging him to stay fit and healthy but for my daughter they were few

and far between," says Elliott. "Women just don't get the coverage they deserve. The commercial UK sponsorship for women's sport is 0.4%. Before the 2012 Olympics it was 0.5% so it's actually a worsening trend which is pitiful and disgusting. People should hang their heads in shame."

During the UCI presidential elections last year, Olympic silver medallist Armitstead voiced her criticism of now-president Brian Cookson, who was formerly at the helm of British Cycling, saying that he hadn't done enough to change the women's side of the sport. Since being elected in September, Cookson has been keen to show that his commitment to women's cycling was "not just manifesto talk".

To that end, the UCI have begun live-streaming World Cup road races while Tracey Gaudry, one of Cookson's three vice-presidents and the first woman to be elected to such a high-level role within cycling's international governing body, has been a regular face at such events. Armitstead said recently that she feels "quite positive about women's cycling right now".

Bertine, though, remains more cautious. "I don't want to dole out too much praise until we see these changes are constant in their development," she says. "I think it's fantastic that Tracey Gaudry was appointed but I don't believe the appointment of a woman changes an entire organisation. If anything, I think we should be very careful that it's not used as a decoy."

With no road academy or programme for British women currently, it is arguably only the most exceptional and determined maverick that can succeed. Armitstead, signed to top Dutch team Boels Dolmans until 2016, is a prime example of a rider with the tenacity and mental strength necessary to progress through the highest echelons of the women's pro ranks.

Scottish rider Claire Thomas has based herself in Belgium for the past three years in a bid to further her cycling career. The 41-year-old from Edinburgh, who rides for Velosport-Pasta Montegrappa and has been named for Team Scotland to compete at Glasgow 2014, is under no illusions about how unlevel the playing field - or rather pavé (cobbles) - can feel.

"Most of us have to work and are juggling that with going to races and training," she says. "The riders who are paid - the likes of Emma Johansson and Marianne Vos - have that support system and can simply focus on their cycling. We are trying to compete with that, working in our day jobs and trying to be as good as we can within the sport.

"Then when you look at the bigger picture, and compare the women with the men, someone like Mark Cavendish will be on 20 times that of Marianne Vos. There is no equality there at all."

Last year former Scottish Cycling head coach Graeme Herd put together a proposal to launch a UCI professional women's team based in Scotland. While the venture has temporarily stalled due to a lack of title sponsor, Herd is convinced of its merit.

"Women's cycling is currently in a bit of a catch 22," he says. "It's one of those situations where you can't get profile for the sport because you can't get money, but you can't get money because you can't get profile. That's starting to change thanks to the Women's Tour and people like Guy Elliott who aren't scared to invest money and time in it.

"As far as I'm concerned women's racing is equal to, or better than, a large proportion of men's. The appetite is there but it will take time to build momentum."

According to Bertine, there is a definite shift in the current. "What is happening now is what is necessary in any social revolution," she says. "The participants need to speak out and women in cycling are doing that. They have realised no one is going to fight for us: we have to fight for ourselves to move the sport forward.

"That is how tennis did it. It took a tennis player, Billie Jean King, to revolutionise the sport: it wasn't a businessman or an organisation. That is what we need now in cycling. I'm honoured to be part of that movement and one of many voices saying: 'We need a changing of the guard'."

Scottish Herald, 8 June 2014
Reproduced with permission of Herald & Times Group

'No one is interested in women's cycling', but we have photographs of stage finishes where the crowds are as big as the men's Tour of Britain

Photo: Rena Schild / Shutterstock.com

Wider world

Photo: sippakorn Shutterstock.com

China's city of lost children brings in shelters for abandoned babies

Shenzhen is introducing what was known in medieval Europe as the Foundling Wheel: a shelter where parents can leave their babies safely and anonymously

By Malcolm Moore, in Shenzhen

SOME ISSUES:

Do you think a shelter is a good or a bad idea?

What other solutions might help the situation?

Should abandoning your baby be a crime?

It is a bustling city of seven million people, many of them drawn from China's rural hinterland to work in its busy factories, neon-lit shops, karaoke parlours and restaurants.

But Shenzhen has another side to its reputation: in the minds of many it has become associated with abandoned babies, a social problem in many countries but one that is particularly acute among the transient workers who come here in pursuit of better job prospects.

For much of the past decade, a baby has been abandoned almost every day somewhere in the city, usually by parents – or just single mothers – who are desperate at the consequences of what may have been an unwanted pregnancy.

In most cases, they are simply unable to afford the medical care needed by babies who are physically or mentally handicapped.

controversy

But now the city is taking a controversial step to protect its unwanted children. It is reintroducing what was known in medieval Europe as the Foundling Wheel: a shelter where parents can leave their babies safely and anonymously.

The shelter, built along the lines of a similar scheme that had been quietly trialled in the northern city of Shijiazhuang, will boast an incubator, blankets, oxygen on standby, and a button for parents to press to alert staff to the new arrival before they left.

The authorities gingerly announced the plan after a shaming flurry of publicity this summer when three babies were abandoned in the space of a few days around June 1, China's "Childrens' Day".

abandoned children

One child was left in a rubbish bin, and had suffered severe organ damage before being discovered and rescued; another was abandoned in a public lavatory; and a third was left lying on a patch of grass outside a hospital.

But the announcement of the baby shelter, literally the "baby abandonment island" in Chinese, provoked a national media outcry, this time with critics claiming that such a scheme would encourage more parents to dump their unwanted children.

In China, as in the UK, it is illegal to abandon a baby, and the mother who left her child outside the hospital in June is have suggested that the number of abandonments will shoot up, others that baby traffickers will lie in wait outside the shelter and steal infants." Six months after the initial announcement, the baby shelter outside Mr Tang's Social Welfare centre remains unfurnished; the public outcry was strong enough to stall its completion.

support

But Mr Tang now has the support of Beijing. Baby shelters will be built nationwide, according to Dou Yupei, the vice minister of the Civil Affairs Bureau.

"Abandoning a baby is a crime in our country," said Peng Xizhe, a professor who abandon their infants at public buildings, such as hospitals. Mr Tang added that there had been pressure in other Chinese cities too, with the number of abandonments in inland provinces now higher than in Shenzhen.

"In Nanjing two infants died, one froze to death after being abandoned in a park and one starved," he said. "The higher-ups have asked us to accelerate our plan and [the nearby city of] Guangzhou is also building a shelter which should be finished in January." He said the shelter would have a second, infra-red, sensor in case parents forget to push the alarm button and that it would be monitored by a guard from a distance.

in Germany, there are over 100 baby shelters, while almost every state in America has an amnesty law which pardons parents who abandon their infants at public buildings, such as hospitals.

still being hunted by the authorities.

"We had been studying how to improve the situation for a long time," said Tang Rongsheng, the recently departed head of the city's Social Welfare centre, where abandoned children, if they are lucky, are taken in and cared for.

opposition

"But when we suggested the baby shelter in June, there was a lot of criticism that I was teaching people how to commit a crime. There have been a lot of wild accusations. Some at Fudan university who specialises in public policy and social development.

"But during the process of committing this crime, babies are the victims. Since the root of the crime which is caused by various complicated issues cannot be solved in the blink of an eye, it is a good option to shift our focus to protecting those victims."

pressure

In Germany, there are over 100 baby shelters, while almost every state in America has an amnesty law which pardons parents While there are apartments overlooking the shelter and CCTV cameras in the streets nearby, he said he hoped it would not deter parents from choosing it as a safer option for abandonment.

"Some people are saying that the shelter will encourage perpetrators to commit crimes. Of all the criticism, this is the only reasonable one," he said. "It is not a question I can easily answer because technically it is true that we are providing a place for the law to be broken. But while the media has hyped this issue, it is not as if people are not already abandoning children." Inside the Social Welfare centre, which functions as the city's orphanage, 560 children, many of whom refer to Mr Tang as "Father Tang", are currently living in dormitories. Nurseries and classrooms are light-filled and well-staffed.

Half of them will eventually be adopted. The other half are too mentally or physically ill for adoptive parents to cope with, Mr Tang said, and will be raised on site until they are adults.

falling numbers

In the last decade, more than 3,500 children have been abandoned here. But there is some good news: abandonments have steadily decreased as China grows wealthier: the centre now only receives between 100 and 200 children a year, down by more than a third from five years ago.

"Usually it is single mothers, migrant workers, who do not know what to do, and who have no husband, money or support, who leave behind their children.

Pregnancy screening also means fewer handicapped children are born," he said.

Mr Tang says the trend confounds the criticism that the shelter will encourage more abandonments.

"I don't think the numbers are going to rise. Parents only abandon their children if they are faced with an insurmountable problem," he said.

Additional reporting by Adam Wu
The Daily Telegraph, 23 December 2013
© Telegraph Media Group Limited 2013

'baby abandonment island' provoked a national media outcry

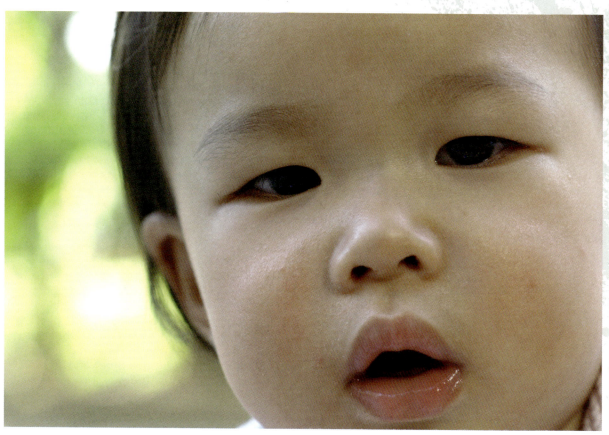

Image posed by model

The frustrating side of life in France

SOME ISSUES:

Why do you think France has so many rules and regulations?

What makes up a national characteristic?

Do you think the writer is being fair to French people and their way of life?

There are times I want to grab my French friends by their shrugging shoulders and slap them forcefully on both cheeks in a parody of the double kiss.

I've never been what you'd call a violent person. My anger has a verbal rather than a physical expression, mainly, truth be told, because I've always been rather terrified someone might slap me back.

Otherwise I might have been tempted to beat the merde out of them. But I'm sick of the resigned acceptance of life that makes up such a huge chunk of the French psyche, encompassed in that familiar shrug and spread of hands.

They, now we, moi, suffocate under tons of forms and procedures demanded by surly, unhelpful, sneering bureaucrats working out their time to early retirement on almost fully salaried pensions.

(That's just the way it is. Shrug.)

They try to set up a little business, maybe employ one or two people, and give up in despair and often bankruptcy, as they are strangled under the rigid social charges demanded in advance and ludicrous claw-backs of the state.

(That's just the way it is. Shrug.)

They allow jumped-up rural mayors to control their attempts to improve their houses. No, not mega-extensions without permission: simple change of shutter colour or a post-box that extends 4cm over their boundary. Then they just half-smile on hearing of the latest four-hour jolly lunch in the county town, involving champagne and les premiers crus, to discuss the area's problems.

(That's just the way it is. Shrug.)

The only time I see the eyes widen is when I compare like-for-like with UK prices in terms of food, white goods, cars, flights … actually, practically everything. After the usual non, c'est pas vrai, and a few emotive hands to cheeks, there comes the shrug (the sad shrug this time) and yes: Ah, that's just the way it is. En France.

Non, non, non. It doesn't have to be. It's both political and arrogant. How often I've used that word when describing life in France. Arrogance is usually a by-product of fear, and fear in a strange way has ruled and still rules France since both world wars.

Protect, protect, and keep her safe and insular while still pretending she has a major role to play on a stage that history tells her children she still dominates. Which is why many are rushing to shelter under the banner of the Front National, but I'm not going there again this week. To us, used to reaping the benefit of a competitive country, it is frustrating and nonsensical to see protectionism at work.

"No-one must be disadvantaged in any way" is the simplified mantra. That means, for example, that even sales are monitored and only permitted on certain weeks during the year.

Woe betides any poor drowning soul who tries to pay the non-negotiable social charges with a quick flash sale. They'd be guaranteed a visit from the police. Choice is limited and prices mainly pegged - barring the newish online discount firms - when buying white goods, televisions etc. It is almost certainly cheaper to buy from American, UK and even Far Eastern sites and pay the delivery charges.

Tyres for my car are delivered within days from Germany, half or less the price here. Parts the same. Spares and parts right down to fan belts for my increasingly decrepit tractor mower are bought online in

the US. What costs, say, €30 online, would cost a whopping €80 to €100 here.

Nick, who sorts my mower, needs a new one himself. The cheapest of the type he wants is pushing €3000 in France. In the UK it would be less than €2000, in the States a

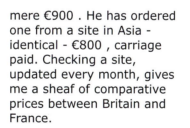

mere €900 . He has ordered one from a site in Asia - identical - €800 , carriage paid. Checking a site, updated every month, gives me a sheaf of comparative prices between Britain and France.

Clothing can be anything from 21 per cent to 40 per cent dearer here. Food is similar. France is cheaper only for wine and cigarettes - our famous cheeses cost us an almighty 41.42 per cent more than you pay in the UK. No wonder expats with families find it cheaper to shop in the UK's food stores and have it delivered to a city near their Gallic idyll.

No wonder there was outrage when M&S decreed clothes could only be bought through their new French site and not delivered from

the UK. They are dearer here and the free delivery doesn't swing it.

Even global brand Ikea is forced to charge more for virtually every item, with delivery charges that are, frankly, ludicrous.

My books come from Amazon UK, not from Amazon France. Simple: cheaper, quicker and easier to navigate.

Of course one wants to support the country in which one lives. But aren't we meant to be in a collective bargaining arena called the European Union?

My French friends become uncomfortable when shown the undisputed facts. Some quickly click on to my recommended sites and glow with the savings.

Others, yes, just shrug and say: Bof! That's the way we do things.

Slap, slap and slap again.

Herald Scotland, 24 May 2014
Reproduced with permission of
Herald & Times Group

ADMIT IT. YOU LOVE CHEAP CLOTHES. AND YOU DON'T CARE ABOUT CHILD SLAVE LABOUR

Companies, western consumers and India are still turning a blind eye to brutal conditions in garment factories

GETHIN CHAMBERLAIN

Until three years ago I did not believe in magic. But that was before I began investigating how western brands perform a conjuring routine that makes the great Indian rope trick pale in comparison. Now I'm beginning to believe someone has cast a spell over the world's consumers.

This is how it works. Well Known Company makes shiny, pretty things in India or China. The Observer reports that the people making the shiny, pretty things are being paid buttons and, what's more, have been using children's nimble little fingers to put them together. There is much outrage, WKC professes its horror that it has been let down by its supply chain and promises to make everything better. And then nothing happens. WKC keeps making shiny, pretty things and people keep buying them. Because they love them. Because they are cheap. And because they have let themselves be bewitched.

I recently revealed how poverty wages in India's tea industry fuel a slave trade in teenage girls whose parents cannot afford to keep them. Tea drinkers were naturally upset. So the ethical bodies that certified Assam tea estates paying a basic 12p an hour were wheeled out to give the impression everything would be made right.

For many consumers, that is enough. They want to feel that they are being ethical. But they don't want to pay more. They are prepared to believe in the brands they love. Companies know this. They know that if they make the right noises about behaving ethically, their customers will turn a blind eye.

So they come down hard on suppliers highlighted by the media. They sign up to the certification schemes – the Ethical Trading Initiative, Fairtrade, the Rainforest Alliance and others. Look, they say, we are good guys now. We audit our factories. We have rules, codes of conduct, mission statements. We are ethical. But they are not. What they have done is purchase an ethical fig leaf.

SOME ISSUES:

Do you know the conditions of the workers who made the clothes you wear?

Should shops have to provide information about working conditions?

Why does it matter what conditions people work in and what they get paid?

Would you pay more for your clothes if you knew workers were getting paid more?

Image: Paul Prescott / Shutterstock.com

We want the shiny, pretty things. And we grumble that times are tight, we can't be expected to pay more and, anyway, those places are very cheap to live in...

In the last few years, companies have got smarter. It is rare now to find children in the top level of the supply chain, because the brands know this is PR suicide. But the wages still stink, the hours are still brutal, and the children are still there, stitching away in the backstreets of the slums.

Drive east out of Delhi for an hour or so into the industrial wasteland of Ghaziabad and take a stroll down some of the back lanes. You might want to watch your step, to avoid falling into the stinking open drains. Take a look through some of the doorways. See the children stitching the fine embroidery and beading? Now take a stroll through your favourite mall and have a look at the shelves. Recognise some of that handiwork? You should.

Suppliers now subcontract work out from the main factory, maybe more than once. The work is done out of sight, the pieces sent back to the main factory to be finished and labelled. And when the auditors come round the factory, they can say that there were no children and all was well. Because audits are part of the act. Often it is as simple as two sets of books, one for the brand, one for themselves. The brand's books say everyone works eight hours a day with a lunch break. The real books show the profits from 16-hour days and no days off all month.

Need fire extinguishers to tick the safety box? Hire them in for the day. The lift is a deathtrap? Stick a sign on it to say it is out of use and the inspector will pass it by. The dark arts thrive in the inspection business. We, the consumers, let them do this because we want the shiny, pretty thing. And we grumble that times are tight, we can't be expected to pay more and, anyway, those places are very cheap to live in.

This is the other part of the magic trick, the western perception of the supplier countries, born of ignorance and embarrassment. India, more than most, knows how to play on this. Governments and celebrities fall over themselves to laud India for its progress. India is on the up, India is booming, India is very

I want people to say to them: "You deceived us. You told us you were ethical. We want you to change."

spiritual, India is vibrant. Sure, the workers are poor, but they are probably happy.

No, they are not. India has made the brands look rank amateurs in the field of public relations. Yes, we know it is protectionist, yes, we know working conditions are often diabolical, but we are in thrall to a country that seems impossibly exotic.

Colonial guilt helps. The British in particular feel awkward about India. We stole their country and plundered their riches. We don't feel able to criticise. But we should. China still gets caught out, but wages have risen and working conditions have improved. India seems content to rely on no one challenging it.

Last week India's powerful planning commission claimed that poverty was at a record low of 21.9% of the population. It did so on the basis that people could live on 26 rupees (29p) a day in rural areas (33 rupees in urban areas). Many inside India baulk at this. Few outside the country did so.

But times are tough, consumers say. This is the most pernicious of the ideas the brands have encouraged. Here's some maths from an Observer investigation last year in Bangalore. We can calculate that women on the absolute legal minimum wage, making jeans for a WKC, get 11p per item. Now wave your own wand and grant them the living monthly wage – the £136 the Asia Floor Wage Alliance calculates is needed to support a family in India today (and bear in mind that the women are often the sole earners). It is going to cost a fortune, right? No. It will cost 15p more on the labour cost of each pair of jeans.

The very fact that wages are so low makes the cost of fixing the problem low, too. Someone has to absorb the hit, be it the brand, supplier, middleman, retailer or consumer. But why make this a bad thing? Why be scared of it?

Here is the shopper, agonising over ethical or cheap. What if they can do both? What if they can pluck two pairs of jeans off the rail and hold them up. One costs £20. One costs £20.15. It has a big label on it, which says "I'm proud to pay 15p more for these jeans. I believe everyone has the right to a decent standard of living. My jeans were made by a happy worker who was paid the fair rate for the job."

Go further. Stitch it on to the jeans themselves. I want those jeans. I want to know I'm not wearing something stitched by kids kept locked in backstreet godowns [warehouses], never seeing the light of day, never getting a penny. I want to feel clean. And I want the big brands and the supermarkets to help me feel clean.

I want people to say to them: "You deceived us. You told us you were ethical. We want you to change. We want you to police your supply chain as if you care. Name your suppliers. Open them to independent inspection. We want to trust you again, we really do, because we love your products. Know what? We don't mind paying a few pennies more if you promise to chip in too."

And here's the best part: I think they would sell more. I think consumers would be happier and workers would be happier. And if I can spend less time trawling through fetid backstreets looking for the truth, I'll be happier.

The Observer, 28 July 2013 © Guardian News & Media 2013

I want those jeans. I want to know I'm not wearing something stitched by kids kept locked in backstreet warehouses, never seeing the light of day, never getting a penny. I want to feel clean. And I want the big brands and the supermarkets to help me feel clean.

The aftermath of the Haiti earthquake, January 2010
Photo © Jan Grarup/laif/Camera Press

A surprising tale of three catastrophic photographs

Cathrine Gyldensted meets world-renowned war photographer Jan Grarup, who includes inspiration and hope in his photographs, to discover how photojournalism has an important role to play in the pursuit of a more constructive media.

SOME ISSUES:

How important do you think photographs are for showing what is happening in a situation?

Are news images sometimes too shocking?

What do you think is the importance of the images in this article?

Should news reporting put more emphasis on pleasant events and less on horrible ones?

For more than two decades Grarup has covered conflict around the world, including the Gulf war, the genocide in Rwanda and Darfur, the siege of Sarajevo, unrest in Somalia and the devastation in Haiti. He's not afraid of getting to the frontlines and beyond in an effort to secure the most impactful and horrific images from wars, famine and natural disasters. If you read Time Magazine, New York Times or Le Monde, you've most certainly come across his photographs, probably on the front page.

Aftermath of the Haiti earthquake in 2010
© Jan Grarup/laif/Camera Press

"To me this was a powerful image of resilience and hope, where you would think there was none to be found"

So you can imagine my surprise when he was suggested to me as a relevant person to interview for my forthcoming textbook on constructive journalism. I'd been drawing mainly from a pool of experienced and insightful colleagues from news journalism - I wanted to explore their insights in order to highlight their best practices to readers of my book. Yet the more I considered Grarup, the more sharing his experiences seemed vital. Here's his tale of three surprising photographs:

"I got to Haiti very early after the earthquake had struck. As you can see, everything lies in ruins in Port-Au-Prince. We know now that more than 300,000 people perished. I knew I had to cover the catastrophe in a more comprehensive and nuanced way than normal.

"I'd already shot images of people looking through the rubble, and of Haitians desperate for food and water, when I noticed this couple walking past. She was nicely dressed, her hair was delicately arranged and they held hands. To me, this was a powerful image of resilience and hope, where you would think there was none to be found.

"In another one from Haiti [p199], I was close to the normally very popular market area, Marché de Fer, and in the background you see the remaining gateway – everything else is destroyed. But suddenly this woman walks by me; tall, proud and with a promise of a new life."

A young girl in a makeshift hospital tent in Kashmir, Pakistan
© Jan Grarup/laif/Camera Press

"For human beings to really become engaged, I find that they need inspiration, hope and a path forward"

"This one is from a makeshift hospital tent in Kashmir where I met and photographed dying and suffering people. In the middle of everything, this little girl lies in a hospital bed, both her legs in plaster from hip to foot, lifted in a hoist. She's obviously badly injured, but surprisingly she has a playful look on her face and stretches her arms toward the ceiling. I intuitively knew that I had a unique image that would encourage people to support the relief effort in the area. It leaves more of an impression on you than the usual death and suffering."

After seeing these images, I asked Grarup why he wanted to add hope, meaning and resilience to his reporting. Why he too is pursuing a more constructive form of reportage, albeit in pictures instead of words.

"For most of my career I believed that the way to get people to take action to better injustice,

killings, poverty and suppression was to show them the ugliest and grimmest side of conflict," he says. "I thought that seeing children killed by a grenade would force people to act. But I found that the reaction from my audience and among power-holders was mostly silence. Nothing happened. Not as much as I had expected, at least.

"Now I realise that people cannot connect to blanket despair, death and hopelessness. For human beings to really become engaged, I find that they need inspiration, hope and a path forward. I always include those elements in my pictures today, and I get much more of a response now from my audiences than previously. I am now portraying a more accurate picture of reality, and isn't that what journalism is for?"

Positive News, 19 February 2014
© positivenews.org.uk

Work

Big business with benefits!

Workforce are told they'll inherit the company!

The multi-millionaire owner of Richer Sounds has a unique way of motivating his employees - they are going to inherit his business

You might have seen one of the 53 Richer Sounds stores or come across the website selling hi-fi, home cinema and TV equipment. The website screams for attention with its bright red and yellow colour scheme. This reflects the original idea of the company's founder Julian Richer expounded in the 'Richer culture' section of the website: "Historically, we have been known for selling budget audio equipment in a 'pile it high and sell it cheap' fashion." This is a business approach borrowed from Tesco and adopted by many retailers. But as the business has grown, the focus has shifted and the Richer approach is different from the big high street electrical stores.

What makes the stores different? There's location - they are purposely not located in the most expensive parts of city centres. There's style - black and white, with a touch of red, they feel cool, slick and welcoming. And there is service - they provide "home-styled demonstration rooms" for you to sample products, aiming at "providing a non-intimidating atmosphere" and "Sales staff are chosen on the criteria of enthusiasm and friendliness" to quote the company website.

The company has a generous and unusual policy to keep its staff enthusiastic. Perks for employees include free trips to company holiday homes in the UK and overseas (regardless of sales performance) and cash to head to the pub and brainstorm ideas. The best ideas are looked at each quarter with the best of the best given a further cash prize.

The company founder, Julian Richer, is the sole owner. This means he has no need to justify his unorthodox business style to share holders or partners. The style may be unconventional but it makes good business sense. Motivated, happy workers provide

SOME ISSUES:

Why might this be a good business model for other companies? Should/could all businesses be run like this?

Will knowing that they will inherit the business affect how staff behave?

What do you predict will happen when the staff inherit the business?

How do you think the decision to leave the business to employees, will affect how staff behave towards the business?

Is this a good business model for other companies?

Perks for employees include free trips to company holiday homes in the UK and overseas (regardless of sales performance) and cash to head to the pub and brainstorm ideas. The best ideas are looked at each quarter with the best of the best given a further cash prize.

the best customer service, which means more happy customers, which means more business.

This positive cycle has got Richer noticed for more than his hi-fis. The word has spread and he has been consulted by large firms on his motivational methods and has shared his ideas in two books "The Richer Way" and "Richer on Leadership" which have earned rave reviews.

Like some other famous entrepreneurs Richer was not a great success at school but started in business remarkably early. At 14, he started buying and selling hi-fi separates. At 17 he was running a record player refurbishment business with a staff of three and by the age of 19 he opened his first store at London Bridge Station. This store is mentioned in the Guinness Book of World Records for having the highest sales, per square foot of space, in the world.

The company is very much his baby and it is entirely up to Julian Richer how he runs it, and what he does with it when he dies. Remarkably, he has decided that when that day comes, ownership of the company will pass to the people who work in it, and the firm's current IT director, Julie Abrahams, will become managing director. This is surely the biggest perk and the biggest incentive that staff could be offered.

He says, "It's important. My life's work is my legacy...the worry is that I'd sell it and someone might sell off all the freeholds or do something terrible to it. So I'd rather leave a team in place."

Like some other famous entrepreneurs Richer was not a great success at school but started in business remarkably early. At 14, he started buying and selling hi-fi separates

He may be joking when he explains, "I haven't got a spoilt child to run the business." But his decision certainly will benefit the workforce who have helped his business thrive. It also mirrors his other interests. He is a committed Christian, was the first patron of the Big Issue Foundation and is a Vice President of the RSPCA. He has founded and funded "ASB Help" a charity for victims of anti-social behavior and "ACTS 435" which enables people to give directly to those in need.

Richer is now 54, so the staff are not likely to be coming into their inheritance any time soon. "I've been there for 35 years; I want to be here for the next 35 years," he says.

In the meantime, staff can continue to enjoy an annual holiday with Julian after five years' service, use of the company holiday homes and drinks in the pub. So there's plenty of incentive for them to want him to stick around!

Sources: Various

Company founder Julian Richer

If the Face(book) fits

How your Facebook profile could make or marr your job prospects

Social networks are just that, aren't they? Social - the clue is in the word. You social-ise. You hang out with your mates. You exchange stupid jokes and videos of kittens. You post a satisfyingly long rant about your day, your boss, the stupid people who get in your way. Or you post intriguingly short messages, "Oh,no!", just to get a conversation started. But you don't expect a future employer to go poking about amongst the drinking games and unflattering selfies.

But increasingly that is what is happening. Employers are screening candidates for jobs by looking at their social network profiles - and it means that some people fail their job interview before they even know they are being considered.

It is perfectly lawful for a prospective employer to take a look at your public profile as long as they use the same basis for decisions that they would if they were recruiting in any other way. They must not discriminate on the grounds of age, sex, religion, sexual orientation or political belief. But what if an employer was considering Philip Brown for a job, and then found out from Facebook that he was an active member of Greenpeace. If the boss decided not to interview him because of that, would Philip even know?

The Chartered Institute of Professional Development is a professional body which aims to improve working practices for people and organisations. It has produced a guide for employers who want to view a candidate's social media profile. As well as the legal requirements not to discriminate, it suggests:

> Employers should only look for specific information relevant to a job, not trawl through someone's profile for any random information.

> A candidate should know right from the start if online sources are going to be used

> They should be given the chance to respond if something in their profile affects the decision

SOME ISSUES:

Do you think it is right that potential employers judge people based on their online profiles?

What does your online profile reveal about you?

Should you consider potential careers when posting online?

Posting inappropriate pictures or comments was mentioned by 50% of employers

The CIPD says that employers should have a clear policy about using social media in recruitment and that the professional network LinkedIn is a legitimate source of information while Facebook is not.

However, research seems to bear out what we all suspect - that employers can and do make judgements based on social media. One US firm which helps people manage their social image conducted a small survey of 300 people involved in recruitment. 91% of them said they used social networking sites to screen potential employees. 47% did this screening after receiving an application and before speaking to the candidate. A large proportion, 69%, said they had rejected a candidate because of what they saw about them on a site.

The basis for those rejections varied but posting inappropriate pictures or comments was mentioned by 50% of employers in a 2013 survey by Careerbuilder, a UK online jobsite. It was not specific about exactly what inappropriate meant or who should be the judge. Comments about drinking or drug use had ruined prospects too - mentioned by 48% who spoke to Careerbuilder.

Employers also found other, perhaps more relevant, concerns in their digging into candidates' behaviour. They mentioned finding that job seekers had shared confidential information from previous employment, made discriminatory comments, shown poor communication skills or lied about their qualifications. One deadly mistake was that rant about your boss. 33% in the UK survey had ruled candidates out for badmouthing a previous employer.

But you can't avoid problems by simply not being online. These days that in itself is considered suspicious, the mark of a loner - or worse (the Norwegian mass murderer, Anders Breivik was noted to have no social media presence). It also looks suspicious if what you say on Twitter doesn't match the person you appear to be on Facebook. You need to present yourself consistently, favourably and truthfully on all platforms.

But your site can work for you. What employers are looking for is someone who would be a great addition to their team. While 69% of employers had rejected someone on the basis of something they had seen online, 68% also said they had

hired someone based on their online presence. 39% of them said this was because the site gave a positive impression of personality and organisation. Other positive attributes they found were: creativity, being well-rounded, having awards and accolades, good references from others and good communication skills.

As well as avoiding negative comments and risky photos, you should promote your good points - the charity walks you have done, how you help the local youth sports team, what a reliable baby-sitter you are. Post the pictures of you volunteering as well as the ones of you drinking with friends. Tweet Instagrams of your artwork as well as of your dinner.

Numerous surveys have shown that the thing that people appreciate most about work is not money or job satisfaction, it is the relationship with their colleagues. You need to use social media to show what an interesting, stimulating and yet dependable person you are, how great you are to have around.

An employer who is looking at your Facebook profile is already interested in you and wants to see how you might fit into a group. 'Social' media - the clue is in the name.

Sources: various

Complete Issues

understanding our world

Section names are in capitals and in colour.

Page numbers refer you to the article rather than the specific term.

When you use this index for research it refers to articles within this book. When you enter a search term online using Complete Issues, you can search this volume and previous ones as well as Fact File for related statistics and Key Organisations for relevant contacts.

www.completeissues.co.uk

Index

M

Manchester United 77
Marathon 179
Media see INTERNET & MEDIA
Men see GENDER
MENTAL HEALTH 146-154 & 34, 118
Money see FINANCIAL ISSUES
Mothers 64, 66, 167
Murder 142
Muslims see Islam

N

Nationality 46

O

Obesity 100
Organ donation 116

P

Parents see FAMILY & RELATIONSHIPS
Photography 199
Politics 41, 44, 50, 52, 62, 82, 87
Population 44, 46
Poverty 48, 52, 80, 82, 98
Prejudice 48, 60
Puddington, Reece 124

R

Race 44, 46
Reading 62
RELIGION 155-165 & 91, 94
Richer Sounds 203
Running 179

S

Schizophrenia 152
School 58, 60, 105, 170
Self harm 132
Selfies 134
Sexism 105, 110, 113, 142, 187
Sexting 128
SEXUAL ISSUES 166-177 & 105, 108

Smoking 11, 118
SPORT & LEISURE 178-189 & 31, 62
Social media 41, 64, 74, 122, 124, 128, 132, 134, 139, 147, 205
Sugar 100
Suicide see ASSISTED DYING 22-29 & 147
Sutton, Stephen 124
Swimming 182

T

Tattoos 66
Teen pregnancy 167, 170
Tolerance 156, 163
Toys 110, 113
Transplants 116
Trolls 132
TV 48

U

University 56, 84, 87

V

Violence 142
Vegetarianism 94, 96

W

War 199
Wealth 50, 77, 80, 82, 203
WIDER WORLD 190-201 & 60, 96
Women see GENDER
WORK 202-206 & 44, 50, 52, 56, 58, 72, 82, 84, 110, 196

Y

Young people 20, 28, 41, 60, 64, 84, 87, 105, 132, 167, 170, 172, 174

Published by Carel Press Ltd
4 Hewson St, Carlisle CA2 5AU
Tel +44 (0)1228 538928,
Fax 591816
office@carelpress.co.uk
www.carelpress.co.uk
This collection © 2015
Christine A Shepherd & Chas White

COPYRIGHT NOTICE
Reproduction from this resource is allowed for use within the purchasing school, college or library only. Copyright is strictly reserved for all other purposes and remains with the original copyright holder.

Acknowledgements
Designer: Anne Louise Kershaw
Editorial team: Anne Louise Kershaw, Debbie Maxwell, Christine A Shepherd, Chas White
Subscriptions: Ann Batey (Manager), Brenda Hughes, Anne Maclagan

We wish to thank all those writers, editors, photographers, press agencies and wire services who have given permission to reproduce copyright material. Every effort has been made to trace copyright holders of material but in a few cases this has not been possible. The publishers would be glad to hear from anyone who has not been consulted.

Cover design:
Anne Louise Kershaw
Front cover photo: © Jan Grarup/laif/ Camera Press

British Library
Cataloguing in Publication Data

Essential Articles 2015: The articles you need on the issues that matter
1. Social problems – Study and teaching (Secondary) – Great Britain 2. Social sciences – Study and teaching (Secondary) – Great Britain
I. Shepherd, Christine A
II. White, C
361.00712 41
ISBN 978-1-905600-46-5

Printed by Finemark, Poland